The body of a seven-year-old . . .
discovered by a nine-year-old

"We were looking for blackberries," the little girl later told police. "We knew there were lots of blackberries down that trail because we had picked them before. It was about seven o'clock when we decided to go play at the forest. People dump all sorts of stuff there—leaves and things. We were walking and my friend saw a skate. At least she thought she saw one, but we didn't know for sure. We walked down further and that's when we saw it."

"We were walking side by side," the other little girl confirmed. "We went around to the other side of the bushes, but we couldn't find the skate. On the way back up the trail, I saw a human foot. It was under some grass clippings. It looked like a kid's foot. I screamed, and the other kids came running over."

From his pickup truck, Wesley Coulter heard the screams and saw the two crying girls. "On every other telephone pole in all of Everett, there was a poster of Roxanne Doll. I just had a feeling, so I grabbed my phone and went down to where the kids had been playing. I saw some little toes sticking up out of the grass. I looked at them and I didn't believe they were real."

Coulter grabbed a tree limb and prodded the foot to see if it was indeed real, or that of a doll. It was real. "I was filled with anger when I touched the toes. Then I knew for certain that Roxanne had died."

BOOK YOUR PLACE ON OUR WEBSITE AND MAKE THE READING CONNECTION!

We've created a customized website just for our very special readers, where you can get the inside scoop on everything that's going on with Zebra, Pinnacle and Kensington books.

When you come online, you'll have the exciting opportunity to:

- View covers of upcoming books
- Read sample chapters
- Learn about our future publishing schedule (listed by publication month *and author*)
- Find out when your favorite authors will be visiting a city near you
- Search for and order backlist books from our online catalog
- Check out author bios and background information
- Send e-mail to your favorite authors
- Meet the Kensington staff online
- Join us in weekly chats with authors, readers and other guests
- Get writing guidelines
- AND MUCH MORE!

Visit our website at
http://www.kensingtonbooks.com

BROKEN DOLL

BURL BARER

PINNACLE BOOKS
Kensington Publishing Corp.
http://www.kensingtonbooks.com

Some names have been changed to protect the privacy of individuals connected to this story.

PINNACLE BOOKS are published by

Kensington Publishing Corp.
850 Third Avenue
New York, NY 10022

All Kensington Titles, Imprints, and Distributed Lines are available at special quantity discounts for bulk purchases for sales promotions, premiums, fund-raising, and educational or institutional use. Special book excerpts or customized printings can also be created to fit specific needs. For details, write or phone the office of the Kensington special sales manager: Kensington Publishing Corp., 850 Third Avenue, New York, NY 10022, attn: Special Sales Department, Phone: 1-800-221-2647.

Pinnacle and the P logo Reg. U.S. Pat. & TM Off.

First Printing: May 2004
10 9 8 7 6 5 4 3 2 1

Printed in the United States of America

For Jaja

Acknowledgments

This book is an account of events adapted from trial transcripts, police records, and interviews. Conversations, statements, legal arguments, testimonies, and all other remarks quoted herein are adaptations of such as recalled from memory. For purposes of clarity, concision, and continuity, statements and conversations often necessitated condensation and emendation. All efforts have been made to retain the original intent, and any errors are unintentional.

This book would not have been possible without the exemplary cooperation of the Everett Washington Police Department, and the Snohomish County Prosecutor's Office.

Heartfelt appreciation is expressed to the dedicated health-care professional, Donna McCooke, RGN, of Great Britain, whose views of the issue at hand were of significant value in helping the author retain a sense of perspective.

My editor, the patient and unflappable Michaela Hamilton, deserves credit for the book's readability. Heartfelt gratitude to Charlotte Dial Breeze, my literary agent for a decade, my dear friend for life.

An individual who chooses to surrender to the promptings of his material nature can sink to levels of depravity and bestiality which are abhorrent to the discerning eye, and which are totally unworthy of the human station.

—'Abdu'l-Bahá

The more often the captain of a ship is in the tempest and difficult sailing, the greater his knowledge becomes. Therefore, I am happy that you have had great tribulations and difficulties. . . . Strange it is that I love you and still I am happy that you have sorrows.

—'Abdu'l-Bahá

Prologue

May 28, 1988

On a pleasant spring evening in Everett, Washington, an innocent after-dinner game of hide-and-seek turned traumatic for Angela Rono and her youngest daughter, four-year-old Feather Rahier. "It was about nine P.M.," recalled Rono, "and I had just called my four kids to come in from outside because it was bedtime. They all came right in, except Feather.

"I sent the kids back outside to get her," Rono said, "and they were calling her name and looking all over for her. When they couldn't find her, I sent them to the neighbor's house to ask if they had seen her. Then I sent them across the alley to the Clark residence."

Carol Clark, a kindly woman with a great love of children, had a twenty-year-old nephew named Richard, who often lived there with other members of Carol's family. Richard Clark knew Feather, let her play with his puppy, and even gave her gifts. He primarily stayed in the garage adjacent to the residence. Feather's siblings asked Richard if he'd seen the missing child, and he told them that he hadn't seen her.

Perhaps it was mother's intuition or simple persistence that compelled Rono to send her eldest daughter, Misty, back to Clark's garage. Richard Clark again denied seeing

Feather, but the missing child's desperate sobs were now audible outside his locked garage door.

"When my daughter told me that he had her in there," Rono said, "I went running over, yelling at him to open up and let her out."

"I don't have her," answered Clark from behind the locked door. "I'm trying to sleep. Go away and quit bothering me."

"I know she's in there!" screamed Rono. "I know you have my daughter. Let her out, open the door."

"I can't find the light switch," replied Clark. "I can't find the key."

Unconvinced and outraged, the distraught mother battered more violently on Clark's door, alerting the neighbors. "Let me in!" she screamed. "Let me in right now! I swear to God if you've hurt my daughter, you're going to jail. Open the door right this minute."

When Clark finally fumbled free the heavy chain and padlock, Rono pushed her way inside. There, in what seemed the most vile of environments, she confronted a bone-chilling scene—her four-year-old daughter stood in front of her, face drenched with tears, green socks tied on her wrists, and the rear of her pants pulled down below her buttocks.

"He was trying to pull up her pants with one hand, and trying to get the sock off her wrist with the other hand, "recalled Rono, who grabbed young Feather and hurried her out of the garage. Clark followed her outside, then turned and ran. Two men from the neighborhood aiding in the search for Feather grabbed him at the end of the alley.

When police arrived, they found Richard Mathew Clark standing stoic and silent as Feather's mother beat upon his chest with her fists. On either side of Clark were the two neighbor men, who chose not to intervene on Clark's behalf.

"I was dispatched to the report of a sexual assault," recalled Officer Dwight Snyder. "When I got back in the area, I heard a lot of people yelling and screaming, separated them, and began to talk to each individual to sort out what had occurred. I knew detectives would want to talk with a child that young—I didn't want to get too detailed—so I just wanted a general idea of what occurred. I was pretty general on my questions. Feather said she had been outside playing," explained Snyder, "and that Mr. Clark had come up and talked to her. And then she looked at me and said, 'He put a sock in my mouth.' And I asked her if she had talked to Mr. Clark, and she said, 'Yes, he gives me things.' She showed me a small, kind-of-statuette, I guess, of a dog that had been given to her. She showed me that, and after she showed me the dog, she looked at me and said, 'He touched me.' And I asked her, at that point, well, how did he touch you? And she would just turn away, look at the TV, and not say anything. So I didn't press the matter. At that point, I decided to arrest Mr. Clark."

"Richard tied me up with socks and tried to put his hand down my pants," said Feather. She didn't simply say it once; she said it repeatedly all the way to the hospital.

Feather's version of events, detailed five days later to Detective Diane Berglund of the Everett Police Department, related that she was happily playing when Richard Clark picked her up and carried her off.

"It was dark in there," she said of his garage. "He put a sock in my mouth and a sock around my wrist and tied it in back," explained Feather, "and a sock over my eyes and another one on my arms—he put the wrist one on first. When Richard put a sock over my mouth, I cried. I was crying and screaming. No one else was in there with me. I knew Misty came over to Richard's house because I could hear her."

Although Feather was assuredly mistreated, she was

not technically sexually violated. He did not put his hands inside her pants, said the child. "He touched me on the outside," explained Feather.

Locking a four-year-old girl in a garage, stuffing a sock in her mouth, and tying her up is against the law in Everett, Washington. Richard Mathew Clark was charged with unlawful imprisonment and convicted of the crime.

The entire horrific event in Clark's dark garage lasted no more than a few minutes, but the effect on Feather was indelible. At the age of four years old, young Feather had now been twice traumatized by inappropriate adult male behavior. Her first sexual molestation was when she was only two years old. The perpetrator didn't live across the alley or down the road. "It was her own father," confirmed Angela Rono.

By the time Feather reached adolescence, the troubled teen no longer lived with her mother. From May 20, 1995, until March 29, 1997, Feather lived with a foster family lovingly headed by matriarch Julie Gelo.

The residual trauma of her violated childhood, the predictable pains of puberty, and the instability engendered by frequent placement in foster care raised Feather into a significantly troubled preteen. The aforementioned afflictions resulted in emotional chaos, fragmented relationships, inconsistent school attendance, and precocious sexuality.

Although the stability and structure of the loving Gelo family provided innumerable benefits and blessings, one horrific event immediately preceding her placement in the Gelo household precipitated a maelstrom of devastating emotional impact—the brutal sex slaying of a seven-year-old Everett girl named Roxanne Doll.

Part 1
MISSING

Chapter 1

On the final night of her life, Roxanne Doll spent the hour before bedtime watching a Disney video with her mother, sister, and brother. It was *Cinderella,* the fairy-tale romance about castles, glass slippers, and an adorable, exploitable young girl rescued by love and magic from a life of mistreatment and toil. Roxanne didn't live to see sunrise.

Sometime during the night, she was abducted from her bed, raped, and stabbed to death. Her body was found on April 8, 1995, dumped down a brushy north Everett hillside. The blond-haired, blue-eyed second grader lay there for a week, partially buried under a heap of grass clippings and other yard debris.

Roxanne's disappearance and death struck a nerve in Snohomish County. Hundreds of people beat the brush around south Everett looking for the missing child near her home. When her body was found, hundreds more openly mourned her. Family, friends, and strangers wept at the funeral—a funeral that her parents, on their own, could ill afford.

"If it wasn't for some very wonderful strangers," said Roxanne's mother, Gail Doll, "Roxanne's funeral would have been nearly impossible to do. So many people gave to us so we could bury her with more dignity and the respect she deserved." A makeshift roadside shrine was erected where two children picking berries discovered her body.

The man arrested, charged, and convicted of this most heinous crime was no stranger to Roxanne Doll or Feather Rahier. According to the newspaper, the twenty-six-year-old suspect lived in a garage on Lombard Street. His name was Richard M. Clark.

Snohomish County prosecutors, seeing similarities between the 1988 incident involving Feather and the 1995 kidnapping/murder of Roxanne Doll, subpoenaed Feather in February 1997. "When it was opened and she read it, she became very angry," recalled Gelo.

"I refuse, I'll not testify. I don't want to be in the courtroom," Feather said. "I don't want to remember what happened to me."

Clark's defense attorneys also wanted a deposition, which she reluctantly provided that very month. During the deposition, Feather repeatedly deflected questions by saying, "I don't remember." In truth, she remembered.

"I knew Feather had disclosed things to me that would have answered some of those questions," recalled Gelo. "And so I asked her, I said, you didn't tell him everything, did you? She hung her head and kind of got tears in her eyes. She said, 'No, I didn't. I could have answered just about all of his questions, but I don't want to remember. I get so scared and I get so sad that I'm afraid of what I might do, and what others might do. I just don't want to think about it; I don't want to talk about it.'"

Feather's anger and resentment soon influenced all aspects of her life. "I started getting telephone calls from her school," recalled Gelo. "They told me that she was losing control in the classrooms, yelling at the teachers, saying that she had to get out of the classroom, that she felt she was being closed in. Then, on Sunday, February twenty-third, she lost control at our house and threatened to hurt herself or to kill herself, and to hurt another child in my home. She ran away, going out her bedroom window."

The police found Feather fifteen miles away—she had walked the entire distance. When Gelo arrived at the Everett Police Department, Feather was in handcuffs because she was still threatening to hurt herself or hurt others.

"At this point," said Gelo, "it was decided to take her to Everett General Hospital. She was released from handcuffs for a while at the hospital and she took a paper clip and was trying to carve in her arm. Two mental-health professionals evaluated her at the hospital that night, and had her transported by ambulance to the Fairfax Psychiatric Hospital in Kirkland, Washington, arriving about five in the morning on Monday the twenty-fourth."

Gelo took Feather to Harborview Hospital for an involuntary-commitment hearing, requesting that the youngster be held for fourteen days for a complete psychiatric evaluation. The involuntary-commitment order was declined, Gelo explained, because "Despite Feather's threats, there had never been any actual harm done to another child in my home, and because the scratching and the carving on her arm had not drawn blood."

The Department of Social and Health Services decided that it would not be safe for Feather to return to Gelo's home until there were other services in place to make sure she would not carry through with her threats.

"At that point, she was placed in a facility called Cedar House from Tuesday, the twenty-fifth of February, until Monday, March third," said Gelo. "I had numerous contacts with her while in Cedar House, and we worked on things such as family reconciliation, and we worked on getting additional services in place to make it possible for Feather to return to my home, which she did on March third."

Feather returned under close supervision and heavy

medication, including twenty milligrams of Prozac, one milligram of Klonopin, and forty milligrams of Ritalin. Near comatose from Klonopin, she sleepwalked through school on Tuesday, March 4, before that medication was removed from her regimen.

"We also had, in addition to once-a-week group therapy sessions, a case manager and outreach worker appointed for her by LifeNet Mental Health," Gelo said. "We had no-harm contracts drawn up between Feather and our household and a crisis-intervention plan was set into place. And with that, she seemed to level off for a little while."

Tuesday, March 11, Feather came home after a session with the outreach worker and told Gelo that she had something to show her. "She took me into the kitchen and showed me that on the inside of her right ankle that she had started to carve initials, initials of a boy. These actually were cut into the skin," Gelo recalled. "It was not a scratch, and it was an actual cut done by a razor blade. We then put into place more precautions at home, locking up all knives, even dinner knives and kitchen knives, taking away all mirrors, everything that we could find that could be potentially dangerous."

The following day, March 12, deputy prosecutor Ronald Doersch sent Feather a fax via Lori Vanderberg at LifeNet Health. The transmission contained an avalanche of embarrassing and troubling questions.

Doersch requested the girl's recollection of how often she was touched, what she felt, what it felt like, what he said before, during and after she was tied up, where she was touched after being tied up, and what parts of Richard Clark's body touched her body. He also asked if Richard touched himself while touching her, and what parts of his body were touched, why and when he stopped touching her, what he did after the touching stopped, and if Richard Clark told her not to tell anyone, or he threatened her in any way.

"Thank you in advance for your cooperation in this matter," wrote Doersch. "We realize how difficult this is for you." It was more difficult than Doersch knew.

"She completely lost her appetite," recalled Gelo. "She was now down to ninety-eight pounds and was being monitored twice a week by the pediatrician because we were really concerned about her weight loss and her not wanting to eat."

A few days after receiving Doersch's fax, Feather requested adoption by Gelo and her husband. "She wanted to be able to use our last name, that she wanted to know that she was going to be safe and in our home forever, and not ever have to leave."

The desire for adoption did not spring fully grown from Feather's heart in a sudden burst of inspiration. Adoption was an ongoing topic at Gelo's, and Feather witnessed the process firsthand. Gelo took Feather's request seriously, advising her to discuss it with her court-appointed guardian.

"Gelo's remarkable sensitivity to Feather's personal issues," said a woman familiar with Gelo's unquestioned dedication to those in her charge, "is well known in the foster-care community. Gelo's own life, and personal challenges, are not only inspirational, but mirror in many ways those of her troubled foster children."

Born and raised in a North Dakota alcoholic home, Gelo was drinking out of her dad's beer bottles as early as she can remember. Her first major drunk was at thirteen. At fourteen, she met her first husband. He was nineteen and on his way to Vietnam for his first of two tours of duty.

Gelo was always with kids older than herself, and by age sixteen, she was spending most of her free time on the college campus drinking three to four nights a week.

When her husband came home after two years in Vietnam, his drinking fit right in with her alcohol-based lifestyle. They partied every weekend, said Gelo, and she did "controlled" drinking a couple of times during the week.

Pregnant at seventeen, she denied the condition until almost her sixth month, and kept up her drinking lifestyle. Two days after Gelo's eighteenth birthday, her first child was born. A daughter, Faith, was only six pounds twelve ounces, and eighteen inches long. All through school and with the subsequent birth of two more children, Gelo realized that Faith was different. She struggled in school and with relationships, but she graduated from high school at nineteen without much special help from the schools.

Gelo stopped drinking when Faith was eight years old, divorced her first husband, and married again five years later to another alcoholic, but one who was in recovery. Moving to Washington State, they became foster parents. Nothing prepared them, however, for the difficulties of their first foster children. One day her second daughter came home from high school and told her about Linda LaFever, a woman from whom she heard about fetal alcohol spectrum disorders. Fetal alcohol syndrome and fetal alcohol effect (FAS/FAE) are disorders of the brain resulting from exposure to alcohol while in the mother's womb. FAS is the most severe form; FAE, although not as physically visible in its outward signs, has equally serious behavioral impact. LaFever's son, Danny, was seriously affected by her drinking during pregnancy.

The most serious characteristics of FAS/FAE are the invisible symptoms of neurological damage, including mental illness, disrupted school experience, incarceration, alcohol/drug abuse, and inappropriate sexual behavior. Almost half of individuals with FAS/FAE between the ages of twelve to twenty commit crimes against persons, such as theft, burglary, assault, murder, domestic violence, running away, and child molestation.

Gelo's young foster children manifested many traits symptomatic of FAS. They were all obstinate and defiant, failed to bond with anyone, had no sense of personal boundaries, and did self-injurious things. Gelo had her two foster boys diagnosed; both had FAS. Faith, Gelo's firstborn child, was also affected.

Feather Rahier was part of the Gelo household in July 1996 when the Gelos adopted two of their foster children, a boy and a girl. The boy was diagnosed with atypical FAS and his sister with neurobehavioral disorder—alcohol and cocaine exposed. They both had a diagnosis of attention deficit hyperactivity disorder (ADHD). The young boy also had reactive attachment disorder, oppositional defiance, and conduct disorder. The female had post-traumatic stress disorder, separation anxiety, and depression.

Soon another child, a boy, was added to the mix. A succession of other foster children came and went before the boy's brother came to live with the Gelos. Two years later, another brother joined the family—a delicate child afflicted with febrile seizures. During the course of getting a CAT scan for the seizures, it was found that he had diffuse atrophy through his entire brain. There was a hole in the left temporal lobe attributed to alcohol exposure.

In June 1995, one month after Feather Rahier moved in, Gelo received a call from a caseworker asking her to take a ten-day-old baby who had been a full-term breech delivery on the streets of Seattle, but the infant only weighed a little over five pounds. He almost suffocated at birth, and tested positive for syphilis. Fetal alcohol syndrome was strongly suspected.

When the child was three months old, a neurologist said that the boy would always be severely retarded. "He may never roll over or even respond to people," reported the specialist. Other doctors speculated that he would not live a full year. "He did not sit up alone until eleven months," recalled Gelo. "He crawled at thirteen months, walked with an orthopedic walker at twenty-two months, and on his second birthday took his first independent steps. He survived and thrived, although his mother didn't."

Shortly after requesting that her parental rights be terminated so the child could be adopted by "the only mom and dad he has ever known," her drinking and drugging took their toll. She had cirrhosis, meningitis, hepatitis, renal failure, sepsis, and had been assaulted and beaten at a party. After two weeks in a coma and on a respirator, she woke up, looked at Julie Gelo and the pictures of her children, and passed on. "She was twenty-eight years old at her death, and both her parents died in their early thirties from alcohol," recalled Gelo. The adoption was completed in October 1995.

Illumed by the above history, Feather Rahier's request for adoption by Gelo would appear both logical and prudent. Seeking outward stability as an anchor for inward instability, Feather sought a situation of inclusive permanence.

Sadly, there was nothing permanent in Feather's immediate future, least of all her own moods. Troubled and volatile, Feather was often found crying in her closet. "The next minute, she could be exploding in anger," said Gelo. "It was very hard on her and on the rest of our family."

The youngster's pediatrician wrote to the prosecutor's office asking, if possible, that Feather be excused from having to testify. "He felt that all of this was having a real negative impact on her mental health," said Gelo. "He was afraid that we would end up losing her totally."

Gelo repeatedly assured Feather that everyone was doing everything in his or her power to keep everything as easy, nontraumatic, and safe for her as possible. These assurances failed to calm Feather's fears.

"I would go in to check on her at night, and sometimes she would be thrashing around in her sleep. If I went to lay my hand on her shoulder, and went to talk with her and say, 'Feather, it's okay,' she would kind of thrash at me with her hands and say, 'Don't touch me, don't touch me, leave me alone.'"

Feather's behavior became more troublesome as the date of Clark's trial grew closer. "She was attempting to draw attention to herself or cry out for help in some ways," said Gelo. "She would come and tell me what she was doing and they were behaviors that she knew would get consequences, or knew would get attention, you know, from me and from the other people in her life. And it was things like accepting a bottle of cider from a winery down the hill from us that had alcohol in it and drinking part of that bottle, but bringing the rest of it home and giving it to me."

Feather also wore very provocative clothing to school—outfits that were not provocative when first purchased. "She was taking all of the new clothing that we had bought her and cutting it up and making it very sexualized—cutting, you know, the pants to be very short, or the T-shirt, so that they would expose her midriff," Gelo said. "That isn't what she would leave the house in the morning with, but she would carry these clothes in her backpack and change. And I would get calls from the school asking that I bring her more appropriate clothing."

One day, Feather vanished from school after first period. Students and teachers overheard her say that she was leaving with two boys. "The story was that they were going to a boy's house," Gelo recalled, "because the boys wanted to do drugs. Feather wanted to go along to do her 'wild thing' that day. She was back in school by the beginning of fourth hour, and didn't appear intoxicated or under the influence of drugs. Feather knew that when she got home, she would be getting consequences at home, and yet she came home straight off the bus."

Advised by Gelo that skipping class was not a prudent decision, and one that entailed consequences, Feather had no objections. "She was not the least defiant," said Gelo. "She was pleasant and cooperative."

Spring break started that day, and Feather was put on restriction. "Again, there was no arguing, not even the sullen look that I would have seen from any of my other teenagers. Saturday morning, she got up very compliant, asked me, 'What can I do to help you today?'"

Feather helped with the children while Gelo went grocery shopping. "She asked if she could go outside and rollerblade, and my husband said it was okay as long as she was on the corner of our house, and not across the street. That was fine with Feather, it seemed. She soon returned, and my husband suggested that they go downstairs and watch a movie together. He went on down and waited for her, but she didn't come down."

He looked upstairs, and out on the deck, but Feather wasn't there. "He looked out the living-room window just in time to see her rollerblading by our house with a backpack on her back and a little bag in her hand. And a few minutes later," said Gelo, "my nineteen-year-old daughter, Faith, came to our house and she had seen Feather down at the 7-Eleven with what looked like a cigarette in her hand. By that time, I had come home, and we went down looking for her and she was gone; we couldn't find her. And," said Julie Gelo, in 1997, "that's the last time anyone has seen or heard from her."

Rather than again relive her childhood trauma, Feather packed basic belongings into a backpack, then rollerbladed down the block, around the corner, and out of sight.

She would never be a witness for the prosecution against the man charged in the brutal, sexually motivated slaying of seven-year-old Roxanne Doll—the big man from the dark garage whose fractured family, abusive upbringing, and interpersonal malaise were tragically similar to her own—a young man who manifested each stereotypical trait of the fetal alcohol spectrum disorders: Richard Mathew Clark.

Chapter 2

Richard Mathew Clark entered the world as the fruit of an adulterous womb, on August 18, 1968, and was the youngest of three children. His mother, Kathleen Ann-Marie Feller, had married George Walter-Burton Clark Jr. when she was fifteen years old and already pregnant. The age at which Kathleen began drinking is unknown, but her adult years were spent ceaselessly under the influence.

"When my mom got pregnant with me," said George Clark II, "her folks didn't approve of my father or my mother's actions, getting pregnant out of wedlock and such. I believe they held it against us, maybe me, but they didn't have much to do with us."

There was an inarguable difference between Richard, his sister, Leslie, and four year older George Clark II. Richard Clark's father was Gordon Nickelson. This parental faux pas contributed to the Clarks' separation when Richard was sixteen months old, and their subsequent divorce. Carol Clark, the children's aunt, good-hearted and protective, often looked after the youngsters.

"She came and stayed with us when Richard was first born," recalled George Clark II. "She was a good cook, and I always had lunch for school."

The home was not long without a father figure or Kathleen without a man. Neither did her reproductive system remain idle. Commuting to the eastern Washington town of Moses Lake to drive a potato truck, Kathleen met Norman Hastings.

"When she came back from Moses Lake, he would come over and visit, stay the weekend," recalled George Clark II, "and that's how my younger sister Jennet Hastings came about."

After the relationship with Hastings petered out, another man entered her life. "He had three kids of his own, so we were kinda like the Brady Bunch," said George. "After him came Bob Smith, and they had kids together too."

Bob Smith was known for continuous consumption of strong drink with his wife, his strong opinions on child training, and his even stronger methods of behavior modification. "He beat us," said George flatly. "He beat us with a belt, a fireplace poker, electrical cords, and his fists. He took a liking to Jennet, and she was spared. His own daughter, Crystal, could do no wrong. But he beat the rest of us—Richard and me more than he beat Leslie. Maybe because we were boys, or maybe because he didn't hate her as much as he hated us."

According to George Clark II, the three kids—Leslie, he, and Richard—would wait in line for their beatings. "We had to watch each other get beat," he recalled. "What made me scream the most was the fireplace poker that he used on us."

Unlike his older brother, Richard Clark didn't scream. "Richard would grit his teeth," said George, "he wouldn't cry until after Bob was gone. Me and Leslie would scream like crazy, but Richard very rarely cried until after it was over."

According to Aunt Carol, shortly after Kathleen married Bob Smith, she picked up Richard Clark for a visit. "I took him home with me for the weekend," said Carol. "He had bruises up and down his back and his legs from being beat with a belt. He cried and couldn't sleep for two days. I wrote his mother a letter. I told Kathleen that if I ever [saw] anything like that again, I would report Bob to the authorities."

Because of that admonition, Carol Clark was not permitted to visit again for three years. "I next saw Richard when he was eight years old," recalled Carol Clark. "My mom and I had gone to the doctor's office for her appointment, and I saw Richard come out of the doctor's room with his mother. And I didn't know if it was Richard or not because he had lost so much weight and his teeth were protruding out of his mouth. Well, at that time I asked Kathleen if I could bring Richard home with me and keep him because he looked so bad. And she thought it over and she did let me bring him home eventually and keep him because of what was going on. He must have been about eight years old at the time," said Carol Clark. "Richard lived with me for two years straight."

Times were always tough in the Bob Smith household. Kathleen broke her neck when Richard was very young and never worked again. Smith did seasonal berry picking, sold marijuana, and poached deer to obtain meat.

"The Clark side of the family was always good to us," recalled George. His aunt Carol verified the accuracy of his assessment. "Members of our family bought food and clothing for the children," she said, "and one time I even went to Richard's school and gave him some money."

Carol desired neither recognition nor praise for this surreptitious expression of honest, loving concern. Sadly, Bob Smith got wind of his stepson's financial windfall. "When Bob found out," recalled George Clark, "Richard was beaten as punishment."

Frequent school absences characterized the Clark brothers' school records. "We were kept home from school," explained George, "because the beating left us so bruised and swollen. Smith didn't want some teacher seeing the signs of severe abuse."

According to George Clark, Smith was continually under the influence of alcohol and/or drugs, and he seemed to concentrate his meager mental efforts on making George, Richard, and Leslie's lives miserable.

"When the family lived in Arlington, Washington," explained George, "we were forced to sleep in a woodshed. When we moved to Darrington, Smith bought a two-bedroom double-wide trailer. Then he built what he called a bunkhouse fifty yards away from the main mobile home. It had electricity, but no heat. That's where Richard and I lived. We were only allowed in the house for meals.

"To keep us kids out of the house," he explained, "Bob would make us go out into the yard and pick up rocks and stack them up into piles. Once we finished that, he had us move the piles around the yard."

According to George Clark II, Bob Smith's treatment of Richard was not only physically painful, but also emotionally humiliating. "There was one event that I'll never forget as long as I live."

Richard and Jennet, young and mischievous, got up in the middle of the night and ate up all of sister Leslie's Camp Fire Girls cookies. "There were dozens of them," said George, "and they ate them all. My mom and Bob were responsible for the money. Bob went down to some store and bought this big cigar, very big around. That night we had roast beef, mashed potatoes, a great big dinner. And Richard had to stand next to the kitchen table with a glass of water, had to eat that cigar while we ate our dinner."

The sight of his younger brother gagging on the cigar diminished George's appetite. "I couldn't eat my dinner, and I don't think any of us kids could. Richard was shaking like a leaf, and Bob was telling him that if he didn't eat it, he was going to get the hell beat out of him."

When asked why Kathleen allowed Bob to beat her children, George gave the question serious consideration. "I figure Mom must have really loved Bob Smith a lot to let him do that to us. That's all I can figure. Mom must have really loved him."

Richard Clark was fourteen years old when his loving yet terminally inebriated mother died in an auto accident on September 19, 1982. "She was full of drugs and alcohol when she died," said Carol. "She hit a bridge on Highway 9."

"The next morning," recalled George, "Leslie took the girls, Jennet and Crystal, out in one corner of the yard, and I took Richard out to the other corner of the yard and told him of our mom's death. I don't know how he was affected by it—I was in shock; Bob was in Alaska. He and our mother were not on good terms at that time."

George Clark telephoned Bob Smith, the man who beat him with a fireplace poker, and told him of Kathleen's death. "When Bob got home, all the kids scattered—left, kind of went our own ways."

After the funeral, Richard Clark went to live with his aunt Carol. "When he came to live with me, he was very upset over his mother's death, but refused to openly grieve," said Carol. "He wouldn't talk about her death. He kept everything inside. I couldn't even get him to cry. Then, one night, he was at the home, and he was outside and he was all upset and he was crying. He said, 'I just want to die.' And that was the time when I told him that I couldn't be his mother. I had to be my son's mother, and that upset him."

Desperate, disoriented, and self-destructive, Richard Mathew Clark attempted suicide three times within twelve months. "He slit his wrists," noted Carol sadly. "He still has the scars."

Richard Clark, still seeking a surrogate mother, moved in with his mother's ex-husband and his new wife, Toni.

"I married George Clark, Richard's father, on November 2, 1974," said Toni Clark. "After Kathleen died, Richard came to live with us for a couple weeks, but it didn't work out because we lived in a two-bedroom house, and we crammed all the kids into one bedroom. It was just so crowded," she said, "that they didn't have sneezing room. Richard had to walk to school, and he didn't like that school too much anyway. So he went to live with his grandma Feller, Kathleen's mom, for a while after that. After that, he moved into the house of his mother's best friend."

Although there was always an open door for him with Aunt Carol, Richard Clark remained disconnected and disenchanted. His teenage years were dissipated, bouncing back and forth between a hodgepodge of particularly unimpressive associates who shared his fascination with intoxication. Moments of semiclarity only accompanied the occasional respite with compassionate relatives, none of whom could replace his tragically taken mother. He simply could not bond with any of them.

From that point on, Richard Clark's primary passion was conspicuous consumption of alcohol; his highest educational attainment was seventh or eighth grade. His sadly predictable life-trajectory of emotional distancing and personal boundary violation via burglaries and car thefts escalated in 1988.

At the age of twenty, his inappropriate behavior reached an apparent peak when he locked four-year-old Feather Rahier in Aunt Carol's garage, tied her with socks, and touched her in ways that made her perpetually uncomfortable. He was still under thirty in 1995 when released from the Snohomish County Jail for unpaid traffic tickets. Clark devoted his postincarceration lifestyle to drinking, drugging, and other self-destructive activities classified as "partying."

"I met Richard Clark at a party," recalled Roxanne'

father, Tim Iffrig. "It was just a casual acquaintance. Two years before he murdered my daughter, I attended a party hosted by Clark's aunt, Vicki Smith."

Anyone who met Tim Iffrig came away with the same impression—immediately likable. Good-natured, outgoing, and adept at overlooking the faults of others, Tim Iffrig was the guy you can't help but like because, as one person said, "he is so darn affable."

Gail Doll, with her cherubic face that manifested good upbringing and essential innocence, was never a "party person." Unlike many of her generation, she never crossed the line of light social drinking, nor did she trespass beyond typical teenage experimentation with pot. "In fact, when they took me out for my twenty-first birthday, I didn't order a drink because I was still nursing Roxanne," she said.

"People thought Tim and I were a real mismatch," said Gail. "When I told my best friend, Kim Hammond, that I was getting married, she asked me who in the world I was marrying. She just couldn't picture Tim and I together."

"I was so upset at first about Tim and she getting married," confessed Hammond. "I actually called *Ricki Lake* and tried to get on TV. They were having a show, 'Do you have a friend who you want to keep from making the biggest mistake of his or her life?' Well, I called *Ricki Lake* three times trying to get on that show to keep Tim and Gail from getting married. But as I told Gail, if she does marry Tim, I'll be supportive of her decision, and supportive of their marriage."

"I had a problem with Tim's drinking," said Gail, "but he was never abusive nor mean. In fact, quite the opposite. He's one of those guys who starts out in a good mood and just gets in a better mood. Drinking and such were just something he grew up with, whereas I didn't. He has always been the most wonderful and attentive of fathers."

"As for Richard Clark," said Gail Doll, "the man who kidnapped, raped, and murdered our daughter, I never liked him from the minute we met. I told Tim that Richard made me uncomfortable. There was something icky about him, and I would never, ever leave him alone with my kids. Maybe it was mother's intuition or something, but Tim couldn't see it. To him, I guess, Richard was just a sometime drinking buddy. And because the house is just as much Tim's as it is mine, I felt Tim was entitled to have his friends over."

Richard Clark visited Tim and Gail on Friday night, March 31, 1995. The next morning, eight-year-old Nicholas Doll walked into his parents' bedroom and spoke four words that precipitated an avalanche of terror, trauma, and sorrow. "I can't find Roxanne," he said, and the nightmare began.

Chapter 3

"Richard Clark took his sick and twisted need for control and gratification out on a bright and promising child," said Roxanne's mother several years later. "He didn't need to take my child. He didn't need to find power in killing her, but he did."

In retrospect, there was as much precognitive irony as perverted tragedy in the death of Roxanne Doll. The month prior to her kidnapping, a policeman lectured her class at Fairmont Elementary School on the dangers of child abduction. "If someone tries to kidnap you," said the police officer, "kick and yell."

"When we were by the slide and the trees," recalled playmate Melissa Greenman, "Roxanne said that she was afraid that if she were kidnapped, she would be sad. She would like to be home. She worried about being kidnapped in her sleep. I taught her how to kick and punch."

The two weeks before her death, Roxy's mood and demeanor took a downturn. "She was afraid of a man who was giving her gifts, a man who she was very uncomfortable with," affirmed commentary entered in her school records. The man who gave her gifts, the man who groomed her for abduction, was Richard M. Clark.

He utilized the same methodology with Feather Rahier. A puppy enchants the child; gifts soften her up. In both episodes, neither technique overcame the child's apprehension or revulsion. For whatever reason, Richard Clark named his new puppy "Misty"—the name of Feather Rahier's sister, the one who summoned Angela Rono to pull her daughter from the dark garage.

"Roxanne was a very pretty girl and always friendly to everyone," recalled Gail Doll. "She wasn't afraid of new people or things. She loved to read and play with her sisters. The month just before her death, Roxy mastered riding her bike."

In truth, Roxy was blossoming in physical grace and personal accomplishment. Her school records reveal a child of resolve, charm, and dedication. Faced with early challenges in certain skills, she not only overcame her initial difficulties, but also surpassed expectations.

"Roxy would go to the school's library instead of playing on the playground most of the time," said Gail. "She wouldn't just read picture books, she would read books that had lots of words and very few pictures, and she read her older sisters' books too.

"Roxy loved pets and animals in general. She would play with our cats and they would allow her to wrap them in baby-doll clothes, blankets, and put them to sleep in her doll buggy. They never clawed or fussed.

"After her death, her favorite cat left, I guess to go find her. I don't know, but when she was gone, so was he. Roxy had always loved to play with her dolls. When asked what she wanted to be when she grew up, she said she wanted to be a mommy."

Fascinated with infants, Roxanne delighted in the presence of younger children. "She loved it when her baby cousins came over," her mother recalled. "She would carry them around and feed them their bottle, play with them. At school, family functions, or Scouts, she would locate the families that had babies just so she could play with them."

Easygoing, charmingly feminine, and innately musical, Roxanne loved singing. "Roxy knew a lot of songs from Disney movies and church," recalled Gail. "She would sing them in the car or to her baby dolls. She was a very easygoing child that knew what she wanted in life and would tell you—she wanted to be a mommy and have twelve children. She would get up every morning and do her hair in braids or ponytails and she wore dresses even in the winter months. It was a fight to get her to wear pants. She had very good manners and crossed her legs 'like the movie stars did.'"

Gail tucked her daughters in bed that Friday night, and naturally anticipated seeing them in the morning. Roxanne went to sleep wearing a brand-new nightgown. When young Nicholas said he couldn't find Roxanne, Gail was understandably concerned. The new nightgown was atop the bedroom dresser.

"Long before I called 911," remembered Gail, "I searched everywhere for my daughter. I looked in Nick's room. I looked everywhere. I called the neighbors and Roxanne's friends. Then I went next door to Shawn Angilley's and asked her if she had seen Roxanne. I called my sister Trish, called my friend Kim and told her that I couldn't find Roxanne." Gail also called her mother, Willa Doll, and her eldest daughter, Jennifer, in the nearby town of Arlington. "I even went back again to Shawn's. Finally, at about ten-thirty in the morning, I called 911."

The responding officer, Daniel Johnson, was no stranger to missing persons investigations. A police officer with the city of Everett, Johnson had close to sixteen years' experience the day he responded to Gail Doll's desperate call.

"Almost every missing persons call that I have been involved in," recalled Johnson, "they have all been found in various places. They were either at the neighbors' playing, or I found them sleeping under beds, in closets, in the car, or they went to the grocery store with Mom—and Dad didn't know it. Or they were at the park and went walking on the beach and the parents didn't see them go, but they were always found."

When Johnson arrived, he found an understandably upset Gail Doll. "I immediately started asking questions, like where she might be, where is the dad—I was trying to see if she might have gone with somebody, got up early and went playing.

"The father, Tim Iffrig, had left early in the morning on a camping excursion," recalled Johnson. "Also scheduled to go along was Roxanne's grandmother Neila D'alexander. It was highly possible that the girl had, at the last minute, been included in the camping party. I advised that we should wait and see if we could find her husband because maybe Roxanne had gone with him."

Gail Doll and Officer Johnson agreed on a simple plan: "We decided the best thing to do," said Johnson, "was to contact Tim Iffrig's mother because she was going to go on the camping trip also. Gail called the mother-in-law and she still had not been picked up. We were going to wait until Mr. Iffrig arrived at his mother's to pick her up to determine whether or not Roxanne was with him."

Officer Johnson returned to the Doll-Iffrig home shortly after one o'clock. "That's when I found out that Mr. Iffrig had never picked up his mother, and that it would be a good idea to send somebody up to where he had gone camping to see whether or not Roxanne was with him."

When Gail discovered via telephone that her husband and Richard Clark were seen heading to the campsite without Roxanne aboard the van, Johnson immediately called a conference with Sergeant Jerry Zillmer and other superiors who had followed him back to the Doll-Iffrig residence.

"Initially," Sergeant James Stillman of the Everett Police Department later commented, "I was called on April first when it came to the police department's attention that Roxanne Doll was missing. Our watch commander assumed duty in the early afternoon of April first. He, in turn, called me because he was aware that I was the acting lieutenant of the criminal investigations unit. He asked for my response, and I responded by going to the Doll residence. There were numerous others there by then also," said Stillman, "including Officer Johnson and other uniformed patrol officers, and Jerry Zillmer, a sergeant with the patrol division."

Detective Lloyd Herndon responded to the victim's residence at 4:35 P.M. after being contacted at home by Lieutenant Peter Hegge, the watch commander at the Everett Police Department. "When I arrived—and Detective Kiser arrived also—I made contact with Sergeant Zillmer, who was on the scene directing a search of the nearby woods."

"Herndon and Kiser had gathered quite a bit of information prior to me getting there," recalled Stillman, "and attempts were made to talk with everyone who was present at the Doll residence. The detectives had to determine who actually had been at the Doll residence before it was first noticed that Roxanne was missing. Unfortunately, some of those who had been at that residence the day prior to her going to bed that night and throughout the night were not present, such as Richard Clark."

"We seriously began to locate anyone and everyone," said Detective Herndon, "who might have had even an opportunity to be at the residence, or might have had some type of knowledge or connection to Roxanne Doll."

Kiser and Herndon were told to focus their efforts on Richard Clark and the other campers accompanying Tim Iffrig. Sergeant Stillman and Detective Costa went to Arlington, Washington, a small town not far from Everett, to locate Willa Doll, Roxanne's grandmother.

"We wanted to know if she had any information or

knowledge as to where the child might be," Stillman said. "We did locate Willa Doll and spoke to her, and also Gail's eldest daughter, Jennifer, who was there also. We found nothing of any value there, as far as information."

Meanwhile, back at the Doll-Iffrig residence, Detective Costa took responsibility for organizing the manpower and plans for the extensive search expanding outward from the home. "He gathered the assistance of Explorer personnel," said Stillman. "Those are teenagers involved in law enforcement, a Scouting-type program. We garnered the assistance of the Snohomish County Sheriff's Office and their resources."

"We had called in the south end and central police units," confirmed Officer Johnson. "We notified dispatch to contact the K-9 units, and we had two K-9 units respond. There was a wooded area; there were several abandoned houses to the west of the residence. We searched every one of those abandoned houses; we searched every car in the used-car lot to the north. Even the trunks of every car were checked. We checked Pilchuck Sports, all of the boats, all of the buildings outside of there."

Johnson personally searched the entire Doll-Iffrig residence, room by room. "Inside the home, with a flashlight, I checked under beds, in closets, moved stuff around, and made sure that she wasn't somewhere in the house. We checked the car outside. There was a trailer and a garage-type thing, and everything was checked, including the neighbors'. We handed out flyers that we made, and we gave flyers to all the neighbors."

Gail Doll, her best friend, Kim Hammond, and brother-in-law William D'alexander drove up to the campsite to find Tim, Richard Clark, and the other camping companions. "At two o'clock," recalled Gail Doll, "we got in Kim's car and went to find Tim."

"We drove up to Granite Falls," recalled Kim. "They were camping up toward Red Bridge and we went up there to try to locate them. We spotted a sheriff's car in the area at one of the campsites up there and we talked to the deputy and told him who we were and asked him to help us. We gave him a description of the van, and gave him a description of Tim. He said he would help us.

"The deputy went one way, and we went the other," Kim said. "We turned around and were heading back up the hill when the deputy flashed his lights and we pulled over. He said that he found them and that they were just up the road."

Kim, Bill D'alexander, and Gail Doll arrived at the campsite to notify Tim of Roxanne's disappearance. "When we first pulled up," recalled Kim, "I really didn't see much of anything because I stayed in the car. I didn't even get out, just Gail and Tim's brother got out of the car. And then Tim and a couple other people came walking up from the river."

"I didn't believe Gail at first when she told me about Roxy," said Tim Iffrig. "I thought it was an April Fools' joke, but then I glanced down and I seen this flyer in her hand and I started to believe. I was scared, and pissed off, and hurt—I don't know, so emotional that—I just really don't know what my emotion exactly was. I just heard my daughter is missing, you know. I was just all stressed out."

Gail Doll, although preoccupied with her daughter's disappearance, noticed that Richard Clark looked different. "He had shaved off his mustache," said Gail, "and he was wearing black-rimmed glasses that I'd never seen on him before." Tim, despite being with Richard Clark on and off since the previous afternoon, noticed nothing.

"I'm not a very observant person," commented Tim Iffrig later, "he could have been bouncing off the walls and I wouldn't have noticed."

The group, shocked by news of Roxy's disappearance, immediately broke camp.

"Everyone was pretty freaked out about what Gail

said," recalled Vicki Smith. "We started packing everything up. As for the sleeping bags, I didn't bother rolling 'em up like normal. I just picked 'em up and folded them in a real hurry and threw them in Richard's van because everyone was concerned with what was going on."

Tim rode home with Gail, and Richard Clark was told to bring Tim's camping gear home in his van. "We stopped at Granite Falls on the way home," said Gail. "We called home and asked if there was any news on Roxy, and to say that Tim was with us and that we were on the way home. We got back about four or five in the afternoon."

"We pulled into the driveway," recalled Iffrig, "and we were lucky to be able to get in there because there were so many police cars, media, and one or two of Gail's friends there. I just got out and I talked to one of the police officers, and if I remember correctly, had somebody else write out my statement with my acknowledgment and my signature because I've got pretty bad handwriting."

Awaiting Iffrig at the house were Detectives Kiser and Herndon of the Everett Police Department. "This wasn't the first time I'd met Tim Iffrig," Herndon recalled. "Shortly after their son, Nicholas, was born, I got called up to the hospital. It seems that Tim had a pet ferret at home. The ferret somehow managed to get out of its cage one night, and it crawled up into Nick's crib." Detectives aren't trained in ferret motivation, Herndon acknowledged, but for whatever reason, the adorable animal found Nicholas's ear an item of interest.

"The ferret didn't make a meal of the ear," recalled Gail, "but the little critter nibbled it enough to draw blood. Nick has little tiny teeth marks on his ear to this day." When Gail and Tim took Nicholas to the hospital, Child Protective Services (CPS), as a matter of routine, was called in as well. The lady from CPS, according to Herndon, told Tim that they were taking away either the ferret or Nicholas—his choice. "I'm keeping the ferret," replied Tim.

"I about cracked up when he said that," admitted Herndon, "because in context it sounded as if he preferred the ferret over his kid, which of course he didn't." Iffrig relented when advised that the ferret was only being taken away "for testing."

"They didn't tell me they were going to kill it; they just said they were going to test it. I really liked that little animal, being my pet and all. I haven't had a ferret since then," said Tim. "I remember that whole thing, but don't recall that it was Herndon who was there—I mean I was more concerned about Nicholas and the ferret than I was with the name of the policeman. It was Herndon, you know, who worked so hard on the case when Roxy was taken," stated Iffrig. "He's a good cop, and a good guy too. Hell of a nice guy, really."

Chapter 4

Outgoing and compassionate, Officer Lloyd Herndon's intended career path led unintentionally to law enforcement. "I never liked cops," Herndon said. "Ever since I was a kid, I didn't like cops. I never thought I would be one. My education prepared me for a career in social work. When it was first suggested to me that I apply for a position with the Everett Police Department, my response was negative. That wasn't what I had in mind as a way of helping those less fortunate than myself.

"Some people struggle all their lives," he explained. "But I never did. I had it easy. My parents weren't wealthy, but they owned a business in eastern Washington. When I got my driver's license, my mom gave me a brand-new car. I went in the service when I was eighteen, and then stayed on unemployment as long as I could. That was my goal—I was gonna party as long as I could until I started college. I went to Edmonds Community College and was working part-time at an auto parts store in north Seattle. The boss was great," Herndon said. "He said that college was very important and he would give me whatever hours I wanted."

Herndon went to school on the GI Bill, and earned his degree in social work. "Right after I graduated, the city of Everett was hiring community service officers—a civilian position. I was hired, and there were five of us. After about fifteen months on the job, it was suggested to me that I become a cop. He kept going on and on about it, and finally I went to the mailbox one day and there was an application. The chief of police had been my sergeant at the time I'd been hired. He told me that if I passed the test, I'd be hired."

Hired, he was. And for nine years, Lloyd Herndon worked patrol. "Then I went right inside, which today is unheard of," he said. "There were four detectives, and within a year or two, the other three retired. So, all of a sudden, I was the senior detective. That's when the Doll case was tossed at me.

"My own daughter, Megan, was the same age as Rox-anne Doll," recalled Herndon, "so the entire matter had a lot of emotional impact on me. Actually, it shouldn't have been my case. It should have been handed over to the Crimes against Children Division. As soon as I real-ized that I went to Sergeant Stillman, but I was told to handle it. Some of the guys in Crimes against Children were a bit miffed about that I guess."

From Herndon's perspective as an experienced police officer, Richard Clark spun his malevolent web of per-verted sexuality and intoxicated ill intent, albeit haphazardly, well before the night of March 31.

"You can get a more clear picture of events, and the relationships between these people," related Herndon, "if you go back to before we got the missing child report on Saturday. When we did our initial investigation, of course, we retraced the steps of everyone involved going back to the previous day and even further.

"The first people we spoke to were the parents, Gail Doll and her husband, Tim Iffrig," said Herndon. "At first, everyone was a suspect. Following the sequence of events, you get good insight into the lifestyles, relation-ships, and how Clark ingratiated himself—how he put himself in a position to commit this horrid crime."

"Richard Clark gave gifts to my children and my

mother," recalled Roxanne's father. "It was only a couple weeks earlier, on the eighteenth or nineteenth, that Richard Clark came over and mentioned that he had some stuffed animals in his van. He asked my permission to give them to the kids. I said that I didn't mind, and he handed me three stuffed animals. I handed all three to Roxanne and she gave her brother and sister two to choose between themselves because she picked one out for herself first."

"He gave me a stuffed raccoon," recalled Roxanne's grandmother, Neila D'alexander. "Prior to this, he had given all of the kids Power Ranger toys."

Neila D'alexander lived with her son, Timothy Michael Iffrig, and his wife, Gail Doll, in a small house just off busy Highway 99 in Everett, Washington. Also in the modest residence were the Doll-Iffrig's three youngest offspring: Nicholas, Kristena, and Roxanne.

Iffrig, industrious and hardworking, put in long hours at the Howatt Company in Everett making interior mats for Kenworth and Peterbuilt trucks. "I was running a dye press ninety-nine percent of the time," said Iffrig. "Every now and then, I would have to go back in the glue room and make glue mats for Kenworth and Peterbuilt trucks."

His workday started at 6:30 A.M. on March 31, 1995. "We were working lots of overtime because we fell behind due to a lack of materials. On that morning, I started an hour early and worked all day."

At the workday's end, Iffrig got a lift home from his production supervisor. "Work was just down the road from my house," said Iffrig. "I got off work about four-ten, so I was home by four-fifteen or four-twenty. When I got home, it was just my mom and the kids and Gail, my wife."

"Tim was just getting home from work," recalled Gail, "when I left with my friend Kim Hammond in her car to go walk laps at Cascade High School."

Tim Iffrig's after-work itinerary usually consisted of changing clothes and immediately picking up around the house or in the yard. "I'm constantly cleaning around the house. I come home; I go straight to picking up the yard or the house or whatever. So, I was either changing my clothes or cleaning, one of the two, when Richard Clark showed up with his younger half brother, twenty-seven-year-old Jimmy Miller."

Gail Doll and Kim Hammond walked two or three laps around the Cascade High School track, then came back home. "It must have been between five and five-thirty when I got out of Kim's car and saw that Richard Clark had arrived in his van. With him was Jimmy Miller. I walked over to the van and talked to Tim, Richard, and Jimmy about the upcoming camping trip," Gail revealed.

"Richard Clark came by to confirm our plans," said Iffrig. "While we were standing there talking, Richard suggested that the three of us—me, Jimmy, and him—go up the street to the Amber Light Tavern and shoot a game of pool. I know it was Richard's idea because it wasn't mine, and Jimmy was too drunk to think of it."

Iffrig, the dutiful husband, asked his wife if he could be excused for a game of pool. "Gail told me that unless my mom would watch the kids, I couldn't go. I asked my mom, but she said no. Then Richard went in and told my mom that he would give her a ride if she would watch the kids while we ran up there to shoot pool."

Neila D'alexander agreed to watch the kids; Tim Iffrig, Clark, and the inebriated Jimmy clattered off in Clark's van to the Amber Light Tavern. "It was a bit embarrassing 'cause Jimmy was falling-down slobbering drunk, and the tavern wouldn't serve him," remembered Iffrig. "Richard and I shot a quick game of pool and came right back home. The tavern was only about three minutes up the road, so we were not gone very long. When we got back, I ran in and told my mom that

Richard was ready to go. She got in the van with Richard and Jimmy and they took off."

"That was at about six-thirty P.M.," confirmed Gail Doll. Tim Iffrig spent time relaxing with his wife and kids before he went next door to visit with neighbors Patrick Casey and his female housemate, Shawn Angilley.

"Actually," recalled Shawn, "I didn't know Tim came over then because I was in bed asleep. I'd been getting up for work every morning at four-thirty. At one point, I was awakened by somebody blasting his horn next door."

While Angilley was still sleeping undisturbed, Tim Iffrig and Pat Casey shared light beers over equally light conversation—typical blue-collar Friday-night camaraderie. "After I drank a beer with Pat, I went back to my house," said Iffrig. The two homes were only a few feet apart. "Every time I left their place, it was always straight back to my house to see whether my house is intact, tell my wife what I'm doing, and so on.

"When I got back from Pat Casey's," Iffrig explained, "Gail and the kids were all together watching *Cinderella*. I went to the back room to sit down, relax, and have a smoke.

"In a bit, after getting the kids off to bed, Gail came back and started talking to me about the upcoming camping trip and her own plans for the evening. She and her friend were going to the movies."

"When the video was over, it was over around eight-thirty," Gail Doll told detectives. "I told the kids to go to bed. Nick went to his room, and the girls went to their room around nine o'clock. I heard the little girls talking and giggling, and I told them to go to sleep."

A loud horn honk in front of the Iffrig house awakened neighbor Shawn Angilley at approximately 9:00 P.M. "When it woke her up," recalled Pat Casey, "she asked me what was going on, and I told her it was someone next door. I looked out the window and saw this yellow van at Tim's, but I didn't know who it belonged to at that time."

"I'd seen that van before," said Angilley. "For the previous two to three days, it was parked over in the field across from the house when I came home from work."

"She was very mad," recalled Casey. "We sat down together and watched some TV, and just then a knock came at the door. I said, 'Come in,' and it was Tim. He asked if it was okay for his friend to come in with him."

Richard Clark's yellow van arrived as Iffrig was walking next door. Tim wouldn't take him to Casey's without permission. "I said that it was okay," recalled Casey, "and that's when he introduced me to Richard Clark. We talked for about fifteen minutes and they left."

"At the time Tim introduced me to Richard," Shawn Angilley said, "I asked him if he was the one with the yellow van. When he said that he was, I told him, 'You're lucky you didn't get your horn shoved up your ass.' He apologized for waking me up."

It was only a few minutes later that Gail Doll drove over to Kim Hammond's. "I left the house, locking it," confirmed Gail, "and went next door to tell my husband that I was leaving for the movies and gave him the keys. After I left, I stopped at the am/pm to get gas, and then went to my friend Kim Hammond's house. Kim, her mother, Sandra Collins, and I went to the Act Three theaters in Sandy's car. The movie started at ten-oh-five P.M. We watched *Muriel's Wedding*."

When Gail left for the film, Tim lingered with Casey and Clark for only a few minutes before both he and Clark went. "He said he was leaving because he didn't want the kids alone in the house," Casey recalled, "and he wanted to make himself something to eat. Richard Clark said that he was hungry too and that he was going to go out and get himself something."

"Richard Clark and I were together the whole time he

was there at Casey's," Iffrig said. "I went home to check on the kids—Richard went with me—then we walked back next door for a minute. I told Pat that I should stay home with the kids, plus I wanted to have something to eat. Richard said that he was leaving to get something to eat too."

The two men walked outside together. "He turned off toward his van," Iffrig said, "and I kept walking toward my house. I saw Richard Clark get into his van and pull it forward, but I didn't actually see him leave because I went into the house."

Tim Iffrig easily admitted that he was slightly intoxicated that evening. "I was feeling quite a buzz going," he said. "I remember I was having problems opening and unlocking my door. I'd had a few drinks, so I wasn't feeling any pain. Now I am not sure, but I think I did check on the kids when I first came home to get something to eat, but I did it just like Gail did. All we ever do is crack the door open, flick the light on real quick, and flick it off. And on that top bunk, it was real easy to think that you are seeing two people if they got a group of blankets or pillows or anything up there."

Tim put some Cajun-style steak in a frying pan, put the burner on low, and sat down on the couch. Tim fell asleep; the steak burned. Detective Herndon's report stated that Gail Doll's husband "passed out on the couch."

"No, I didn't pass out," insisted Iffrig. "I dozed off. I was tired. We are looking at nine-thirty or ten at night after working hard since six-thirty A.M. The intoxication may have helped me fall asleep, but I wasn't passed-out drunk."

After the movie, Gail returned to Kim Hammond's, got into her own vehicle, and arrived home at 12:05 A.M. "The Cajun-style steak was blackened all right—to charcoal. The house was hazy with smoke; Tim was asleep on the couch," Gail recounted to Detective Herndon. "I immediately went into my kitchen and took the pan off the stove. Next, I went to my son's room, turned on the light, and saw he was asleep."

What Gail Doll next said would prove a source of confusion, accusations, and intense legal argumentation. "I went into the girls' room, turned on the light, and saw Roxanne and Kristena asleep in the top bunk. I shut off the light, then slapped the bottom of Tim's foot to wake him up and scolded him for leaving a pan on the stove."

"When Gail entered the residence," reported Detective Herndon, "she checked on the children by opening the door and looking into the room. She stood in the hallway, peeked in, but did not tuck them in or make direct contact with them. After checking on the children, Gail Doll awoke her husband and had a discussion about the burned steak and other problems in their lives, including a lawsuit that was pending against Tim Iffrig. This lawsuit was apparently generated from an insurance company who was suing Iffrig for a vehicle accident which occurred some time ago."

"We sat there on the couch talking and stuff," confirmed Gail Doll, "until about one A.M. when we saw Richard Clark drive up."

"I figure it was at one o'clock," agreed Tim Iffrig. "I don't wear a watch. Anytime I do, I wind up breaking it, so I never know what time it is. But I know that Gail usually gets home about midnight when she goes to the movies."

Gail stayed up and talked to both of them until two o'clock. "I told them that I was going to bed," said Gail. "I put in a movie to help me fall asleep, and I woke up at seven-thirty to Tim telling me good-bye.

"I asked Tim why he was leaving so soon," Gail recalled, "and he told me that Richard had to go get his check and do some more errands for the trip." Gail asked Tim to make breakfast for the children. "He told me that only Nick was up. I suggested that he put cereal in bowls for the kids, and Nick could pour milk for the girls when they got up." When a significant cereal shortage was noticed, Gail said she would make breakfast for all the kids at about 8:30 A.M.

"Tim left, and I got a call from his mother asking me to tell Tim where she was. I told her that he had already left, hung up with her, and got another call from my friend Tammy about a yard sale I was supposed to have this weekend, but I told her that it was called off on account of rain."

The cataloging of seemingly inconsequential details may, at first glance, seem irrelevant to kidnap, rape, and murder. It was upon the accurate recounting of such mundane matters, however, that hinged the eventual capturing and conviction of the person responsible for Roxanne's disappearance.

"The telephone conversation lasted till about eight o'clock," said Gail, "I watched a few minutes of cartoons. That's when Nick said, 'Roxy isn't here.' I got up, asked him what he was talking about, and started looking for her. I called the neighbors' house to see if she was there, and I called Roxanne's little friend Amanda's house and talked with her mother. I called Sarah Austin, another classmate of Roxy's at Fairmont Elementary School. Parents of both kids told me that their kids hadn't seen or spoken with Roxanne today. Then I called my mother, who said to look outside, to search the yard, the trailer, and the camper, which I did."

Gail also called Kim Hammond, her brother-in-law, William D'alexander, her sisters, Patricia Doll and Katherine Martin, before heading back outside to resume what was rapidly becoming a frantic search.

"Gail first called me at about eight-thirty in the morning," said neighbor Shawn Angilley. "She asked me if Roxanne was over here. Twenty minutes later, Gail was knocking on the front door. She asked if I had seen

Roxanne. I told her that I just now unbolted the door Then I called her about a half hour later to make sure she found Roxy, but she hadn't. By that time, Gail's friend Kim Hammond showed up."

Kim and Gail had known each other for thirteen years and were best friends. "Since we are very close, we talk to each other about everything," said Kim to detectives. "Gail and I went to the movies last night. It started at five after ten and we were back at my place about midnight. She went right home. I didn't hear from her again until eight-thirty this morning when she phoned me, and said that she couldn't find her daughter Roxanne. I then came right over."

"Kim and I went out looking and calling for Roxanne," recalled Shawn Angilley. "I never stopped looking for her and handing out flyers until eight-thirty P.M."

"Roxanne Doll was kidnapped out of her bed between the time Tim Iffrig fell asleep on the couch and when Gail Doll got home from the movies," said Herndon. "But with everyone intoxicated or asleep at the time, it was initially difficult to put all the pieces together.

"It was more than an hour or so after Gail and Tim returned from the campsite," Herndon recalled, "and Richard Clark still hadn't shown up. I waited around the victim residence until approximately six P.M. because I wanted to speak to him and any other witnesses who had been involved with the family prior to the disappearance.

"After Clark failed to show, I contacted the station and asked to check computer records for any information on a Richard Clark. According to the father, Tim Iffrig, Richard Clark had just gotten out of jail recently. I was able to narrow down the list of Richard Clarks to three possibilities—in other words, three guys named Richard Clark showed up in our database. Based on prior information obtained from Tim Iffrig, I determined that this

Richard Clark's last known address was on Lombard Street."

It was 6:00 P.M. when Detectives Kiser and Herndon left the victim's residence and drove seven miles to Richard Clark's last-known address on Lombard. "We took Tim Iffrig and his brother, William D'alexander, along with us, since we were going to drive back up to the campsite to check for any possible evidence or signs of the victim."

Iffrig, highly upset, couldn't recall the campsite's exact location, but his brother, William D'alexander, said he could lead the detectives to it with no problem at all.

"First I contacted Carol Clark at her home on Lombard," reported Herndon, "and asked if Richard Clark still lived there at that residence. According to her, Richard did stay there on occasion, but he had not been there on that day. Carol Clark stated that Richard might be at his father's house in Marysville, Washington. I gave her my card and pager number and instructed her to have Richard call me as soon as possible."

The entourage of Herndon, Kiser, Iffrig, and D'alexander headed for the campsite, stopping along the way at the George Clark residence in Marysville, Washington.

"If you're looking for Richard, you just missed him," said George Clark Sr. "He was here earlier, but I don't know if we'll be hearing from him anytime soon." Herndon provided his pager number. "Please have Richard call me as soon as possible," asked the detective, and George Clark promised to do so.

Herndon radioed the police station and asked for an all vehicles registered report. "I soon learned that Mr. Clark's van was a 1978 Dodge with Washington State plates. I advised dispatch to put an attempt to locate on this vehicle, adding that I needed to speak to Mr. Clark and the occupants regarding Roxanne Doll's disappearance."

Thanks to D'alexander, the Red Bridge/Coal Creek

campground site used by Iffrig, Clark, and party was easily found. "It could be best described," recalled Herndon, "as an undeveloped, unauthorized campsite along the main highway. We checked the area with flashlights and could not locate any pertinent evidence, or Roxanne Doll. At that time, there were no other campers in the area, although Iffrig stated that another party of two had been camping near their campsite."

The other party to which Iffrig referred was that of Bruce Hawkins. "I saw this Dodge Van—sort of tan or rust in color—pull into my camp. The driver was a white male with slightly curly, shoulder-length light-colored hair. He was wearing wire glasses," said Hawkins, describing Richard Clark. "There was another guy who said he was the missing girl's uncle," he continued. "He had long hair in back, short on the sides, and a Fu Manchu mustache. The fellow, who might have been the girl's father, since I saw the sheriff drive off with him, had long, dark hair. He was slim, but looked in shape. Then there was a woman, a large woman with a loud voice. She talked real loud. And then there was a Native American Indian, who, I believe, had some top teeth missing.

"Anyway," explained Hawkins, "these folks showed up at my site and they pissed my dogs off, and started saying stuff like 'Don't mess with me or I'll kick your ass.' I grabbed my two very large dogs and I told them to leave. The uncle and I did have a brief scuffle. I did indulge in about half a fifth of Black Velvet at this time," Hawkins acknowledged, "and that's about all."

The detectives returned Iffrig and D'alexander to Iffrig's residence. "Tim was understandably an emotional wreck, as any father would be. He was terribly distraught over the disappearance of his little girl. Of course, everyone at his house was very emotional. Gail Doll, completely drained and exhausted, was out cold on the couch."

On their way back to the police station, Detectives

Kiser and Herndon learned that Richard Clark and his aunt Vicki Smith drove to the police station in Everett, where they spoke briefly with Lieutenant Peter Hegge.

"Before going to the police station, Richard drove Jimmy Miller and his girlfriend, Lisa, back to the house," said Vicki. "I went in the house, but then I said to Richard that I wanted to go into town with him. All my stuff and Tim's stuff was still in the van."

"Vicki Smith was heavily intoxicated at that time," recalled Lieutenant Hegge. "She smelled of alcohol; her eyes were watery; she had trouble walking, and also had the odor of wood smoke, which I attributed to the camping experience. Clark did not seem to be intoxicated."

Hegge told Clark and Smith that detectives were at the Doll-Iffrig residence interviewing everyone who might have information relevant to the search for Doll. He asked Smith and Clark to go to the Doll-Iffrig house and talk to the detectives. Clark agreed to drive Smith and himself there.

Clark drove by the Doll-Iffrig house, but he didn't stop. Vicki Smith personally didn't want to go there. "I figured I would just be in the way," she said. "When Richard saw all the cops there, he just kept driving." Richard Mathew Clark never arrived at the Iffrig residence. After leaving the police station, Richard drove his alcoholically altered aunt Vicki to Carol's house on Lombard. Vicki Smith and he stayed, she said, about four hours.

Vicki told detectives that Richard Clark later gave her a ride to Aaron's Restaurant in Everett. "He just left me there in the cocktail lounge. I don't know where he went or what he did after he left me at Aaron's," said Vicki. "I walked to my daughter's house after the bar closed, and I didn't see Richard again until Sunday."

"I think the next time Gail Doll saw Richard Clark," commented Detective Herndon, "was when he was on trial for murdering her child."

Chapter 5

Vicki Smith's recollections of April 1 are both somewhat accurate and moderately befogged. It is true that she and Richard stayed at Aunt Carol's until late in the evening, but prior to attending Aaron's, the slightly sloshed Smith/Clark duo's destination was the Sports Center. It was there that Clark and his aunt Vicki encountered Richard's longtime associate and occasional criminal cohort, Michael Jaaskela.

"Richard Clark and I are old pals," Jaaskela said. Years of friendly association with Richard Clark provided Jaaskela with a plethora of pleasant memories. "We've done crime together; we've drank together; we've done drugs together. And without getting myself in trouble, we robbed a rental place out in Marysville, and we took a cherry picker and a bunch of tools and other shit.

"We done lots of crime," he said, "lots of bad stuff, lots of drugs, lots of drinking, yes. We partied together many of years—many a times. As for Richard being a big drinker, he's a real hard-core alcoholic. He also does cocaine, methamphetamines, marijuana, LSD, and basically about everything.

"I seen him the night after the abduction of Roxanne Doll," he recalled. "Yes, I seen him at the Sports Center, downtown Everett. I know it was Saturday night, April first, because my lady has the receipt that we got money.

I loaned him money that night and I have a receipt that says the second, that was seven minutes after midnight, so it would be Sunday, so I know it was Saturday night that I saw him."

Despite his acknowledged intoxication, Jaaskela's recollection was remarkably clear. "The Sports Center was closing, so it must have been at least ten or ten-thirty, thereabouts. I know the time because the bartender took a half hour to get me a beer. I was sitting there and I asked Kevin for another beer, but he wouldn't serve me because I was already drunk. I ordered a beer and it took about a half hour before he would give it to me."

The loquacious inebriant downed his beer and was preparing to stumble toward the door when his old pal Richard "Animal" Clark came in. "He had his aunt Vicki with him," recalled Jaaskela. "They were told that they couldn't order a drink 'cause the place was closing.

"The three of us proceeded to go down to the Aaron's Restaurant and Lounge so we could have some drinks down there. It was me, Richard, and Vicki, and we probably got there between ten-thirty and quarter to eleven. We stayed long enough for two drinks," explained Jaaskela. Realizing not everyone conceptualizes time in relation to alcohol consumption, he added, "About half an hour is approximately enough for two drinks.

"Actually, to be precise," he clarified, "I had one drink, Richard had a beer and a straight shot of tequila, and Vicki had a beer, two rum and Cokes, I think. I'm pretty sure. I had a rum and Coke myself."

Richard Clark and Mike Jaaskela left Aaron's together. "We were walking by the First Interstate Bank and I asked Richard, 'Should you be leaving your aunt alone?' I asked if she had any money, and he said she did. I asked him if she had a hundred, you know, he said no. I said, 'Well, she have two hundred?' He said no. I said, 'Well, does she have three hundred?' And he said yeah, she has about three hundred dollars, and I said, 'Well, you're leaving her with some guy down at the bar that you know that could peel her for all her money'. I said she's about three-sheets-to-the-wind drunk, she's literally plastered. And I said, 'Well, why don't we go back and peel her for her three hundred dollars? Let's scam her or steal her three hundred dollars.'"

Richard's response, Jaaskela reported, was uncharacteristically conservative. "He seemed really distant or something. He didn't want to do it. That struck me strange because other times he would have took it. *Boom!* He would jump at the chance to rip somebody off for three hundred dollars, you know."

Perhaps the prospect of peeling his beloved Aunt Vicki violated Clark's moral code. "Oh no, that wasn't it," said Jaaskela. "He don't have one of those. Anyway, I kept on trying to get him to come back and try to go get Aunt Vicki. Why leave her there with three hundred dollars? I stopped him about three times to make sure that he didn't want to go back."

The main reason for Richard Clark's reluctance, Jaaskela believed, was Clark's increased paranoia of the Everett police. "He said he was just afraid the police might get him or pull him over. He was really paranoid at this point about the police pulling him over. He's never been paranoid before about being pulled over, you know, because he don't have a driver's license, he don't have no insurance. He had nothin' to worry about anyway, but he just didn't want to see the police. He didn't want to see the police, period, at all.

"Now, by this time, he was really buzzed. He was pretty well drunk. He was legally drunk," asserted Jaaskela. "From that point, we kept on walking down to his aunt Carol's house and we got in his van and he chopped up some crystal meth and shared it with me.

"I don't remember what he used to chop it up. It was

pretty dark. I do remember that little dog whining and whimpering soon as I got in the van. I do remember the dog just whining and wouldn't shut up the whole time and everything, and Richard picked it up. Like the dog was really freaked out or something. I mean, I don't know what was wrong with it, it just kept on whining and whining the whole twenty minutes I was in the van. That dog was freaked out about something. I don't know. The dog just kept on whining and whining. It was happy to see Richard, but when Richard picked it up, the little black puppy was still whining."

Clark and Jaaskela each snorted a line of meth. "Yes, we did. We both did a line, but maybe close to a half gram of crystal meth. I did a line and he did a way much bigger line. He said that when we were previously at the Sports Center that he had been up the night before doing crystal meth then too. You know, he had not just been up that day; you know, he was up since at least six Friday morning."

The average person, according to Jaaskela, will stay awake for twenty-four to thirty hours after snorting a line of meth. "You just don't go to sleep." Finished snorting meth, Clark and Jaaskela then went to the Buzz Inn Tavern in search of Jasskela's friend Mike. "I had a pitcher of beer, and then me and Richard went over to my house to get some money. My ol' lady only had twenty dollars on her, and Richard wanted to borrow a twenty, but I needed some money too. So my girlfriend, Angela Caudle, took Richard, her, and the van up to the bank."

When Angela Caudle mentioned a ride to the Safeway store, Clark thought she said "south Everett"—the area in which the Doll-Iffrig residence was located. "He said no, and seemed really wigged out about it," recalled Jaaskela. "There was no way that he could go to south Everett. He didn't indicate why or, or any reason, you know, why he couldn't go to south Everett. He was trippin' out or he seemed weird about it, apparently, whatever you want to call it. He made that point clear, you know. He was not giving a ride to south Everett."

At approximately ten minutes before midnight, Richard Clark drove the five to seven minutes required to get back to the First Interstate Bank. "And five minutes to get back," Jaaskela said. "The bank receipt said, like, seven minutes after twelve on Sunday morning."

Twenty bucks was lent to Richard Clark, he returned Angela home, and Jaaskela and he drove back to the Buzz Inn. The object of the exercise was for the three men to go in together on some cocaine.

"My friend Mike was playing a game of pool, and we sat there twenty minutes, and Richard seemed all nervous. He wanted Mike to hurry up because he wanted to go eat, and he wanted to hurry up and go, and we just wanted Mike to hurry up, *hurry, hurry, hurry,* period. You know, just kept on saying, 'Hurry 'em up, hurry 'em up, hurry 'em up. Let's go, let's go, let's go.' I don't know why he was in such a hurry," said Jaaskela. "It seemed really strange that he was in a hurry. Hurry to go somewhere. But he was going nowhere. He was waitin' for his cocaine."

The three men—Clark, Jaaskela, and Mike—all went in on a half gram of cocaine that they purchased from a friend at the Buzz Inn. The three men went out to Clark's van. Mike got in front with Richard, and Jaaskela climbed into the back of the van.

"It was then, when I got in the back of the van, that I got hit by the smell—it almost turned my stomach. It wasn't the smell of dog poop, or dog pee, or dirty socks," he said. "It was kind of like urine, except a hell of a lot stronger and real sick-sort-of smelling. I couldn't tell what it was, but it was bad—really bad. It smelled like fuckin' death back there."

Wincing from the noxious odor, Jaaskela tried to make himself comfortable. "I sat down on some kind of plastic material back there. It was a tarp or a tent, I guess." Even though the van was dark, the lights from the Buzz Inn parking lot provided sufficient illumination for Jaaskela to see what he described as a blue or gray plastic tarp.

The three men went to Mike's house, and down to the basement to do the rest of the cocaine and meth. "We all shared," remarked Jaaskela proudly. "We didn't say much of anything, just sat there and talked about Mike's mom and dad coming downstairs and busting us up and calling Hawaii Five-O on us—the cops. So we took out of there and went upstairs, we got in Richard's van and went back to the Buzz Inn."

Jaaskela and Mike exited the van. "By the time we turned around, Richard was gone," said an irked Jaaskela. "He hadn't said anything to me or Mike about going anywhere, but he sure was in a hurry." Clark ditched his friends outside the Buzz Inn between 1:30 and 1:45 A.M., leaving them to walk home.

Such behavior was uncharacteristic for Clark, according to Jaaskela. "But the whole night he wasn't like himself at all. He was way different—distant, quiet—not at all like he usually is. As a rule, he's real jabber-jaws. You can't get Richard to shut up. Ya know, *yak yak yak*. All the time, flappin' his jaws."

Saturday night, April 1, Richard Mathew Clark was markedly different. "Dead quiet. Like he wasn't there. Weird." Looking back on his former friend's demeanor, Jaaskela was most troubled by Clark's complete silence on the topic of Roxanne Doll.

"He said nothing about the missing child, Roxanne Doll," recalled Jaaskela. "He said nothing of having been camping with Roxanne's father, or that he even knew the girl and the family. He never said nothing about the little girl being missing or anything. He didn't tell me that he had gone camping the previous night with a friend named Tim, or nothing."

Clark's silence, especially regarding the missing Roxanne Doll, preyed heavily on Jaaskela's mind. "Everybody knew that little girl was missing—it was on the news and everybody was talking about it. And Richard, who knew the girl and the family and all that, didn't say a single word about it all the time we were together.

"Why wouldn't he say something to me about some little girl being missing, unless he had something to hide from me?" asked Jaaskela. "You would think he would say something about it right away to his friends. Hell, maybe I might have seen her, or maybe somebody else seen her.

"He never indicated that he went camping up with the little girl's father, Tim," said an exasperated Jaaskela. "We were together four hours and he never said a word to me about nothin'. In fact, he seemed real quiet and, you know, seemed distant that night. Didn't seem the same Richard. It seemed like he was out in left field waiting for a ball that wasn't coming. Seemed like he felt a little guilty. He was just like he was there, but he wasn't."

Following his drug and drink interaction on April 1 with the uncharacteristically distant Richard Clark, Jaaskela discovered an unwelcome memento of their time together—peculiar reddish brown stains all over the back of his pants.

"I noticed that on the back of my ass there was a big mud stain. There were mud stains from about the middle of my back leg right up to the back of my pocket. There was nowhere I was that I could get mud all over my ass like that," he insisted. "I wasn't sittin' nowhere in mud, all time sittin' in booths, chairs or, you know, I wasn't sittin' outside in the mud. I put them pants on clean that day, that morning. I think the stain came from Richard Clark's van. Ya know, when I sat in the back on top of the tarp or the tent, or whatever it was that smelled bad, on that Saturday night, April first."

* * *

April 2, 1995

Detectives and other police personnel returned to the Iffrig residence at 9:00 A.M. to resume investigation. A half hour later, Detective Herndon's pager went off. It was Richard Clark.

"Clark had been instructed by his aunt and his father to call me as soon as possible," Herndon said. "Clark told me that he was at his aunt's house and would wait there for me.

"The first thing I noticed when I met him," said Herndon, "was that Clark had my name and pager number written on his hand. I asked him why he didn't come to the residence like he was asked to, and he told me that he did not stop because he was low on gas and could not make it out to the house. Then I asked him why he didn't page me. Clark responded he did not want to hassle with the police. I asked him if I could search his van, and he said it was okay with him, so I took a good look. I didn't see anything obvious that would belong to Roxanne."

Herndon said years later, "I admit that I had tunnel vision in that search. I wasn't looking for trace evidence. I was looking for something more substantial—shoes, clothes, toys—something that belonged to Roxanne. And I didn't find anything of that nature. I saw two black puppies. There was a small portion of feces on a mattress that was located in the back of the van. The van was also loaded with sleeping bags and camping equipment, which apparently belonged to both Clark and Iffrig."

In recounting his activities the night of March 31 and on April 1, Richard Clark said that the only time he left the Casey residence during the "party" was when Pat Casey and he went out to Casey's garage and looked at an airplane that Casey had disassembled.

"Me, Tim, Shawn, and Pat partied until approximately seven-thirty in the morning," Clark said. "But Shawn's kid woke up and it was time for us to leave. Tim and I walked back to Tim's house and I sat on the couch while he said good-bye to his wife and collected his camping gear. Gail Doll's eight-year-old son, Nicholas, came out of his room and sat on the couch with me," said Clark. "The door to the girls' room was shut and Nick was the only kid I seen. Tim and I left and drove to the north Everett area looking for Neila D'alexander, Tim's mom, who was going to go camping with the rest of us."

"Richard Clark told us," recalled Herndon, "that he and Tim Iffrig had planned a camping trip the following morning and that he was to pick up his brother Jimmy Miller, who was now out on the reservation; Jimmy's girlfriend, Lisa, and Vicki Smith, who was Richard's aunt. They were also supposed to pick up Tim Iffrig's mother, Neila. According to Richard, they could not find Neila D'alexander, so they drove to the Indian reservation, where they picked up Vicki Smith, Jimmy Miller, and Lisa Rader, who is Jimmy's girlfriend. After waiting around at Vicki Smith's for several hours, all drove to the Everett area in Richard's van, where they picked up Vicki Smith's check at Carol Clark's house on Lombard. They then drove to U.S. Bank on Hewitt and cashed the check. After stopping at Rocky's Gas and Grocery for beer and gas, Richard drove to the campsite."

Herndon admitted years later, "I was suspicious of Richard Clark. Everyone was a suspect, and we hadn't eliminated others, of course. But I had strong suspicions of Clark, and not just because he didn't show up at the Doll residence like he was supposed to, or just because he didn't page me. When I ran a check on him, I found out about the incident with Feather Rahier back in 1988. Now that fact wasn't evidence against him in any way. It also wasn't any indication that he was involved in the disappearance of Roxanne Doll. It just gave me what you might call stimulus for reasonable suspicion."

Herndon asked Clark if he would be willing to take a polygraph test concerning the disappearance of Roxanne Doll. "Yeah," said Clark, "but I promised to help my friend Andy do some landscaping in the Marysville area later this afternoon, but I can do it tomorrow."

"I asked him how I could contact him if the polygraph examiner was available later in the afternoon, and he didn't hesitate to tell me that I could contact his aunt Vicki or his father in Marysville, who lives nearby. They could get him a message about the polygraph test."

A quick conversation with the polygraph test administrator revealed that April 3 actually would be more convenient, since the examiner was going to speak to the parents first. At 11:00 A.M., the detectives returned to the Doll-Iffrig residence, and Kiser took extensive photos, including the interior and exterior of the home. Herndon also took VHS video recordings of the residence and surrounding area.

"If you look at the videotape," said Herndon, "you'll see one part where the camera comes around into the girls' room and Roxanne's sister is holding a doll that's almost the same size that she is, and it has lifelike hair. It would be very easy to mistake that doll's head in the bed for another child—specifically Roxanne."

Looking over the photographs of the home's interior, Herndon noticed a smoke detector in the hallway just outside Roxanne and Kristena's bedroom. "I went back to the house specifically to see if that smoke detector was operational," said Herndon.

If the smoke detector was in working order, it should have awakened Tim Iffrig and his children when the house filled with smoke from his burned steak. "The family never mentioned a smoke detector going off," Herndon said. "Well, if someone is sleeping on the couch and steak is burned on the stove, you think a smoke detector would go off and wake that person up."

Standing on a chair, Herndon took the cover off the smoke detector. "There was no battery in it, and it was obvious the battery had been out for some time. The whole inside of the smoke detector had sooted over, or had that nicotine brown residual-type coating on it. And I asked Neila D'alexander about it; she really couldn't provide me with any information with regards to when it was last in operation. But Nicholas said that his father had taken the battery out of it over a year prior, after it had gone off from steam coming out of the bathroom. When that sort of thing happens, it's not uncommon for folks to forget to put the smoke detector back in working order."

Gail Doll and Tim Iffrig were escorted to the Everett Police Department at 1:00 P.M. for polygraph tests. Detective Barry Fagan of the Snohomish County Sheriff's Office interviewed Tim Iffrig; Special Agent Ray Lauer of the FBI interviewed Gail.

While Tim and Gail took polygraph tests, specialist Kelly Bradley interviewed their five-year-old daughter, Kristena. "Kristena was accompanied to the police station by her grandmother Neila," Bradley noted, "and her brother, Nicholas. They were not present, however, during the interview."

Bradley asked, "Can you tell me your full name?" The child answered, "Kristena."

"Do you know your last name?"

"No," she replied, but she was aware that she was five and lived in a blue house with her mom, dad, grandmother, and brother. She also knew that Roxanne was gone.

"Is there anything that happens in your house that you wish you could stop?" Bradley asked.

"I don't know what it is," said Kristena, playing with Bradley's marking pens, "but this color smells good."

"What's the best thing about your daddy?"

"He plays Barbies with me. We play house. He's the dad and I'm the mommy."

"What happens when you play house with your dad?"

"We take care of the kids. Feed them and dress them."

"What is the one thing you don't want your dad to do?"

"Get mad," said Kristena. Asked what happened when Tim Iffrig got mad, his daughter answered, "You go to your room and wait awhile."

Bradley also questioned Nicholas Doll. Neither child gave any indication of unpleasant or inappropriate behavior in the home.

"Kristena's parents were polygraphed that day, as were Kim Hammond and William D'alexander," said Herndon. "I was very eager to hear the results."

Gail's polygraph test lasted much longer than Kim's. "It seemed to me," said Gail, "that Kim's took fifteen minutes and mine took three hours. That might be an exaggeration, but if so, it's not much of one. The guy interviewing me seemed obsessed with the erroneous concept that I kidnapped my own daughter and had her stashed somewhere. They even speculated that I had her hidden her with relatives in Nebraska." Recalling, the event in 2003, Gail Doll shook her head in disbelief. "I leave the house at nine-fifteen and return at midnight, and I'm supposed to have spirited her out of state? The guy kept insinuating that I was lying about Roxanne's disappearance. Maybe that is the technique they use or something, but I found it insulting and offensive."

The polygraphists reported to Herndon that Gail and Tim were both truthful, as were Kim Hammond and William D'alexander. Four individuals were thus eliminated as suspects.

"I contacted Pat Casey and Shawn Angilley, the next-door neighbors, at about six P.M.," recalled Herndon. "They were very cooperative and terribly concerned."

"Tim and his friend Richard returned to our house between twelve-twenty and one A.M.," Angilley told police. "We sat and talked for about forty-five minutes to an hour about Pat's plane. Then Pat and Richard went to the garage to see it. They were out there for about a half hour while Tim and I sat inside and talked. When Pat and Richard came back in, we all sat around talking until around six-thirty in the morning. We were kind of loud, and we woke up my son. Once he was up," she said, "we asked them to go.

"When they left, Pat locked the door behind them. We then went into our room to watch TV. Pat fell asleep and I was watching TV until about eight-thirty when Gail called to see if Roxy was here playing with my son, Chris."

Twenty minutes later, Gail was knocking on Angilley's door. "Again she was asking about Roxy. I called her back in a half hour to make sure she found Roxanne, but she hadn't."

"Casey and Angilley suggested I talk to a thirteen-year-old boy down the street," reported Herndon. The youngster was known as "Bad Boy Roy" and was not welcome at the Casey residence.

Detectives Herndon and Kiser met with the boy briefly and quickly determined that he was not involved in the incident. Returning to the Iffrig residence, evidence was gathered from the victim's bedroom. Detective Kiser was able to lift three latent prints from the exterior of the victim's window located on the North side of the residence.

"Gail Doll took me into Roxanne's bedroom," recalled Kiser "and I observed some things in the bedroom. She pointed out a nightgown that Roxanne had been wearing and some other items."

"I was one of the responding officers that met detectives at the residence," recalled Sgt. Boyd Bryant. "Gail Doll told us that Roxanne regularly wet her bed in the middle of the night. I reached down and felt her mattress. It was dry to the touch. From that, we reasoned that unless she remained dry that night, she had been missing for several hours."

"A couple of hours later," added Kiser, "we began searching around the outside. I believe it was Detective Herndon that decided that maybe we should try to collect some fingerprints, if there were any available, and then we went to the back side of the house, which would be the north side."

It was already dark outside when Herndon and the other detectives made the fingerprint discovery. "Herndon had his flashlight with him—he carried the flashlight, and together we went to the back of the house, on the north side."

A large friendly dog, tethered with a rope, wagged its tail at the officers while they examined the rear of the house. "The dog's presence explained all the muddy smudges on the wall below the kid's bedroom window," said Kiser. "There are four windows on that side of the house. Two of them slide open. The far left window was Roxanne Doll's bedroom window, and we carefully examined it for fingerprints."

Kiser noticed a clear print on the outside of the bedroom window. "Once I noticed it, I took out the fingerprint powder and a brush—it's a very fine brush. And you sprinkle powder, it's a black powder on the area you want to lift the print from, and that's what I did in this case.

"Sometimes when I dust a print," explained Kiser, "I can actually make two lifts from the same print because there is enough powder on there, and that's what I did— I made one lift; then I decided that I would try it again to see if maybe the next time it will be more clear. I was able to make the same lift twice of that one individual fingerprint."

Detective Kiser's fingerprint proficiency ended with

efficient recovery. "I don't have any expertise in reading prints," admitted Kiser. "I submit the fingerprints to someone else. In the Roxanne Doll investigation, as with all others, we submitted the fingerprints to someone especially trained in that science." The "someone else" was James Luthy.

Hired by the Washington State Patrol in May 1988, he classified, compared, and searched fingerprints via the automated fingerprint identification system. "That's a computerized system that allows for rapid searching of fingerprints," he explained. "Also, at that time, I began assisting latent-print examiners with processing evidence in crime scenes for latent prints."

In March 1993, Luthy was assigned to the missing and unidentified persons unit, where he assisted coroners and medical examiners in identifying the deceased. One year later, he was assigned to the Latent Print Unit. Latent means hidden.

"A latent fingerprint generally means a fingerprint left on an object when that object is touched," explained Luthy. "It generally requires processing with powders or with chemicals or with alternative light sources before it can be seen. That doesn't have to be done all the time, but that's typically what needs to be done, and that's why they call it latent.

"There are a variety of methods used in retrieving and comparing fingerprints," said Luthy. "One way is to just photograph it, and then you have a permanent record of it. You can also process it with powders, lightly dusting it with powder and then lifting it, or putting a piece of tape over it, lifting the tape and placing that tape on a white card that would provide for you a permanent record of that impression. You may also develop it with chemicals so it can be enhanced, so you can photograph it and record it that way."

Fingerprints are compared and identified, Luthy

explained, "because the friction ridge skin that we have on the palms of our hands and also on the bottom of our feet is unique to each individual. The ridges that are formed there have unique characteristics—ridges that stop, or perhaps they will fork or divide into two. We call it bifurcation when they divide like that.

"We compare the ridge endings and the bifurcations of one print to the ridge endings and bifurcations of another. That's basically what we do; we compare fingerprints looking for ones that match."

Luthy received the fingerprint lifted from Roxanne Doll's bedroom window. The results of his comparisons wouldn't be known immediately, if at all. "If the person who made that print doesn't have his or her fingerprints on file," he said, "you're not going to find a match."

"The best we could hope," said Herndon, "is that whoever left that print on the bedroom window was the perpetrator, and that the perpetrator either had a print on file, or we would find the person responsible and get a print from them at that time."

Herndon and Kiser packed up all items of evidence, provided or recovered. Included were one roll of 35mm film containing photos of the exterior and interior of the house, two fingerprint cards of the latent prints lifted from the exterior bedroom window by Detective Kiser, one pink Barbie-type nightgown—the last-known item worn by Roxanne Doll found atop the victim's dresser—and one second-grade class photograph of Roxanne and her classmates, plus one note to "Michael" from Roxanne. It simply said, "I need some fun."

When the police drove away, the distraught parents sat outside on the front porch. "It's Richard," said Gail. "I just know it."

Chapter 6

April 3, 1995

The day began with two important telephone calls: Detective Lloyd Herndon called Richard Clark and scheduled him for a polygraph test that afternoon. In turn, Clark placed a call to half brother Elza Clark. The topic of conversation: bloodstains in Richard Clark's van.

Ask Elza Clark how Richard and he are related, and his reply will be as blunt as a bottle and equally reflective. "I dunno. He supposedly is my dad's child. I've known him all my life, and he's almost like a brother." Elza saw Richard Clark on Friday, March 31, 1995, at about noon.

"I was living with my folks. I lived with them for twenty-one years. I had just got up," recalled Elza. "I wasn't feeling good because I had a hangover, and I had been sick for about three days. Richard wanted me to go out with him, but I didn't want to go because I just got paid. I figured he just wanted to go out drinking on my money. Anyway, on Monday, April third, Richard calls on the telephone and said if anybody like the detectives or anybody called, to lie about bloodstains in the van and say that they came from a poached deer."

Poaching deer was illegal. Were Elza to tell police, "Oh, I poached a deer and got blood on the inside of Richard's van," he would be confessing to a criminal act. Elza refused his half brother's request.

"I told Richard I wasn't gonna lie for nobody," said Elza, although he acknowledged that Richard and he had poached numerous deer over the years, and that he had poached one only a few days earlier.

"That day, April third, Richard Clark came to the police department right on time, as promised," confirmed Herndon, "and he gave a further statement to Detective Kiser in addition to the one he gave at his aunt Carol's house."

"I have known Tim Iffrig and his wife, Gail, for about two and a half years," Clark stated to the detective. "About a week ago, Tim and I planned a camping trip. It was the kind of deal where whoever wanted to go could. On March 31, 1995, Friday, I was over at Tim's house putting together our supplies. I left about six-thirty P.M., after being there about two hours. I gave Tim's mom, Neila D'alexander, a ride into north Everett. My half brother, Jim Miller, was with me."

In complete contradiction of known facts, Richard Clark told detectives that Jimmy Miller and he "went back out to Tim's place, arriving at about nine P.M. We picked Tim up and went to the Amber Light Tavern, where we drank some beer and shot some pool. We were gone about an hour. We went back to Tim's and dropped him off. I took Jim out to his girlfriend Lisa's house on the reservation.

"I then met up with Neila at the Dog House Tavern in Everett," stated Clark. "I got back out to Tim's place about quarter to one. At about one A.M., I was talking to Tim and Gail, and I told her who all was going on the camping trip, including my aunt Vicki. Vicki and Tim had an affair in the past and Gail knew it. She told Tim that he had better buy some rubbers. She didn't seem upset and I didn't see them arguing.

"He and I went to his neighbors' house, Pat and Shawn, where we stayed partying until about six A.M. We went back to Tim's house, picked up his camping gear. I remember his son coming out of his bedroom and Tim going into his own bedroom. We left and went looking for Neila, but couldn't find her. We went out to the reservation and picked up Jim Miller, his girlfriend, Lisa, and my aunt Vicki. We made it out to the campsite about two-thirty P.M. About two and a half hours later, Gail and Kim and Bill showed up and told us about the missing girl."

Keep in mind: No one is ever obligated to answer questions by the police, the FBI, or any law enforcement officer. No one is obligated to consent to a search of his or her person or property.

It makes no difference if one is under arrest or not—no American is obligated to even show identification unless they are operating a motor vehicle, or in an establishment that serves alcoholic beverages. The Everett Police Department was not serving alcohol, and Richard Clark was not driving during his interview.

It was at about 10:30 A.M. that Special Agent Ray Lauer of the FBI interviewed Clark in preparation for the polygraph test. The interview took place on the third floor of the Everett Police Department in a little room about ten square feet. The door to the room was unlocked during the interview, and Agent Lauer was not wearing any type of uniform and did not display a weapon.

Clark was told that he was not under arrest and that he was free to leave anytime. Agent Lauer went through a "consent to interview with polygraph form" with Clark, and he also advised him of his Miranda rights using a preprinted form. Clark read the rights form aloud.

The form indicated that Clark had the following rights: he had the right to remain silent; anything he said could be used against him in court; he had the right to talk to a lawyer for advice before questioning and that to have a lawyer with him during questioning and that if he could not afford a lawyer, one would be appointed for him before questioning, if he wished; and that he had the right to stop answering questions anytime.

"During the interview," recalled Special Agent Lauer, "it was pretty much of a question/answer arrangement. There came a point when I challenged Mr. Clark's story. I told him that he wasn't being truthful with me and that he needed to clarify some points and be honest. I talked to him for about an hour from that point on.

"I would like to think that I was friendly toward him," said Lauer, "but at the same time, I was telling him that he wasn't being honest with me, and that he needed to be truthful."

It was the exceptionally muddled middle of Clark's narrative summary of activities, whereabouts, and companions that triggered distrust by Agent Lauer. "He kept saying that he was uncertain about several things," explained the FBI agent. "He was uncertain that he was with Jim Miller and Vicki Smith up to certain points. And then he was certain he was with Neila at the Dog House Tavern, and he was certain that he was with Tim at the Amber Light between nine and ten P.M."

When he dropped off his brother, Richard Clark "wasn't certain" which grandparent was baby-sitting the kids at the Doll-Iffrig house, how many times he ran into Neila that night, or whether it was just Jim Miller who accompanied him March 31 to the Doll-Iffrig residence, or if Vicki Smith was there also.

"He told me that at about four P.M. he went to the Iffrigs' with Jim Miller and Vicki Smith," recalled Agent Lauer, "and that he stayed there until about six P.M., and then went to Marysville to visit Mr. Clark, described as his father. Stayed there for about a half hour, and then went about a block away to see a friend named Andy," said Lauer. "He never mentioned that he went to Pat Casey and Shawn Angilley's house."

"I urged Mr. Clark to tell me the truth," said Agent

Lauer. "During the last hour that we were together, the only thing he said, other than 'I want an attorney,' was 'I didn't hurt her,' or words to that effect. He said it two or four times during that hour."

Lauer performed three polygraph tests on Richard Clark. All three came back as deceptive. "I wasn't surprised that the tests showed deception," said Herndon years later, "but I was pretty surprised to hear Clark's new version of where he was and who was with him on March thirty-first.

"That stuff about Vicki Smith and the Amber Light was completely inconsistent with all the other information we had from other witnesses," said Herndon, "and it completely contradicted Clark's previous statements as well. I mean, it was just totally out of left field. What possible reason could he have for so drastically altering his story? Why suddenly invent the presence of Vicki Smith?"

A possible explanation is that if Vicki Smith had been present that night, he would be eliminated as a suspect. This impromptu addition, wildly divergent from his version of events related that same day, would only stand if Vicki Smith confirmed it. "More than that," said Herndon, "everyone from Tim and Gail to Neila, Shawn, and Pat would have to place Vicki Smith there, and they don't.

"Richard Clark had been at the victim's residence prior to Gail Doll leaving for the movie, and had been with Tim prior to him passing out on the couch," reasoned Herndon. "It was obvious to me that Clark had the opportunity to remove Roxanne Doll from the residence. Besides that, his previous statements provided to investigating officers regarding time and place were not consistent with the times provided by the victim's parents and other witnesses. I knew that he'd been with Tim over at Pat Casey's, that he was at their residence prior to Gail Doll leaving for the movie at approximately nine P.M. Clark did not tell us that when he gave his statement."

Knowing the polygraph results, Herndon placed Richard Clark in an interview room and questioned him again. "The first thing I asked him," said the detective, "was to provide me with the names and any other pertinent information regarding witnesses that had been with him on the camping trip the day of Roxanne's disappearance. Clark told me that his aunt's name was Vicki Smith, and her age and her pager number. Then he told me that his stepbrother was Jimmy Miller, twenty-seven, who lived next door to Vicki Smith on the Indian reservation. Jimmy Miller was apparently living with his girlfriend, Lisa. According to Richard," reported Herndon, "he, Jimmy, and Vicki had gone to the victim's residence at four P.M. on March 31, 1995, to see if Tim was still going camping the following day. He told me that Tim and Gail were not home, but Neila was there with the kids, including Roxanne. Neila told Richard that she wanted to go camping too."

Richard Clark then told Herndon the same new version of events he related to the FBI agent. When the detective admonished Clark for his blatant deviations from previous statements, Richard Clark again asked for an attorney. Herndon left the room, and the next man to enter was not an attorney, but another FBI agent.

Agent Vanderberry attempted to trick Clark into believing that he was Clark's attorney. He told Clark that he was "counsel" and that the police thought Clark knew something about Roxanne's disappearance. If Roxanne were still alive, said Vanderberry, this information could benefit Clark with the police. Clark told Vanderberry that he did not know where she was; Agent Vanderberry then left the interview room and Detective Herndon returned. After speaking briefly with Herndon again, Richard Clark left the police department. "Vanderberry attempted to deceive Clark for the limited purpose of determining if Roxanne Doll were still alive," stated the

Snohomish County Prosecutor's Office, "and, if she were, where she was located."

Prior to this act of deception, investigators sought the advice of Snohomish County chief deputy prosecutor Jim Townsend. He told them that he was troubled by their proposed ruse and advised them that any information they got from Clark could not be used against him.

"I can only advise. I can't order," he said of the police. "But the truth is, I said, 'Go for it.' I felt it was worth the risk. Generally, I think people are pretty much in favor of trying to save people if they can."

Bob Stiles, Everett deputy police chief, said his investigators' decision to try to trick Clark into revealing Roxanne's whereabouts was based on a belief that the child still could be found alive. "The tactic hasn't been repeated since, nor is it likely to be soon. It was highly unusual in a highly unusual case," he said. "Police make their own decisions on investigative tactics and rely on prosecutors for advice only."

The rationale for not honoring Clark's request to speak to an attorney, later advanced by deputy prosecutor Ronald Doersch, was that since Clark was not under arrest, the police were not obligated to honor his request for a lawyer. "A suspect who is in custody and is to be questioned has that right, but Clark was not in custody and was free to go at any time."

"What Doersch said about them not being obligated," explained assistant chief criminal deputy prosecutor Seth Fine in 2003, "is actually the law, as strange as it may sound on the face of it."

"Based on the polygraph results, and his previous criminal history," recounted Herndon, "it was decided that Clark's van should be seized pursuant to a search warrant, which I was to obtain through Everett District Court. When we seized the van, Clark called me on the telephone and asked why we did that. I explained to him that I was obtaining a search warrant for his van, and that it would be returned as soon as our investigation was completed. He was at the point of anger, so I referred him to my supervisor, Deputy Chief Pat Slack. Clark seemed very angry about it."

Detective Herndon completed a telephonic search warrant and was granted approval by Everett District Court judge Roger Fisher at 6:04 P.M. "Sergeant Stillman and I determined that the van would be processed by crime scene team members of the FBI, and the search was to be directed by Detectives Evers and Burgess of the Everett Police Department's Crimes Against Children unit."

"I was provided with the license plate, and discovered it on the twenty-five hundred block of Lombard Avenue," John Burgess said. "I took photographs of the van, I sealed the doors with evidence tape to indicate that no entry should be made, and also to show that with this tape that seals it, that if the seal isn't broken, then nobody has entered after it was sealed. I impounded the vehicle and requested that a tow truck come to the scene. The van was towed to our vehicle service area for the city of Everett."

Special Agent John Reikes of the FBI, based in Seattle, was part of the evidence response team. "At the onset of a missing or potentially abducted individual case, we will respond to assist the local police departments," he explained. "In my experience as an investigator for twenty-eight years and working with missing children cases, in many instances, unfortunately, we find that they have either been sexually assaulted or killed, and we look for hairs; we look for fibers; we look for blood residue; we look for other particular matter. And all this is done microscopically and beyond the capacity of the naked eye."

In the processing of Clark's van, Agent Reikes's naked eye did notice items of significant interest. "There were actually a number of items that were visibly stained," recalled Reikes. "There were stains in the sleeping bag, and discolorations on the sleeping bag, and we discussed having those analyzed."

There was also a pillow and pillowcase, numerous blankets, and other items in the van that were wrapped and sealed in evidence bags, and initialed by Agent Reikes. "We do that for two reasons," he explained. "The first is to preserve the integrity of the evidence. If any hairs or fibers fall off, they'll be contained in the wrapper. And the second is to protect the chain of custody so I can come back and identify the particular item."

Also on the evidence response team was Agent Mark Meinecke of the FBI. "My specific assignment on April third was the taking of photographs and assisting in the search of the vehicle. We took various samples of carpet and drapes and insulation from the van, and we typically obtain samples of this nature for hair and fiber examination later on.

"Typically," said Meinecke, "these samples contain various fibers for hair and materials, and those items would be sent in for examination in the laboratory to match any fibers or hairs that were recovered later."

When Meinecke took drape, carpet, and insulation samples, he had no idea which of them, if any, would be of evidentiary value. "None of the samples taken from the van were selected because we could specifically identify them as being valuable evidence. We took the samples to test for hairs and fibers that might possibly be of evidence."

In addition to FBI agents and Everett police, Michael Paul Croteau of the Washington State Patrol Crime Laboratory contributed his experience as a forensic scientist to the investigation. Trained in biochemistry, Croteau is knowledgeable in blood spatter patterns, and received on-the-job training at numerous crime scenes.

"I examined Richard Clark's van with Ingrid Dearmore, a forensic scientist from our laboratory. We brought two different types of chemical tests for blood. One of them is used for taking a little swab of a suspected bloodstain and testing it, and the other one that you spray—the end product is a bright green color that shows up against lots of surfaces.

"When we go to a crime scene and we are conducting a presumptive test, we are trying to figure out if a stain that looks like blood is really blood. The lab technicians back at the lab will do the actual determination of whether it's human blood or animal blood."

Croteau and Dearmore conducted such presumptive tests on Richard Clark's van. "We removed all manner of items so that the entire inside of the van could be sprayed," recalled Croteau.

While the FBI was processing Clark's van, Herndon returned to the Doll residence. "My purpose was to collect any comparison evidence, such as hair, saliva, et cetera, which could be compared to any physical evidence removed from the van," said Herndon. "I met with Gail Doll at approximately eight P.M. and she provided me with a fingerprint card that had been completed on Roxanne at her elementary school."

Gail also provided an elastic hair tie that contained strands of the victim's hair and Roxanne's toothbrush. Also present was Gail's brother-in-law, William D'alexander, who told the detective that Richard Clark called him that afternoon complaining about his van being impounded.

"He said how screwed it was that he wasn't able to have his van," said D'alexander. "Richard also asked how come everyone thinks that he's involved in everything. He told me that Tim's tent was still in the van. He said that one of the cops told him that he was a definite suspect."

If the cops were suspicious of Richard Clark, he was equally suspicious of them. A man with something to hide needs a place to hide it, and when that something is the truth, the best place to hide is behind a lie. Richard Clark's truth needed more than one lie, and more than one friend or relative willing to manufacture excuses and explanations.

That following day, and for the above-mentioned purpose, Richard Clark paid a personal visit to half brother Elza. "I was outside working on a lawn mower with my dad," said Elza. "Richard and Carol and Jesse and Grandpa all pulled up in Carol's car. Richard again asked me to say that there was deer blood in his van from a poached deer, but I refused. I told him not to talk to me about it anymore. I'm not going to lie. I told him that if anyone came to talk to me about it, I would tell them that I didn't have no deer in that van."

According to Elza, Carol Clark asked him to grant Richard's request and verify the poached-deer story. "I told her the same thing that I told him," said Elza. "I told her that I wasn't gonna say nothing about no deer blood in Richard's van."

Detectives knew nothing of these conversations until four o'clock that afternoon when Jimmy Miller contacted Lloyd Herndon of the Everett Police Department. "Elza told Jimmy and Jimmy told us," recalled Herndon. "According to Jimmy, Richard Clark and Carol Clark had driven to Elza's residence and again had told Elza to tell us about deer blood in the van. According to Jimmy, Carol Clark also emphasized the same thing in regards to the blood. Jimmy added that his parents had told him that Richard had left his white pair of tennis shoes at their house on the evening of April 1, 1995. These white tennis shoes had apparently been left in George Clark's grandson's bedroom. Toni Clark and George Clark observed pinkish or red stains on the tennis shoes. Richard Clark apparently left his white tennis shoes and took his father's black tennis shoes from the residence. According to Jimmy, the tennis shoes had also been damaged. The last time the parents saw those shoes, they were not damaged at all."

Based on prior information, Detective Burgess drove out to the Clark residence and interviewed both parents and Elza. "I drafted a second search warrant," recalled Herndon, "requesting the white tennis shoes located in a bag outside the residence. Richard Clark did his best to hustle up alibis and backup for various versions of his activities and whereabouts on the night of March thirty-first. He was under surveillance by both the Everett police and the FBI."

Chapter 7

"After Mr. Clark's van was impounded," said Detective Herndon, "we called in Vicki Smith for a witness statement. I was pretty sure that she wasn't going to confirm Clark's story that she was along for the ride on March thirty-first, and she didn't."

"I was watching the news on channel eleven at eleven o'clock," Smith told detectives. "Richard and Jimmy pulled in with Richard's van, so it was between eleven and eleven-thirty. They were both pretty intoxicated."

Vicki Smith, admittedly tipsy during the interview, insisted that she was sober the night of March thirty-first. "I wasn't drinking because I don't drink that much, you know, and I was pretty broke, 'cause Saturday's the first of the month and that's when my check comes in. I get monthly grants from public assistance, or DHS or IAU, because I'm a disability from work from eleven and a half years of fishing.

"When Jimmy came in," said Smith, "I told him that his girlfriend, Lisa, was up at the house and he was all excited because he would be seeing her. He stayed there at the house with her, and then Richard turned around and stayed maybe twenty minutes; then he left. That was around midnight. He didn't say where he was going. He asked me if I wanted to go with him, and I said, 'I ain't climbin' in that van with you; you're intoxicated man— you could wipe out somebody and kill me too,' you know."

Smith recounted the drive-by avoidance of the Doll residence following the return from the abruptly ended camping trip, plus her Saturday-night foray to Aaron's Restaurant. "I slept the night at my daughter's house, there on the couch," said Vicki Smith. The following morning, Kenny, her boyfriend, picked her up and took her to Carol's. When she went to retrieve her two sleeping bags from Richard Clark's van, one of them was missing. "I kinda wondered, 'What the hell?'"

She then told detectives about a matter of more-than-minor importance that transpired on Sunday, April 2.

"Jimmy Miller and me, we got a ride to the store," said Vicki. "We went in and got a case of beer, and then we stood out there by a telephone pole." Noticing her listeners' quizzical expressions, Vicki Smith politely explained the telephone pole's potentially lifesaving feature. "Ya see, if you step up by the telephone pole and you stick your thumb out, they have a chance to pull over to pick you up. Okay? Drivers just can't stop in a fifty-or-forty-five-mile-an-hour zone. If they stop all of a sudden, that's gonna cause a wreck, you know?"

As fate would have it, the vehicle graciously pulling over by the telephone pole contained Richard Clark, Carol Clark, seven-year-old Jesse Clark, and Richard's senile grandpa. "It was Richard's aunt's car, I think it's, uh, a Grand Prix," said Vicki. "Carol's dad is real, real old. Man, he's senile. He don't know anything, you know. The little boy was laying down in the seat, and when I climbed in, I kinda put his little feet, you know, over my legs.

"So, he picked me up and I go, like, 'Whoa, what's all this? What are you doing out this way?' And he goes, 'Well, the cops . . . *blah, blah, blah.*'"

"You have to be more clear, Vicki," prompted Detective Herndon. "*Blah, blah, blah,* isn't quite specific enough."

"Well," she responded, "that was it, you know?"

They didn't know; they asked.

"Okay," she said wearily. "He said somethin' like cops are lookin' for him or somethin' like that; I'm goin', 'What the fuck for?' And he says, 'Well, they think I'm the suspect for doing something to Roxanne,' and stuff like that. He seemed kinda nervous and worried. He was just, you know, babbling on and stuff; well, see it's hard for me now because I'm drunk, you know, kinda. But he didn't seem himself, though; he seemed kinda worried, strange, stressed, yeah, that's how you'd say it, stressed, just not himself. And I'm going, 'What?' 'Cause see, I wasn't told at the time about Roxanne Doll, and I didn't know about that other little girl either," she said, referring to Feather Rahier.

It was Jimmy Miller who, earlier that day, asked her if she knew about what Richard did to Feather Rahier back in 1988. She didn't know; Jimmy told her. "What do you think happened back in '88 when Richard abducted that five-year-old?" Herndon asked her.

"Oh, my God." Vicki began sobbing.

"I wonder whose sleeping bag he took that time? Of course," continued the detective, "he didn't have a chance to use a sleeping bag."

Vicki Smith cried harder, imagining what horrid things Richard Clark perpetrated upon Feather and, most recently, upon young Roxanne Doll.

"I'm just a person, okay? And Jim's just a person, and I can't . . ." She couldn't finish the sentence.

"Listen, Vicki," Herndon said, "let me speak, okay? I can't read minds; I wasn't there; I don't know what happened to this little girl. If I knew . . ."

"If somebody did something like that to my daughter, I'd shoot 'em," declared Vicki through her tears. "There wouldn't be any fuckin' jail."

"That's right," agreed Herndon, "and I'd do that; I'd do that if somebody did that to my child too."

"It could happen to my grandson," said Vicki, "and he's not even a three-month-old baby yet."

"That's right, it happens all the time. There are many sick people out here. They don't walk around with a big tattoo on their head saying 'I'm a pervert,' or 'I'm a pedophile'; they're just everyday people."

Vicki Smith controlled her tears, composed herself, and asked Detective Herndon an insightful question: "How did my daughter know?"

"What do you mean?"

"She told me when she was fourteen years old," explained Vicki. "She said, 'I don't trust Richard, Mom. I asked her why and she says, 'I just don't trust him, Mom.' Nobody had ever told me about that little Feather girl. Nobody, nobody, told me about her until this morning. Jimmy told me. He said, 'Aunt Vicki, do you know anything about what Richard did to that little five-year-old little girl?'"

"Would you cover for Richard?"

"I wouldn't cover for anybody that would do anything like that to a little girl. I wouldn't. If Richard did do it, he needs to get some help."

"That's right, he does. And . . . and he doesn't need people covering up for him. Right, Vicki?"

"That's right," she agreed through tears. "I'm not going to cover up for nobody."

"And you're willing to take a polygraph test? Okay, the sleeping bag, you're willing to show us the sleeping bag that matches the one missing from the van and possibly turn it over to us?"

"You can have it," she said willingly. "You can have it. Anything to help, okay? You can have it. It's in the back of my truck, where I put it after I took it out of Richard's van that Sunday morning. It's locked. My boyfriend, Kenny, has the keys. If you meet us over there in a little while, you can have it. It has not been out of that truck since I put it out of the van into the truck."

The tearful Vicki Smith left the Everett Police Department after providing a taped, transcribed, and signed statement. "We originally were going to polygraph her that day, but we didn't do it," recalled Herndon. Her honest emotions bespoke volumes, and detectives had other urgent evidentiary matters. "Our next stop," said Herndon, "was Carol Clark's house."

Carol Clark answered the door and allowed officers into the residence. "She also provided keys to the garage and shed," Herndon recalled, "which was searched by the Washington State Patrol and Detective Olafson."

"They were taking pictures of our home; they were out in the garage," recalled Carol Clark. "They were knocking at the door, they were taking pictures of my car and everything, and they were seizing things. The police came and searched the garage, I think, three times, and the house once."

"Detective Kiser and I went through Richard Clark's clothing and attempted to locate any that had possible stains present," said Herndon. "According to Carol Clark, she had washed all the clothes, but we did locate some clothing with stains on them. These were secured, packaged, and impounded. While on the scene, it was determined that Carol Clark's vehicle should be searched for any trace/evidence."

This vehicle was not included on the initial warrant, but Carol Clark voluntarily consented to a complete search of her vehicle. All evidence located by Detectives Herndon and Kiser was located to the southwest corner of the residence. "Apparently, Richard Clark maintained a dresser by the washer and dryer that contained his clothing, and several boxes were on top of this dresser," Herndon reported.

Clark's Dodge van, held at the Everett service center, would undergo yet another round of scientific scrutiny the following day, subsequent to another search warrant, and Detectives Burgess and Phillips were dispatched to the residence of Toni and George Clark to collect one pair of white tennis shoes left there by Richard Clark on the night of March 31.

There was other surveillance shadowing Richard Clark in addition to local law enforcement and FBI agents. Representatives of Everett area media were also tracking the "likely suspect," Richard Clark.

"The attention her family was receiving from the media," said Detective Burgess, "was very upsetting to Carol Clark. In fact, she called and complained to the Everett Police Department. I wasn't available when she called, so she left a message. On April fifth, I called her back. She didn't come to the phone, but Richard Clark did."

"My aunt Carol isn't available," Clark said. Burgess then asked Clark if he had been in touch with an attorney. "I've got an appointment with one at three o'clock."

"If the news media is bothering you," Burgess told him "and if the news media are causing problems in regards to contacting an attorney, I can arrange transportation for you."

"Well, at this point, I don't need no transportation, but I'll get back to you if I need that, okay?" The conversation concluded, Burgess went about his business. A few minutes later, he received a phone call from Richard Clark.

"When they searched my van," asked Clark, "did they find any evidence?"

"I can't comment on that, Mr. Clark," replied Burgess, and the conversation ended. Clark, however, had another important conversation on his agenda—a face-to-face sit-down with Tim Iffrig's part-time paramour, Clark's aunt, Vicki Smith.

"It was between five and six in the afternoon," recalled Vicki. "I was doing laundry. Richard and his aunt Carol arrived in her car. She waited in the car; he got out and started walking over toward me. That little puppy of his was tagging along."

Smith was carrying a basket of laundry from the house toward the clothesline behind her trailer. "I walked right past Richard without saying a word to him," she said, "and he asked 'What's the matter, you mad at me or something?'"

Smith replied honestly, "Yeah, I am mad at you. I had to go to the police station to fill out a statement." She didn't tell him of her tearful conversation with detectives regarding her shock of hearing about the Feather Rahier incident, nor her fears that Richard Clark kidnapped Roxanne Doll. Her statement, of course, contradicted Clark's sudden improvisation to Agent Lauer that she was with him all of Friday afternoon and evening.

"What did you say to them?" Richard asked Vicki.

"The truth."

"You did?" Richard was visibly disappointed. "Did you tell them that I was with you Friday night?"

"No," said Smith. "I wasn't with you Friday night because you were drunk, and I don't ride with nobody when they're drunk."

She later commented, "I was mad at him because I felt that he wanted me to lie for him. I looked him in the eye and I said, 'Richard, did you do something to that little girl?' He didn't answer me. He just stood there with this scared look on his face."

Just then, Jimmy Miller and his girlfriend, Lisa, showed up. Vicki had already shared with Jimmy and Lisa her concerns about Richard and her conversations with Detective Herndon. Richard, perhaps seeking comfort, acceptance, or camaraderie from his brother's girlfriend, followed Lisa into the house. If acceptance was his goal, it was not achieved. Lisa turned on him with unmistakable disgust. "Leave," she demanded harshly. "Leave right now and don't ever come back."

Richard Clark said nothing in response. He stood there as stoic and silent as when Angela Rono beat upon his chest. He reached down, picked up his puppy, walked out of the house, got into Carol's car, and they drove away.

"Surveillance team members informed us that Richard Clark had gone to Vicki Smith's residence on April fifth at approximately four P.M., along with his aunt Carol Clark," said Herndon. "We drove out there and spoke with both Vicki Smith and Jimmy Miller, asking them about Richard's visit. To say they were not exactly thrilled to see him would be an understatement.

"The way we heard it, Richard told Vicki that she had been with him Friday evening on March 31, 1995. Vicki told Richard Clark that, no, she had not been with him Friday night and for him not to ask her to lie, and, I guess, Lisa went up to Richard and told him to get the hell out of there."

The question of blood in the van was again raised at 5:15 P.M. when the Washington State Patrol crime scene team reported that their examination of Richard Clark's van revealed numerous bloodstains. "They told us that this was a presumptive test," said Herndon, "and we wouldn't know until the next day if this blood was of an animal, such as from a poached deer, or human, as from Roxanne Doll."

Meanwhile, the physical search for Roxanne Doll continued unabated in an area of woods close to both the Doll-Iffrig residence and Tim Iffrig's place of employment. "Richard Clark had knowledge of this area," Herndon reported, "and both he and Tim had been in this area cutting wood in the past."

The woods surrendered neither Roxanne nor clues to her whereabouts. The physical trail from Doll's bedroom window to her current location was nonexistent. Each passing day reduced hope of finding her alive.

"Everyone was doing all they could; everyone was co-operative," said Herndon. "But there was definite confusion as to Jimmy Miller's presence with Richard Clark at various times in the evening. For example, Clark mentioned picking up Jimmy Miller hitchhiking, and he even told Jimmy the same thing. None of this corresponded to other witness statements."

It was time for a more intensive interview with the seldom-sober Jimmy Miller. "We needed to reconstruct Richard Clark's time line of activities on that Friday night/Saturday morning," recalled Herndon, "and Jimmy was supposedly along for the ride just about everywhere."

April 7, 1995

Jimmy Miller, the man too drunk to be served, gave police his best shot at cooperation. "I had drank about a case of beer," said Miller. "I don't remember going to Tim's house, the Amber Light, the Dog House, or being with Richard that entire evening. He may have dropped me off," Miller said with a shrug. "I may have left on my own and he could have picked me up on the street, or found me hitchhiking.

"I remember getting to my aunt's," he said as if pleased at the accomplishment, "but I don't know what time I got there. Later, Vicki and Lisa told me that it was about eleven or eleven-thirty P.M.

"The reason I don't remember nothing is I was drunk," stated Jimmy Miller reasonably. "I was so drunk that I blacked out the whole evening. I can't honestly say what happened."

His honesty in the matter was unquestionable. His

prior proven alcoholic behavior, substantiated by friends and family members, attested to Miller's veracity. "Oh yes," confirmed his mother, "he's had them blackouts while drinking right here in the house."

As a matter of record, his drinking began once he left his parents' house on March 31. "They don't allow no drinking in the house anymore," said Miller. "I was over at my folks'—Toni and George Clark—doing some laundry and watching the soaps when Richard showed up about two in the afternoon."

It was common for Clark and Miller to go out "drinking and driving whenever we had the money," said Miller. It was usually Clark who financed these absurd excursions in irresponsibility by "pawning stuff, unless he got the money some way," explained Miller. As for drug use: "We might have smoked a little pot if we had it, but it would depend if there was enough money after buying the alcohol." Purchasing alcohol, confirmed Miller, was always the number one priority.

"As far as I could tell," Miller told the detectives, "Richard had been drinking before he came to my parents' house. Me and him drank pretty much the same amount, as far as I could tell, unless he had a head start on me. But after we hooked up, I drank about half the whiskey, and he drank about half the whiskey, and we shared a case of beer."

With no particular place to go, the two men simply got drunk behind the wheel of Clark's van. Miller's tolerance prior to unconsciousness was significantly less than Clark's. Two hours later, when Tim Iffrig came home from work, the two inebriants showed up. According to all accounts, Jimmy Miller was already "falling-down drunk." Richard Clark, however, seemed unfazed by his equal ingestion.

Miller's memory of events receded into an alcohol-induced fog—he only recalled leaving home with Clark, drinking with Clark, and arriving back home around

11:00 P.M. "The next time I seen Richard was about eleven the next morning when he pulls up in his van with Tim for us to go camping."

"Miller couldn't tell us anything," said Herndon. "And he couldn't confirm anything in terms of time or whereabouts due to his condition on that night." At approximately two-fifteen P.M. the Washington State Crime Lab's Greg Frank called with an important message—the two bloodstains in Richard Clark's van were of human origin. "This blood," said Franks, "was located on a piece of carpeting in front of the van's cargo doors on the passenger side and on a pair of socks, which were located balled up in the van."

This new information gave Everett police exactly what they needed to place Richard Mathew Clark under arrest. "Based on the conversation that Richard had with Elza regarding him telling police that any bloodstains were from a deer, and the fact that this blood that had been located in the van was from a human, it was determined the he would be arrested for tampering with a witness; that witness being his own brother."

The Snohomish County prosecutor prepared the arrest warrant, and Detective Herndon located Richard Clark at, of all places, the Department of Corrections. "He was sitting in the lobby," recalled Herndon, "I arrived with Captain Lenny Amundson, Officer Rick Wolfington, Sergeant Zillmer, Sergeant Stillman, and Detective Phillips."

If Clark thought it was mere coincidence that some of the most significant individuals in Everett law enforcement happened to enter the DOC, such fantasies were soon dispelled.

"We told him that he was under arrest for tampering with a witness," said Herndon. "Then I read him his rights, and he told me that he wanted to consult with an attorney and did not want to speak with me." As Clark was under arrest, his request was honored.

"Officer Wolfington transported Clark to the Snohomish County Jail, seized all of Clark's clothing, and turned that clothing over to Detective Duvall, who impounded it. Following the booking of Richard Clark," Herndon reported, "myself and Detective Phillips contacted Carol because she also spoke to Elza Clark about the alleged deer blood."

"Richard did not say that Elza was to tell police that any bloodstains were from a poached deer," insisted Carol. "Richard told him to get rid of any venison from their house before the police bust Elza for possession."

"Carol denied saying anything to Elza about deer blood," said Herndon, "and the interview was terminated after she became very upset and uncooperative. We left and returned to the police station where, at about seven-thirty P.M., I got a phone call from Chris Legaros, a reporter with KIRO-TV in Seattle.

"Legaros had received a voice mail from a male stating that a letter was being sent and that a hair was in the letter," recalled Herndon. "The caller also stated something about a knife, but was not specific. Legaros stated that after receiving this voice mail, he went to his mailbox and discovered a letter with no return address. Legaros opened this letter and discovered a second envelope inside."

Legaros stated that he would dub a copy of his voice mail onto a cassette tape and would have that delivered to Herndon the following day. Despite being behind bars, Richard Clark had plans for the following day as well—he was going to give Elza Clark a piece of his mind.

April 8, 1995

"Will you accept a collect call from an inmate at the Snohomish County Jail?" Richard Clark placed the call from jail to George and Toni Clark in Marysville.

"Well, he mostly wanted to talk to Elza," recalled Toni Clark. "He wanted me to tell Elza that he was a liar about the bloodstains, 'cause he never asked Elza to lie for him about the bloodstain. And then he started talking to me about deer blood. He said that he didn't say anything about deer blood to Elza, and then he says something to me about, I better get the deer meat out of the house, and I said, 'Richard, there's not any deer meat in this house; there never has been. 'Cause it hasn't been since hunting season. And then he wanted me to have Elza get ahold of his attorney and tell his attorney that it was a misunderstanding in their conversation about the blood in the van and that Richard never said nothing about that."

Toni told Richard that Elza was not going to honor that request. Richard Clark's reaction was immediate—he started yelling. "He was yelling about all sorts of things," she said. "I couldn't hear them all. I set down the phone and ran into the other room and turned on the recorder on the message machine to catch it all. He was really yelling."

When Richard calmed down, Toni Clark asked him about the bloody sock found in his van. "How did they know how it got bloody?" said Richard. "It could be that I cut my ankle or something."

"Well, a DNA test will find out if it's your blood or not," replied Toni.

"Richard was real quiet for a little while," she told detectives, "and then he said, 'Yeah, I guess they will. The truth will come out sometime.'"

Later that same day, April 8, Wesley Coulter saw children running up from the wooded area across East Grand. Two little girls were screaming and crying. Their sobs didn't result from sudden fall or a friendship fall-out. They cried because they had found the dead body of Roxanne Doll.

Part 2
MURDER

Chapter 8

"We were looking for blackberries," one little girl later told police. "We knew there were lots of blackberries down that trail because we had picked them before."

"It was about seven o'clock when we decided to go play at the forest-kind-of-type thing," said nine-year-old Sheena Tobias, referring to herself and playmate Siobian Kubesh. "First we went to Garfield Park and then we were going to go over to another friend's, but Siobian didn't want to go there, so we went down to that forest place. People dump all sorts of stuff there—leaves and things like that. Well, we were walking down and Siobian saw a skate—a roller skate or something. At least she thought she saw one, but we didn't know if it was a skate or not. We walked down further and that's when we saw it."

"Sheena and I were walking side by side," added Siobian. "I thought I saw a skate. We went around to the other side of the bushes, but we couldn't find the skate. On the way back up the trail, I saw this human's foot. It was under some grass clippings," she said. "It looked like a kid's foot. I screamed, and there was other kids on the other side that we just came from and they heard me scream and they asked what was wrong and I told them that I saw a foot, and they came running over.

"Sheena was standing next to me," the youngster recalled, "and I didn't know what to do. I was just standing there. Sheena pulled me out of the bushes and said, 'Get on your bike, we're going home.'

"We did go home, and we were in tears all the way. There was these people that saw and they called in to the police before us, because they could get home before us."

Wesley Coulter stood atop his pickup truck, keeping an eye on his friend's kids who were playing down the hill. He heard the screams and saw the two crying girls accompanied by his friend's sons.

"A mechanic friend of mine lives near there," said Coulter. "We were working on a transmission for a car of mine. I was asked to keep an eye on my friend's children—his kids were down the hill looking for their bicycle helmets, I was standing in the back of my truck, because that was the only angle I could get to see where they were at. And I guess that's how I saw what I saw," Coulter said. "There was some kids playing on the hill that drops down toward where the train tracks are. I saw two girls come up the hill, and they sort of were coming toward me, and then I saw my friend's two boys come up the hill toward me. And as the girls got closer, I saw that they were kind of hysterical, crying, and looked upset. And then my friend's kids came to me and kind of looked—well, his oldest son sort of looked perplexed, not so much upset, but just confused. I asked them what was going on. He told me that they had seen a foot. I asked him if it were a real foot, and he gave me a weird look and told me that he certainly thought so.

"On about every other telephone pole in all of Everett, there was a poster of Roxanne Doll on it, so I just had a feeling; so I grabbed my phone out of my truck and I went down to where they were playing at, and then my friend's son, Kyle, showed me down the path to where, where this person was. I saw some little toes sticking up out of the grass. I looked at them, didn't believe that they were real."

Coulter grabbed a tree limb and prodded the foot to see if it was indeed real, or that of a doll. It was real. "I was filled with anger when I touched the toes and I knew for certain that Roxanne had died."

Officer Anthony Britton was the first Everett police officer on the scene. "I didn't approach the body a that time," he said. "I saw a brushy, leafy area of sticks and debris, with a partial human foot sticking up out of the dirt. What I saw that day was five toes. I didn't see any further down the foot than the ball of the foot. The foot appeared to be of a small young human, I would say seven or eight years old. It was very white, not pinkish skin like we would see on a live person. It was what I would expect to see of a dead person's limb," reported Britton.

Sheena and Siobian returned to the site with their mothers and talked to the police. Awaiting them was a television news crew. The cameraman took pictures of the two young girls—pictures that were repeatedly broadcast on the Seattle-area television news.

"After their faces were on television," said Mrs. Kubesh, "they were scared and worried that someone would come after them. For quite a while, they didn't want to leave the house. My daughter was very afraid."

While the youngsters gave statements to the police, Officer Britton did his duty with utmost efficiency. "My area of responsibility at that time was to make everything stop—preserve that scene and make sure nobody goes in there and make sure nothing is disturbed. I suspected whose body it was," Officer Britton said. "The entire community was enthralled by this thing, and the way the dispatch had come out, and the fact that the sergeant of the major crime unit was going to be the second going in, indicated that there was something going on."

The site was not completely unfamiliar to Officer Britton. "It's a hillside that takes you down to Burlington Northern property down there," he said. "It's completely wooded and, I guess, it's an area where kids play in that neighborhood. They have paths and stuff that go down to the tracks and they had bridges and stuff that went across the ditches down below. It's just a place to go and ride their bikes, I guess."

Five minutes after Britton arrived, Sergeant Peter Grassi was on the scene. "I was advised of where the possible body was," said Grassi, "so then I walked down to that area. There is a path that led over to the bank. Initially I went in by myself—they pointed out where it was and they kind of described where it was located, so I went in myself and looked."

As a trained professional, Grassi took precautions not to contaminate the scene. "You try to take and walk down the area that you figure any suspect might not walk down," Grassi explained. "So with this path, there was a well-defined path there, so I walked off to the side of the path, along the edge, so there wouldn't be any disturbing of any possible evidence that was on the path.

"What I did next," said Grassi, "as I couldn't get real close to it—it was down over a little embankment—I found a piece of an old branch that had been discarded there and took it and used it to prod the foot. And from doing that, then I could tell that it was a foot of a human. I carefully backed out of the area. I advised the other officers that were there at the scene that there would be no more entrance into the area and that we were going to start putting up barrier tape to seal off the crime scene. I had Officer Lineberry take some photographs of the general area, and Officer Britton put up the crime scene tape. We also called in the crime scene team members, and also requested assistance from Snohomish County Sheriff's Major Crimes Unit, the Washington State Patrol, and search and rescue—we were going to use their helicopter to get some initial overview scene photographs that night."

"As requested," recalled Britton, "I took steps to secure the area. My first responsibility was to keep people out of the area," he recalled. "I set flares a block out in all directions, and I blocked the intersections of Twenty-second, Twenty-third, and Twenty-fourth and Grand."

Britton took out police tape and set an inner perimeter by tying it around street poles, cars, and any other physical item that served the purpose. "We wrapped it around telephone poles through street signs, whatever we had, over to the school bus stop and eventually we went way down. Our flares were burning out, so we needed to set something solid.

"Once those perimeters had been set," Britton explained, "I took on the responsibility of opening a major scene log. That's a log that everyone has to sign as they come into the crime scene so we know who's been there, why they were there, when they came, and when they left. And it was my responsibility to sign everybody in and everyone out.

"Sergeant Grassi pretty much had his hands full," Britton said. Sergeant Stillman came on the scene and Britton signed the log over to him. "I was then reassigned to the east side of the area. That's down where I spoke about, with the Burlington property, as it goes down the hill, the tracks and all that are down there. I was assigned just to hold perimeter down there. Detectives had not set the perimeter through the woods yet, and I was assigned down there just to keep anybody out and just to protect that. That's my area of responsibility. We set up lights down there so that the hillside was lit up so we could see. And I believe, I was probably there about two hours—until about ten or so when Officer Atwood came and relieved me of that duty and I went back on patrol."

After all the detectives and different agencies arrived, Sergeant Peter Grassi held a briefing. "At that point, everybody was given what assignments they were going to have to do at the crime scene," he recalled. "I was involved in that. On our crime scene response team, I usually call in a team leader. That person is responsible for the actual hands-on work of the crime scene people and I'm there to facilitate. At that point, it was essentially Detective Woodburn who took over."

The body, true to professional crime investigation protocol, was not removed. All professional law enforcement personnel know that you don't move the body until absolutely necessary. "You only get one chance to study the victim's body in the context of the crime scene," explained Detective Herndon, "and once the body is moved, that opportunity is lost forever. You secure the scene, you guard the scene, and you process the entire crime scene, including the body, in the clear light of day."

Key to the investigation of a violent sex crime is the science and art of profiling both the crime scene and the offender from the physical and psychological evidence. The methodology is based on Locard's Principle of Exchange; anyone who enters the scene both takes something of the scene with them and leaves something of them behind. This means that what you recover from a crime scene gives you an impression of the individual who committed the crime.

According to forensic pathologist Brent Turvey, profiling the crime scene may give investigators a more narrowed pool of suspects, insight into motive, and linkages of a given crime to other similar crimes. "The opportunity to profile an unsolved crime," insisted Turvey, "is not to be ignored or wasted."

"The chances of destroying or disturbing any type of evidence must be avoided," said Grassi. "We decided to wait until the light of the next morning before processing the crime scene."

Gail Doll and Tim Iffrig knew about the gruesome discovery on East Grand prior to official notification by Everett police. "Somebody from the *Seattle Times* called to ask me if I knew why Officer Woodburn had left his dinner table to go to East Grand. After that, Detective

Herndon came out and informed me that they had found a foot and that they didn't know if it were Roxanne or not, but there were no other children missing in that area at that time."

"Yes, that is exactly correct," confirmed Herndon. "The fact that we had no other small children missing, myself and a police chaplain went to the victim's residence and advised the family that we believed we had found their daughter, but it wasn't positive."

The further processing of the crime scene began in earnest the morning of April 9. Sergeant Grassi arrived at 4:00 A.M. "Going back that early, what I did was start setting up, getting equipment ready. The detectives were not due back until about six A.M."

Present on-site the morning of the ninth was Dr. Eric Kiesel, the pathologist who would perform the autopsy on Roxanne Doll. "The feet were visible. It was still difficult to see the body because it was covered with dirt and vegetation, but parts of the body were exposed."

Dr. Kiesel didn't notice much blood, either on or around the body. "Regarding the lack of blood, well, the body was covered with vegetable matter and dirt, so I really wasn't seeing much blood at all, and I didn't examine the surrounding foliage or whatever was underneath or near her to determine if there was any blood present. The process of packaging the body, especially in a scene like this, is to package the body in a way not to disturb what's beneath her too much; this is why we rolled her and placed the evidence sheet as we did, and rolled her and lifted her."

When the body was carefully examined on-site, an identification bracelet was clearly visible on the body's wrist. The name on the bracelet was Roxanne Doll. "Roxanne's ID bracelet says 'I love you' in several different languages," recalled Gail Doll. "She had picked it out in September of that year. They sent out a flyer on them from school."

"The presumptive identification of the body," confirmed Dr. Kiesel, "was done by the ID bracelet, the physical description; the clothing, and the fact that we only had one little girl that age missing at this point in time. So we made a presumptive identification, and we always look for a more objective method to confirm our presumptive IDs, since visual identification would be difficult, because of the decomposition."

"After that excavation, and the observation of the ID bracelet on the victim's wrist," recalled Detective Herndon, "Detective Stillman and I went back to the victim's house and spoke with the family."

Herndon acknowledged that he was very uncomfortable at the time of this contact. "No one enjoys telling a family that you've found their child dead—and I have never, ever been comfortable delivering notification of death. I just wanted to get out of there as soon as I could.

"Stillman and I got out to the house, and it was full of people—family and friends being supportive—and Gail asks, 'Did you find her? Did you find her?' and I said, 'Yes, I think we found Roxanne.' Well, everyone is asking a hundred questions and I just wanted to get out of there."

Herndon and Stillman were about to walk out the door when Gail Doll called out, "Detective Herndon, may I ask one last question?"

"Sure," he replied, "what is it?"

"Do we get the reward money?"

Gail Doll's question, seemingly shocking and situationally incongruous, was not an expression of greed, or avarice, but resigned practicality.

"Roxanne had been missing for over a week," said Gail. "By then, I felt in my heart that if they found her at all, she still wouldn't be coming home. I knew they were looking for her body—a precious, little body that we couldn't even afford to bury. We had severe financial problems. I had no idea how we could pay for her funeral," she said. "The reward money, if ours, would allow Roxanne to be buried in a deserving manner. I thank God that many people, compassionate people, came forward and helped us out. Baxter's South, a local tavern, did a fund-raiser for us to help us cover expenses.

"In addition to the cost of the funeral itself," said Gail, "the children had no formal clothes appropriate for a funeral. Kim, bless her heart, got me out of the house and down to the Bon Marche in the mall to pick out clothes for Nicholas and Kristena to wear to the funeral."

Customers, recognizing Gail Doll from television news coverage, made disparaging remarks that she easily overheard. "They were saying things such as 'Her daughter's been murdered and she's out shopping.' My God, what was I supposed to do?"

"It's true," confirmed Herndon. "I got calls from customers at the Bon who told me that they thought Gail was involved in her daughter's death because they saw her shopping."

"I was numb, not only from the horror and shock of my baby being kidnapped and murdered, but from the hate mail and phone calls we received," stated Gail.

The insensitive and the unstable heaped abuse on Roxanne's family. "There is only one person responsible for my daughter's death, and that's Richard Clark," said Gail. "The fact that I went to a movie that night, or that Tim fell asleep on the couch, had nothing to do with the acts and actions of Richard Clark. If he hadn't done it that night, he would have done it another night. He came in through the bedroom window, abducted her in her sleep, and took her away. Tim and I could have been in bed in the next room and it wouldn't have made any difference.

"We were criticized for not crying enough on TV," recalled Gail sadly. "The worst hate mail we received," she said, "was directed at my husband. Tim was devastated by what happened to Roxanne, and it really hurt him to get hate mail accusing him of raping and murdering his own little girl."

The hate mail, hurtful and cruel, added emotional insult to the personal pain of child loss. Caring and compassionate, however, were the outpourings of support and sensitivity. Some of it was poetic.

Doll
I've seen her picture for days
Roxanne Doll, age 7,
school photo beaming brightly with an unforced smile,
teeth erratically spaced,
with big, blue, painless eyes like warm blueberries,
hair thin and blonde, long in back.
Unlike the coloured TV picture,
the Xeroxed black and white flyer is stark.
Bright bouquets reduced to shades of grey on a white dress,
matching ribbon around her neck.
Yesterday 2 little girls found her body
in a shallow grave
under thick trees
dirty and torn.
Cause of death was multiple stab wounds to the neck.
No more smiling photos lace the screen
they are replaced by film taken
of a small thick yellow body bag
tied to a stretcher with heavy black belts.
Cut to her mother; tear flushed
and cursing the arrested family friend
who pleaded with his brother to lie to the police
to say that the blood in his van
belonged to a poached deer.

—Rü Lindenberger

"I received a lovely thank-you note from Gail Doll," said the poetess, "after her daughter saw my poem on my

Web site." There were other poems as well and a song for Roxanne, featured on a CD popular in the Northwest.

April 9, 1995

The autopsy of Roxanne Doll revealed bruising and tearing in her vagina, with two lacerations measuring two and three centimeters long. These injuries, according to Dr. Eric Kiesel, examining pathologist, were caused by the insertion of something the size of an adult penis.

"These injuries alone were enough to cause her death," he explained, noting the significant blood loss. "Roxanne Doll died, however, due to at least seven stab wounds to her neck, one of which severed her left internal jugular vein.

"Actually, all of the injuries in combination are potentially life threatening," said Dr. Kiesel. "Clearly, the one that transected the left internal jugular vein was a life-threatening wound. The reason they are all potentially life threatening is because the head and neck area is very vascular, but the head in general has a very large blood supply relative to a child's size. It's a fairly large area. All of these wounds, even the superficial ones into the skin, will bleed."

Blood loss, especially when you are dealing with this number of wounds, can be significant and life threatening. "The more superficial ones you don't generally think of as being life threatening," Kiesel said, "but we start getting into the wounds that enter the muscle, those are going to bleed. But again, you may be able to stop that bleeding by putting pressure on it. But if nothing is done to stop the bleeding, there isn't much you can do to save her life. Theoretically, even the transected jugular vein, with proper and rapid-enough medical treatment, is potentially a survivable wound."

Potential is one thing, action another. There was no treatment or medical aid summoned for Roxanne Doll by the person who stabbed her. "This person died," stated Kiesel, "because no such treatment was provided. As far as telling you how long it took for Roxanne Doll to die, I believe there are too many variables because you can' t tell how rapidly these wounds were being caused, or which order they came in.

"If you cut the jugular first," he explained, "death is going to be quicker than if you have so many subcutaneous wounds, because you are going to be bleeding faster. Clearly, I think from the blood loss, though, you are probably talking on the order of minutes, at most up to a half an hour."

There was no indication that death was caused by any method other than multiple stab wounds—no strangulation or suffocation.

"There are a couple of things that we use to try to determine the nature of the weapon itself," he commented. "One is to look at the nature of the wound. Does it have smooth edges or are the edges scalped? That could tell us if we have a straight edge knife or a scalloped knife, if we are dealing with a knife. You try to proximate the wounds; that is, pull the margins together and look at either corner to see if you got a sharp edge and a blunt edge. This might tell you if you are dealing with a double-edge knife or whether you are dealing with a sharp edge and a blunt edge on a knife."

Part of Kiesel's examination was an attempt to discern as much about the wounds as possible, and thereby determine the nature of the weapon. "It is interesting in finding out where the wound track is, what did this wound hit, what was the direction of the wound—was it up, down, sideways, front to back, back to front? And the other thing we try to do," he said, "is determine what the estimated depth is. And I say estimated depth as opposed to actual depth, because the depth that I measured can vary because of the skin flexibility, the body cavity flexibility, and because of that ability to compress. All we can do is estimate at the depth. What that does is help narrow down what type of weapon you might be looking for. It can't identify the weapon specifically, but it can help rule in, and out, various weapons."

Kiesel was quick to explain that the depth of a wound did not tell you the minimum length of the blade, assuming a knife was used. "If you have a long knife, you can stick the knife in only a little bit, so you can have a relatively short weapon. If you got a wound, I'm going to exaggerate, twelve inches deep, you are probably not going to create that with a blade that's three inches long. That's not reasonable. But you may be able to create a wound that's four inches long, possibly even five inches long, with a three-inch blade. So, by itself, it's helpful in ruling certain weapons in or out, but you can't distinguish exactly what weapon did it, without—that would require other testing.

"The body appears that she had been dead clearly over a week. But we know she was alive somewhere on the thirty-first, so we know death had to occur after that point," said Kiesel. The condition of decomposition begins at death, and as to the question whether she was dead someplace else for a considerable amount of time before being placed at the recovery site, Dr. Kiesel did not find that highly probable due to the body condition and body posture.

"I don't believe this was dramatically changed from where she was at the time of death. There is certain changes that occur after death, settling of the blood within the body. . . . [These things] are consistent with her body's position at the recovery site. Wherever she was prior, she was very likely laying on her back."

The size and shape of the wounds, according to Dr.

Kiesel, were consistent with a small, single-edged blade
such as a pocketknife. Roxanne's hands also displayed
knife wounds, and it was unclear whether the wounds
were defensive or intentionally inflicted.

"A number of knives were recovered during the course
of the investigation," reported Herndon. "Various knives
were found by officers around the Everett area during the
course of the week that Roxanne Doll was missing. One
knife was found on Broadway, and there was another located by patrol approximately four blocks from the body
recovery site, north on East Grand. And I believe there was
maybe one removed from Clark's van during the search
conducted under the search warrant. There were five
knives taken from Clark's residence on Lombard Street
under a search warrant served on April ninth. All knives
were submitted to the crime lab for testing and analysis."

Chapter 9

While evidence recovered from the body's exterior, autopsy, and the body site itself was being cataloged and sent for analysis, Detective Herndon was checking another site for evidence—the body of Richard M. Clark.

"Detective Jim Phillips, Detective James Duvall, and I went to the Snohomish County Jail medical unit, where we met with Mr. Clark and served him with a search warrant," reported Herndon. "The purpose of this search warrant was to collect blood, saliva, and hair to include pubic, head, facial, and body hair. We wanted to gather evidence to compare with trace evidence expected to be recovered from the victim."

When Detective Kiser requested the warrant, he also asked for permission to photograph in detail the entire nude body of Richard Clark. This was to determine if any injuries existed, such as scratches, bruises, and lacerations that could have been sustained by Richard Clark during the assault on the victim or disposal and concealment of the body.

The investigating officers shot a roll of film, mostly of Clark's legs. "The reason we took pictures of his legs," Herndon explained, "was that we were looking for any injuries. The place where the body was found had plenty

of blackberry bushes that could have scratched him u
pretty good.

"If you look at the photos," commented Herndor
"you'll see numerous scratches of that nature from h
knee area down to his ankles. There was also a scratc
healing on his chin.

"I'm not an expert on injuries," said the detectiv
"but what do you see when you look at the pictures c
Richard Clark's legs? To me, it looks like he tangled wit
thick blackberry bushes and a feisty seven-year-old girl

April 11, 1995

"Did you kill that little girl?" It was Toni Clark askin
her stepson the most direct of all possible questions.

"No, I didn't do it," answered Richard. "I don't kno
who did."

The conversation took place when Richard Clar
called collect from Snohomish County Jail. He spok
with Toni while George Clark Sr. listened in on the e
tension phone.

"Did you rape her?"

"I don't know."

"Did you kidnap her?"

"I don't think so."

"What do you mean, you don't think so?" asked Ton
"Either you did or you didn't."

"Well, I don't remember everything that night."

When Toni asked him why he didn't remembe
Richard Clark said it was because of all the alcohol an
"crank" (methamphetamine) he'd used that night.

"Don't grieve for me if I get the death penalty," sai
Richard Clark, "don't grieve for me."

Richard Clark never lived with Toni and George Clar
for any extended period of time, especially in his adul

years. "He would stay here maybe one or two days at a time, but we didn't want him living with us," acknowledged Toni Clark, "because of his drinking."

The majority of time between the disappearance of Roxanne Doll and his arrest, Richard Mathew Clark primarily lived with his aunt Carol on Lombard Street—a residence searched numerous times with the same meticulous care with which forensic scientist George Johnston of the Washington Sate Crime Lab in Seattle treated the trace evidence recovered from the body of Roxanne Doll.

Johnston held a bachelor of science degree with his major course of study in science from the University of Mississippi. "After graduating from college," he recalled, "I worked for one year in my hometown, a research facility, not a forensic lab, but a different type of laboratory. And I worked for three years in the Houston, Texas, Crime Lab Department."

In November 1980, Johnston moved to Seattle and began work with the Washington system. His established area of expertise was trace evidence; he had testified in over one hundred cases, and carried a most impressive list of professional credentials.

"I attended the FBI Academy on three or four occasions," he said, "once to study basic serology, other courses of examination of forensics, hair and fiber evidence, another time on paint evidence. I received training in microscopy and advanced microscopy, which is an institution that examines microscopic evidence, extensive on-the-job training in various courses and workshops from our professional organizations and associations. It is also part of my job to teach and train other forensic scientists in hair examination and fiber examinations."

He also was a respected member of the Northwest Association of Forensic Scientists, the American Academy of Forensic Scientists, a diplomat and fellow of the American Board of Criminalistics, and also a laboratory inspector for the American Society of Crime Laboratory Directors. "Part of that job," explained Johnston, "is to go to other laboratories and to inspect and to do an audit basically on their operations to make sure that they are fulfilling the needs of forensic science."

Ask Johnston what he does with a piece of evidence, and you'll get an understandable introduction into the art of forensic science. "A piece of trace evidence or piece of debris evidence is basically something that can be transferred very easily from person to person, or from thing to a person. Part of my job is to examine debris evidence or full pieces of evidence, collect that debris and then examine that microscopically either using a variety of visual methods, stereomicroscopic methods, or compound microscopic methods of comparison between those pieces of evidence.

"Trace evidence is not evidence that is used to identify a particular item," explained Johnston. "It's not possible for us, for instance, to identify a fiber as coming from one specific piece of evidence. There are millions, I'm sure, of carpets or clothes made of those same fibers. So what we try to do is determine if there is a link between this piece of miscellaneous evidence and a controlled sample of the carpet or of a coat or something like that. We do a similar type of thing with hair evidence or paint evidence, for that matter. We take the unknown piece, the questioned piece of evidence, compare that using microscopic and instrumental methods and try to determine if it could have come from a particular source or if indeed it did not come from that source."

According to Johnston, there is no way to say a paint chip came from one particular car, based on chemical examinations. Nor can you determine if a hair came from a certain individual, or if a fiber came from a particular piece of clothing.

"The strongest conclusion you can make on these examinations," he said, "is that this questioned piece of evidence has the same microscopic instrumental characteristic as the control sample and could have come from that control sample, or another sample with those characteristics. And as I say, we employed microscopic methods. That's part of our microanalysis or trace evidence section. But we can use instrument evidence to compare or further examine evidence as we need to.

"When it came time for me to examine the evidence in this particular case, I went to our evidence vault, took the evidence, took it to my work area, and examined it."

Included in that evidence, he said, was "trace debris from a training bra, a disposable diaper, several autopsy items that were submitted to me, head hair control samples from both Richard Clark and Roxanne Doll, and carpet control samples from several carpets, from a van, also an insulation control sample, and, I believe, the sample of drapery from a van."

While scientists examined microscopic evidence, detectives pursued the macroscopic. The successful solving of a case may hinge on any manner of evidence, be it a drop of blood, a carpet fiber, or something much larger, such as the location of a big old Dodge van. Richard Mathew Clark covered a lot of physical territory on March 31, 1995, and Detective Herndon was determined to construct an accurate time line of Clark's whereabouts the night Roxanne Doll died.

Richard Clark's seemingly mindless meanderings between leaving the Casey home at approximately 9:30 to 9:45 P.M. and his returning to the Doll-Iffrig residence at 1:00 A.M. were detailed to detectives during his initial questioning. There existed a window of opportunity—a section of time during which he entered the home via the girls' bedroom window, abducted Roxanne, and raped her. Either then, or later, he killed her in his van. At

12:45 A.M., he dumped her body on that Everett hillside, then returned to her parents' home.

"He spent the balance of the evening socializing with the parents and friends of the girl he had just raped and murdered," recalled Herndon, "and then went camping with the father.

"The only way to know where that window was created was to reconstruct Clark's exact whereabouts that night, and build a time line," explained Herndon. "Was he really where he said he was, and at the times he claimed? We retraced his path on the night of March thirty-first, speaking with everyone who saw Richard Clark that night between nine at night and one-fifteen in the morning. We compared his statement with their statements, and that brought the truth to light.

"The first place Clark supposedly went after he brought Tim Iffrig back from playing pool," said Detective Herndon, "was to the Dog House Tavern with, depending on the various versions of his story, Jimmy Miller, Neila D'alexander, and even Vicki Smith. No one else said anything about Vicki being with Clark on Friday night. In fact, he didn't include her when he gave his statement to us when we interviewed him at his aunt Carol's house, or when we spoke to him at the police station. For some reason, he added her when talking to the FBI agent. Vicki Smith, of course, was not with him that Friday night."

"I left the house with Richard Clark and Jimmy Miller at about six-forty-five P.M.," confirmed Neila D'alexander, making no mention of Vicki Smith, "and we went to the Dog House Tavern. The bartender wouldn't give Jimmy Miller a drink because he was too drunk. Richard and I had a beer that Richard only took one drink out of before he and Jimmy left at about seven-forty-five P.M. Richard came back in about an hour later without Jimmy and asked me if I wanted a ride back home—to Tim and

Gail. I told him that I was going over to Randy Winders at Twenty-fourth and Colby."

Neila walked over to Winders's, but he wasn't home. She returned to the Dog House, where she helped Dan Webster celebrate his birthday. "I visited with numerous people," she said, "until I left with Dan Webster at twelve-thirty A.M."

Neila D'alexander's lifelong friend Linda Hein was already sitting in the Dog House Tavern when Neila arrived. "I've known Neila D'alexander ever since we were in grade school. We pretty much grew up together," said Hein. It was between 7:30 and 8:00 P.M., recalled Hein, when a man known as Animal came into the bar. Animal was the tavern nickname for Richard M. Clark.

"I don't remember him leaving, but I think he came back about half past midnight," Hein recalled.

"When Richard left the Dog House, supposedly to take Jimmy Miller back to the reservation," restated Neila D'alexander, "he didn't come back and talk to me after midnight. I left at twelve-thirty with Dan Webster and hadn't seen Richard Clark since earlier."

Cheryle Galloway, the Dog House bartender, had recollections more in line with Neila D'alexander's. "I came on shift at four o'clock and worked until two," she reported. "I remember Richard Clark and Jimmy Miller coming into the tavern just as Neila said. They ordered three schooners and I refused to serve Jimmy because he was on his lips. Richard and Neila had a schooner of beer, and then Neila went over and talked with one of her friends. Richard finished his beer and left with Jimmy. They were not there very long."

She recalled Richard returning, but much earlier than the 12:30 A.M. asserted by customer Hein. "It was only maybe three hours later, I imagine around ten-thirty," she said. "I walked up to him and asked him if he needed anything, if he wanted another schooner. He said no. I offered him a cup of coffee, and he just sat quietly at the end of the bar and drank his cup of coffee. He was only there for about fifteen minutes. While he was there, he asked me if he could put his van up for sale in the tavern, and I told him that I couldn't authorize that without talking to the owner."

The change in Clark's appearance and demeanor, coupled with his interest in selling his van, signaled that the abduction and rape of Roxanne Doll, and most likely her murder, were already completed by 10:30 P.M. Jimmy Miller, passed out in the passenger seat, was certainly unaware that he was companion to a corpse.

Richard Clark was unaccounted for between 9:30 and 10:15 P.M. when he showed up again at the Dog House wearing glasses, staying only long enough for a cup of coffee, and asking if he could sell his van. It was most likely that Roxanne Doll, dead or alive, was in Clark's van, bound and gagged with socks, when Clark was sipping coffee at the Dog House Tavern and when he showed up at the home of family friends, Wendy and Andy Urness, in Marysville at 10:45 P.M. on March 31.

"I was on the couch," recalled Wendy Urness, "when Richard Clark knocked on the front door. I was watching TV, watching a news program, probably something like *20/20*. We usually don't have people come over that late, so it was somewhat strange that someone was pulling into the driveway, so I kind of looked at the clock to see what time it was—it was ten forty-five P.M."

"My wife watches *20/20*," recalled Andy Urness. "That show starts at ten P.M., and it was toward the end of the show, where they had like a flash that comes on and they ask you a dateline question, which is usually at the end of the program. I was washing dishes inside the kitchen and I looked at the microwave and the time was ten forty-five."

Richard Clark went into the kitchen to speak with Wendy's husband, Andy. "I heard him ask Andy if he had any money for gas, and Andy told him no. Richard kept asking for money, and Andy said maybe come back tomorrow. Then Richard asked him if he had any beer, and Andy said that he didn't have any beer. 'Are you sure? I really need something—money, beer.' He was very persistent."

Wendy heard Clark say that Jimmy was drunk and passed out in the van. "Richard told me that on his way back from Everett he picked up Jimmy hitchhiking," said Andy. "I looked out the kitchen window, but it was dark, and I didn't stop to look outside my shades or anything. The only thing I noticed different about him was that he was wearing glasses. He left a little later than ten-fifty."

"Richard didn't seem to be really intoxicated or anything, not that I noticed," said Wendy. "But I've only met him briefly a couple times in the past. Richard was wearing glasses," she said. "I had never seen him wear glasses before. He was just in and out, and acted somewhat nervous. He didn't appear to be drunk or high, and was quiet and soft-spoken, but persistent."

Not long after leaving the Urness home, Richard Clark returned Jimmy Miller to the Tulalip Indian Reservation just past eleven o'clock. He was there about forty-five minutes, according to Vicki Clark.

"I can't say exactly when," remarked Detective Herndon, "but sometime between when he left the Casey residence at nine-fifteen to nine-thirty P.M., and when Gail Doll returned at midnight, Richard Clark raped and killed Roxanne Doll. As for Jimmy Miller, even he doesn't know where he was or what he was doing that night, or what time he went anywhere. He was pretty much passed out on his feet even when he walked into the Dog House Tavern."

"Jimmy Miller was bombed," agreed Neila D'alexander. "He even passed out with his face against the van window on the way to the Dog House."

"One thing we know timewise," asserted Herndon,

"is that Richard Clark was dumping the body of Roxanne Doll in the blackberry bushes below East Grand at quarter to one, the early morning of April first. We know that because the van was brought to a woman's attention by, of all things, a cat."

"I watched a cat run right behind the tire of a rusty yellow-colored older American-made van parked on East Grand," said Janice Cliatt, an employee of Safeco in Seattle's University District. "There were no lights on in the van, and no movement that I could see." Cliatt got off work at 12:15 A.M. The Safeco building is only a block or two from the I-5 Freeway entrance. "I takes me twenty-six minutes to reach Marine View Drive in Everett, from where I enter the I-5 freeway when I get off work," she said. "I got on the freeway at exactly twelve-twenty, took a right turn off the Marine View Drive exit, and I was going south on East Grand. Before I reached twenty-third, a cat ran from the west side of the road to the east side and went right under that van."

April 13, 1995

First-degree murder and first-degree kidnapping charges were filed against Richard Mathew Clark in Everett District Court. "We are waiting for the results of blood, fiber, and hair tests," said Jim Townsend, chief deputy prosecutor, "before making decisions on additional charges such as rape. Roxanne Doll died of multiple stab wounds to the neck that were probably inflicted the night of her abduction."

As for facing the death penalty, the prosecutor explained that it was too soon to determine whether Clark would be charged with aggravated murder, a death penalty offense. "Clark is currently being held on one-million-dollar bail on a witness-tampering charge," said

Townsend, referring to the allegation that Clark asked his "brother," Elza, to lie to police regarding bloodstains in his van.

The day after Richard Clark was charged with murder was the day that Detective Herndon heard important news from the Marysville Crime Lab.

April 14, 1995

"The bloodstains on the socks, the ones taken from the van," Mike Grubb of the Marysville Crime Lab said to Detective Herndon, "the balled-up socks, you know, with the bloodstains on them, and the sleeping bag—well, the blood didn't come from Roxanne Doll. She has a very rare blood type."

According to Grubb, Roxanne Doll's rare blood type was similar to two other groups. Based on early results, they had eliminated approximately 97 percent of the Caucasian population as a source of these stains.

Herndon was instructed to call back later in the afternoon to find out if semen had been located on the socks, which also contained what appeared to be victim blood.

"That's how the day started," said Herndon. "Then, at four-thirty that afternoon, I made contact with Greg Franks in regards to trace amounts of semen that had been found in some socks, and also the vaginal swabs. At that time, Mr. Frank suggested that I submit these items for further DNA analysis or PCR analysis. Of course, that's exactly what we did."

That same day, Wendy and Andy Urness met detectives at the Buzz-Inn Steak House. The motivation for the meeting: seeing Richard's van on the television news. The couple, at Richard Clark's request, provided a mattress and a sleeping bag for his camping trip with Tim Iffrig.

"I just saw it on the TV," said Andy to detectives when he met them at the restaurant, "and that's what prompted me to call. I saw the van doors open on a TV newscast and there was my mattress and my sleeping bag.

"I couldn't believe it," he said. "It hit me way too close to home, because of what was going on. I have two children, a little girl that's seven and a boy that's four."

The difference between the sleeping bag when Andy last saw it, and the way it looked when detectives showed him a picture of it, was the stains. "My sleeping bag was clean, and I've never noticed stains like that. The stains were not on it when I last saw it."

Mr. and Mrs. Urness were not the only ones shocked by bloodstains. The morning after Clark visited the Urness residence—Saturday morning, April 1—Iffrig and he arrived at Kimberly Morrill's Everett home. Morrill is Tim Iffrig's sister, and Roxanne Doll's aunt.

"I had known Richard Clark for about a year and a half," recalled Kimberly. "I met him because I used to go out with his brother, Jimmy Miller. On Saturday, April first, my brother—Tim Iffrig—and Richard Clark came over to my house about eight-thirty in the morning. Tim's eyes looked dilated; he looked like he had been drinking, so I offered him some coffee.

"As for Richard Clark," she said, "he was grinning like a tissy cat, and he looked like he was wired. His eyes were bloodshot and it looked like he had been up all night. They stayed at my place till about eleven-thirty."

Kimberly confirmed that the only companion of Iffrig and Clark was a black puppy dog. "The folks who were already there was me, my fiancé, Matthew, my brother and him, and my two kids. One of the kids was in my stomach, because I didn't have her at that time. James was in his room, and my daughter was, well, in there," she said, pointing to her abdomen.

"I do not remember what was said or what we talked

about, except that at about eight forty-five. I asked Richard if I could go out to his van and get the puppy. And I went out and got his puppy and that's when I seen the blood.

"I didn't crawl into the van to get the dog," she explained. "The dog was sitting on the mattress and I called the dog's name and the dog came right to me. That was when I saw the blood on the mattress and by the van's door."

Neither Tim nor Kimberly knew of Roxanne's disappearance, but the fresh bloodstains disturbed Morrill. She questioned Clark about the blood, and he gave her a vague excuse about the puppy getting a scratch.

"The stains to which Urness and Merrill referred were bloodstains," said Herndon, "the same type of bloodstains Richard Clark asked his aunt Carol to wash out of his shirt at midnight of March thirty-first. Of course, we didn't know about that until she called us up crying and hysterical on April eighteenth."

Chapter 10

April 18, 1995

A tearful and distraught Carol Clark summoned Detectives Burgess and Herndon on a matter of utmost urgency. The two men arrived at her Lombard Street residence to find Clark in a state of high emotional agitation.

"When we first met with Carol Clark, she was visibly upset, crying," recalled Herndon. "Detective Burgess, who had communicated with Ms. Clark on most occasions, did the talking."

The relationship between Burgess and Carol Clark was not one of mutual high regard. She often accused Burgess of harassing her, badgering her, and other appellatives of equal unpleasantness. Admittedly guarded of her personal privacy, and highly emotional, Carol's animosity toward Burgess was somewhat ameliorated by the current circumstances. Carol Clark feared she was facing arrest.

"Richard Clark was initially arrested for tampering with a witness by asking Elza to say the van's bloodstains were from a poached deer," Herndon said. "Carol made the same request of Elza, and she thought that she was going to be arrested as an accessory for tampering also with a witness. Once we assured her that we had no intention of arresting her, and that we only regarded her as a witness, she calmed down."

Carol provided a taped statement, remaining calm and coherent 99 percent of the time. "When she got to the point of telling us what she observed on the night of the thirty-first, or the early morning of the first, she did get a little upset, but then soon calmed down, for the most part."

What she observed was Richard Clark dropping by her house at midnight wearing a bloodstained shirt. "The blood that you saw on his shirt," asked Detective Burgess, "how close were you when you saw this?"

"He was in front of the washing machine and I was in front of the sink," replied Carol. "Maybe a couple feet away."

"And so when you saw this blood, you asked him about it?"

"Well," Carol answered, "I asked him how he got that on his shirt and he said, 'Well, I've been out poaching a deer.'"

"He looked like he'd been drinking," added Carol. "I don't know if he was on any drugs, 'cause I never took drugs myself. See, I never knew what anybody looked like when they're on drugs." She went on to tell detectives that Richard Clark put the shirt in the laundry, took a shower, changed clothes, and left.

"When she told us that," said Burgess, "I believe it was her son Jesse who ran off into another room and he retrieved it and brought it in and she confirmed that was the shirt Richard Clark left with her to wash."

Detective Burgess stayed with Carol Clark while Herndon obtained another search warrant. "She was going to give us consent," he said, "but I thought, since I had the time, I was going to cover the bases and get a search warrant. Once that search warrant was obtained, I came back and gave Carol Clark a receipt for that shirt. Detective Burgess took the shirt and it was impounded. Even though Carol washed the shirt with detergent and bleach, experts were still able to recover DNA matching that of Roxanne Doll."

The nightmare story of Clark's alleged kidnapping, rape, and murder of little Roxanne Doll was the number one lead story in the newspaper, on radio, and on television. Emotions ran high in Everett, Washington. There were those who, given an opportunity, would have gladly lynched Richard Mathew Clark.

"Well, this here country is America," asserted an honored veteran of foreign wars, "and no matter how guilty that son of a bitch is, he's presumed as innocent as a baby lamb until proven guilty beyond a reasonable doubt in a court of law . . . and then we can kill him."

"There is no way Richard Clark can get a fair trial in Everett, Washington," said award-winning broadcast journalist Chet Rogers. "Media coverage of Roxanne Doll's kidnapping and murder, emotion laden and virtually nonstop since the day she disappeared, has so saturated the community that finding an impartial jury will be an almost herculean task. Were I his defense attorney, I would, for the sake of preserving American justice, assuredly seek a change of venue."

Richard Clark's attorneys felt the same way and petitioned the court to act accordingly and move the trial outside of Snohomish County. "There had been coverage nearly every day," recalled noted appellant's attorney Suzanne Lee Elliott, "and in some instances, two to four stories each day. The defense argued that the venue should be changed because Mr. Clark could not be given a fair trial in light of the publicity in this case."

Before Clark's lawyers would argue that the trial should be held elsewhere, they would argue that his van should not have been held and searched at all. The warrants issued for the searching of his van, they asserted, were illegal.

"They argued that the physical evidence seized from his

van and residence should be suppressed because his van
was impounded without a warrant," recalled deputy pros
ecutor Seth Fine. "They also argued that there was no
probable cause to impound his van because Detective
Herndon performed a search of the van the previous day
and found nothing obviously incriminatory."

The warrant issued subsequent to the impounding
lacked probable cause, according to the defense, because
Detective Herndon's sworn affidavit supporting the war
rant merely mentioned that Clark had a previous criminal
history involving a similar crime, and that Clark had failed
a polygraph test with respect to the Doll disappearance
It was further claimed that the affidavit contained inten
tional or recklessly made material omissions, was merely a
boilerplate affidavit, was overbroad, and lacked particu
larity with respect to evidence to be seized.

Clark's defense attorney wanted every piece of physical
evidence tossed out because the evidence was seized based
on an illegal search warrant. "Since there were four search
warrants in total related to evidence seized from the van
and all had supporting affidavits indistinguishable in basic
form from the first warrant," explained Fine, "the defense
argued that virtually every piece of physical evidence
found should be suppressed as tainted fruit of the illegal
van search."

The state challenged each of these assertions with re
spect to the first affidavit because the validity of the
subsequent affidavits would stand or fall with the first. In
order for a warrant to be issued, there has to be "probable
cause, supported by oath or affirmation, and particularly
describing the place to be searched, and the persons or
things to be seized."

The concept of probable cause required "the exis
tence of reasonable grounds for suspicion supported by
circumstances sufficiently strong to warrant a man of or

linary caution to believe the accused is guilty of the indicated crime."

"It is only the probability of criminal activity," explained Fine, not actual proof, that determined whether
probable cause existed. "The judge is entitled to draw
reasonable inferences from the facts and circumstances
set forth in the affidavit, and the affidavit must be read
in a commonsense manner."

When Herndon telephoned Judge Fisher, he mentioned Richard Clark's 1988 conviction for unlawful
imprisonment of Feather Rahier. He also told the judge
about the polygraph test given Clark and that the FBI
agent who administered the test believed that Clark was
"clearly deceptive in his denials." Herndon also stated to
Fisher that if Roxanne Doll was removed from her house
in the van, there would be trace evidence.

The trial court found that although Detective Herndon did not use the word "kidnap" during the telephone
conversation with Judge Fisher, the latter "knew the
crime with which he was dealing. The police knew that
they were restricted to searching for trace evidence left
behind after a kidnapping."

Clark's lawyers argued that just because Clark was
near the victim's house on the night she disappeared,
had a prior conviction, and supposedly failed a polygraph examination were insufficient bases for probable
cause. However, under Washington State law, "prior
convictions of a suspect are a factor which can be considered in determining whether probable cause exists."
In this situation, Clark's prior conviction was for unlawful imprisonment of a young girl for ostensibly
sexual purposes.

"When I got the warrant by telephone," confirmed
Herndon, "my affidavit set forth that after binding her in
his garage with a pair of socks, Clark groped this girl's
vaginal area outside her clothing." This was a crime of the

same general nature as that in which Detective Herndon was attempting to uncover evidence, and therefore was not only proper but helpful in establishing probable cause.

"Polygraph results are not admissible at trial unless stringent conditions have been met," said Seth Fine, "but the judge can take those results into consideration when making a determination of probable cause. Here Clark' polygraph performance was deemed deceptive by the administering FBI agent."

Clark challenged the conclusion of the FBI agent be cause Detective Herndon's affidavit didn't give the agent's qualifications or any other reason to assume the agent's conclusions were reliable or accurate. (Informa tion from a reliable informant has corroborative value even if the informant's basis of knowledge is not speci fied.) Here the FBI agent's basis of knowledge was the administration of the polygraph and his clinical and commonsense observation of Clark's performance.

"Clark seemed to be claiming that no foundation was laid in the supporting affidavit to support the agent' qualifications," explained Seth Fine. "But the FBI agent wasn't required to submit a résumé or his curriculum vitae to Detective Herndon in order for the agent's con clusions and opinions about the polygraph results to be of value to Judge Fisher in determining whether or not to issue the search warrant.

"It may be correct that, taken individually, these things may not have been enough to establish probable cause," Fine acknowledged. "But taking this information on the whole, Judge Fisher could form reasonable belief that Richard Clark was probably involved in the criminal ac tivity under investigation."

Clark, via his lawyer, also claimed that Detective Hern don made two material omissions or misstatements to Judge Fisher. The first was Herndon not mentioning that he had made a brief but inconclusive search of the van prior to applying for the search warrant. The second was failing to mention that Gail Doll told him she thought she saw Roxanne in bed with her sister when she returned at midnight of April 1, 1995.

Clark contended that had these facts been included in the affidavit, no reasonable magistrate could have found probable cause to issue the search warrant.

In order to invalidate the warrant on this ground, Clark had to show evidence of deliberate material omission or statements made in reckless disregard of the truth. "Allegations of negligence or innocent mistake are insufficient," explained Fine. If Detective Herndon himself had serious doubts about the truth of his own affidavit, or if he had obvious reasons to doubt the honesty or accuracy of an informant, but asked for the warrant anyway, that would be "reckless disregard for the truth."

The trial court ruled: "The omission of details regarding Ms. Doll-Iffrig's statement of her observations is not material. The statement in the affidavit that Ms. Doll-Iffrig was 'unsure' of whether she saw Roxanne is truthful. This was the substance of oral statements made to Detective Herndon by Gail Doll. The progression of Gail's thought processes was indicated by the fact that her second written statement is more vague than her first statement."

The court ruled that Herndon's failure to recite all of Ms. Doll-Iffrig's statements to him was not an intentional or reckless attempt to mislead Judge Fisher. The fact that Herndon also didn't mention his previous quick search of the van on April 3 was, the court decided, not relevant.

"The purpose of the April 3, 1995, search warrant," explained Herndon, "was for trace evidence. During my search on April 2, I didn't notice anything remarkable— I was looking for maybe a tennis shoe or an item of clothing, or something obvious. Just because I took a

look in the van doesn't mean that there would not b
trace evidence in there."

The court decided that Detective Herndon did not a
tempt to deceive the judge by purposely leaving ou
information. "It was like I was being accused of being :
liar," said Herndon later, "but any error on my par
didn't have any sort of nefarious motive. I was just doin
my job to the best of my ability."

With respect to Detective Herndon's statement tha
Doll-Iffrig was unsure whether Roxanne was in bed a
midnight on April 1, 1995, it was an accurate summar
of statements on the matter. Gail Doll turned the ligh
on in her daughter's room only momentarily, and was
upon reflection, unsure whether she saw Roxanne or :
large doll.

"If the court ruled that Herndon should have in
cluded those pieces of information," explained Fine
"then what you do is add the omitted facts to the affi
davit and subtract any misstatements. If probable caus
still exists after you do that, the warrant stands."

Given the difference between a search for trace evi
dence and the simple search for blatant evidenc
conducted by Herndon, and given Doll-Iffrig's numer
ous statements as to her uncertainty whether she sav
Roxanne in bed, the court upheld that there was stil
probable cause to issue the warrants to search Clark'
Dodge van.

There was still another lingering and unresolved issu
regarding whether or not the search warrant was legal
and it was a question that struck to the heart of wha
makes America "the Land of the Free"—the Bill of Rights

"The right of the people to be secure in their persons
houses, papers, and effects, against unreasonabl
searches and seizures," states the Fourth Amendment
"shall not be violated, and no Warrants shall issue, bu
upon probable cause, supported by Oath or affirmation

and particularly describing the place to be searched, and the persons or things to be seized."

To comply with the mandate of the Fourth Amendment particularity clause, a search warrant must be sufficiently definite so that the officer executing the warrant can identify the property sought with reasonable certainty. Thus, search warrants are to be tested and interpreted in a commonsense, practical manner, rather than in a hypertechnical sense. In general, the degree of specificity required varies according to the circumstances and the type of items involved. A description is valid if it is as specific as the circumstances and the nature of the activity or crime under investigation permits.

The fact that a warrant lists generic classifications does not necessarily result in an impermissibly broad warrant. The scope of the search warrant Detective Herndon sought was based on the following language in the affidavit: "If Roxanne was removed from her residence by use of the van, there would be trace evidence from the victim in the van."

Trace evidence means "small items of a foreign material left on another of which there are many possible types." This includes hairs, fibers, and other such items. Due to the inherent size and multiplicity of kinds of trace evidence, their prior identification in a warrant is impossible.

"It therefore appears," ruled the court, "that the April 3, 1995, search warrant was not impermissibly broad, as it limited the search to trace evidence in Clark's van of Roxanne Doll. Merely because the search for trace evidence involved the search of many items in the van for trace evidence, including parts of the walls and floors of the vehicle, does not therefore make the search a 'general, exploratory rummaging in a person's belongings' prohibited by the Fourth Amendment."

"They seized the van without a warrant," said Clark's

attorneys. Seth Fine responded, "A motor vehicle may be impounded if there is probable cause to believe that it was used in the commission of a felony."

Clark's argument that the police lacked probable cause to impound his van was based on the same argument used in asserting that Judge Fisher lacked probable cause to impound the vehicle based on the evidence linking Clark to Roxanne's abduction. This was the same evidence that allowed Judge Fisher to issue a search warrant for the van hours after it was impounded.

The van remained impounded behind a chain link fence in Everett, and Clark continued to be held without bail in the Snohomish County Jail. In theory, Clark's battered van could remain parked in that same spot until it rusted into dust—vehicular death by natural causes. Richard Clark, however, faced a more dire threat. If the Snohomish County prosecutor successfully sought the death penalty, Clark could be executed.

September 19, 1995

After serious consultation and consideration, the Snohomish County Prosecutor's Office decided to pursue the ultimate penalty for Richard Clark—the sentence of death.

When seeking the death penalty, the state is required by law to serve notice upon the defendant and his attorney within thirty days. Neither Clark nor his attorneys, however, personally received this notification until after the time was up. Instead, the state left the notice in the designated box in a restricted area in the prosecutor's office, and the public defender's staff retrieved it, took it to the public defender's office, stamped it received, and left it in the appropriate attorney's mailbox.

The notice was delivered to the defendant's attorney

in the same manner as every other motion served for several years—a method possibly at odds with the law.

Defense attorney William Jaquette did receive a telephone call from a Snohomish County deputy prosecutor advising him that a death penalty notice would be filed regarding Richard M. Clark on January 19, and the notice was filed in the Snohomish County Superior Court on that date.

That same day, pursuant to an agreement between the public defender's office and the prosecutor's office, the notice was left in the public defender's office box in the prosecutor's office with a cover memorandum. The death penalty notice and memorandum were picked up by a public defender's office staff person and carried to that office where they were stamped "Received Sep 20 1995 Sno. Co. Public Defender."

It was a simple system, and one that had been in use for twelve years. "The offices of the prosecuting attorney and the public defender have an agreement for transferring correspondence and other papers," explained Snohomish Country Superior Court judge Richard Thorpe. "Twice each day, a nonattorney staff person of the public defender's office delivers its correspondence and other papers for the prosecuting attorney to the prosecutor's office," Thorpe said, "and retrieves the correspondence and other papers from the prosecuting attorney for the public defender from a box within the prosecutor's office."

The public defender staff picked up and dropped off papers at the prosecutor's office as part of the courthouse run, each day at 9:00 A.M. and 3:00 P.M. The two offices never adopted a special protocol for service of papers in cases involving the death penalty.

The state sought personally to serve the notice on Jaquette on September 29, 1995. Jaquette filed a pretrial motion objecting to what he regarded as an illegal notification of the state's intent to seek the death penalty because neither his client nor he was personally served notification as required by law. After examining the arguments, Judge Richard Thorpe of the Snohomish County Superior Court ruled in favor of the defense.

The trial court concluded the notice was not timely served under the statute because personal service was necessary, and struck the notice, directing the case to "proceed without the possibility of the death penalty."

Seth Fine, assistant chief criminal deputy prosecutor, whose experience included more than sixty cases argued in the Washington State Supreme Court, requested that august body to consider reviewing, and hopefully overturning, Thorpe's decision.

Whether or not the state supreme court would consider the matter was unknown. Hence, everything continued toward trial—a trial the defense wanted moved out of Snohomish County.

Chapter 11

December 28, 1995

Between Christmas and New Year's Day, the court held the initial hearing on the defense's request for a change of venue. At that time, the defense introduced exhibits containing articles from the *Everett Herald,* the *Seattle Times,* the *Seattle Post-Intelligencer,* and videotapes and logs of the coverage from KOMO, KING, and KIRO television, and two circulars used to alert the public when Roxanne Doll was missing.

This media attention, which also included KSTW television in Tacoma, began during the period when Roxanne was missing. Featuring extensive coverage of the massive efforts of the police and volunteers to find her, it also embraced the funeral and memorial services held for the young victim, and the Snohomish County prosecutor's announcement that he would seek the death penalty. In particular, counsel noted that the publicity was calculated to appeal to the emotions.

"Articles focused on the concern of Roxanne's family and friends of the family," recalled attorney Suzanne Lee Elliott. "Counsel cited, as an example, an interview with a coworker of Roxanne's mother, Gail Doll-Iffrig. The coworker stated that she tried to do her crying away from the family because she had to be strong for them. The friend's eleven-year-old son had, according to the news coverage, canceled his birthday party and instead helped spread flyers about Roxanne's disappearance."

Another article described a second-grade girl who was unable to sleep because of Roxanne's disappearance. These and other stories, defense attorneys insisted, were not only calculated to evoke emotional responses, but the stories also presented a great deal of information about Richard Clark and his past criminal record, including details that the defense would move to suppress at trial. "The case was even featured on *America's Most Wanted*," noted Elliott.

"Strangely enough," recalled Detective Herndon, "I didn't watch that episode of *America's Most Wanted*. In fact, I was also on another episode and I didn't watch that either. I try to keep my work life and home life separate—or maybe that type of show just doesn't interest me after doing it all day long."

The court denied the motion for a change of venue, giving two reasons for the ruling: the lapse of time between the news coverage and the actual trial, and the great care that would be exercised in jury selection—care that would assure Clark a fair trial with the presumption of innocence.

"The publicity surrounding the case was not inflammatory," insisted deputy prosecutor Ron Doersch. "For the most part, the publicity had to do with the facts of the case. It was the crime that generated public reaction." The media coverage discussed the impact of the crime on the victim's family, he noted. "Is it really inflammatory to report that a murder victim had a family who loved her and will miss her? These are things likely to cross the mind of any thoughtful person upon hearing of such a death. There is nothing inflammatory about reporting them.

"All of the allegedly emotional reporting was done in April 1995," Doersch said. "Since that time, the news articles have focused on court proceedings. Until we attempt to empanel a jury, we cannot know what the jurors' familiarity with the case is, nor its effect on them. The fact that some of the jurors have knowledge of the case is irrelevant. The correct analysis is whether they have such fixed opinions that they cannot act impartially."

February 15, 1996

The trial of Richard Clark, scheduled to begin in February, was brought to a halt. The Washington State Supreme Court announced that it would review Judge Thorpe's ruling that blocked prosecutors from seeking the death penalty for Richard Clark if he was convicted of murdering Roxanne Doll.

"This decision indefinitely stays Clark's trial," deputy prosecutor Seth Fine told Judge Thorpe. "My guess is that we are looking at a year's delay in the trial."

"A full year?" Judge Thorpe was mildly surprised and openly disappointed. "Can they be convinced to review the case more quickly? Have they ever attempted to expedite things besides Seahawks' issues," chided Thorpe, referring to the Seattle Seahawks football team.

"Yes," Fine said, "but the supreme court follows a deliberate process for reviewing death penalty issues. It likely will take nine to twelve months." Fine was only off by three months.

Arguing before the state supreme court, Seth Fine accused the defense lawyers of engaging in a procedural game. "There is no dispute that notice was actually received," he said. "The real issue is whether or not the notice was served in an effective manner."

The law does not specify how notice must be served. "This is a classic case of rigid compliance with the requirement," said Fine. "The word 'service' can mean twenty different things.

"For twelve years, a messenger service between th prosecutor's office and the public defender's office func tioned regularly without any problems," noted Fine State supreme court justice Charles Johnson asked Fin if mailing or faxing the notice would be okay.

"That is an unlikely scenario," Fine responded, "becaus capital-case defendants are usually in jail, so mailin documents to their house wouldn't be appropriate."

Justice Richard Guy noted that in some counties de fendants are called into open court and served with written notice at that time. William Jaquette, Clark's de fense attorney, pointed out that this was exactly th procedure most recently utilized in the death penalt case of Charles Finch in Snohomish County.

Charles Ben Finch, eventually convicted of a doubl homicide, was notified of the prosecution's intent t seek the death penalty in open court. "There is no am biguity here," asserted Jaquette, "when the law is unclea legal precedence holds that documents must be deli ered personally to defense lawyers or their clients. Thi is not a matter of convenience," Jaquette said. "The stat should do what is required because of the severity of th issue. Let's do the right thing."

The state supreme court, never one to deliberate in heated rush, delivered its verdict within 240 days. On Au gust 8, 1996, the question of Richard Clark facing th death penalty was finally resolved.

August 8, 1996

The state supreme court gave more than a decision; i gave pointed commentary. "This was a close case, an needlessly so. We will not condone sloppy practice," th decision stated, and reprimanded the prosecution. "Th State can easily avoid all the issues discussed in this opir ion by the simple expedient, for instance, of serving the statutory notice upon the defendant or counsel in open court, on the record. The State should be aware," continued the supreme court, ". . . that anything less than a punctilious approach toward the filing and service of the statutory notice in a death penalty case is a risky practice. Especially when the ultimate penalty is involved, this Court's duty is to ensure the defendant receives every statutory protection the Legislature has provided.

"Clark's lawyer noted that the State did not physically bring the papers inside the Public Defender Office. But where the delivery was effected according to the method chosen and controlled by the Public Defender Office and the Public Defender Office assumed physical control of the notice before it even left the Prosecutor's office, it was a reliable method of service meeting the requirements."

In other words, despite "sloppy" and/or "risky" practice, the notification was ruled valid—Richard Clark faced death. Clark asked for reconsideration, but the state supreme court denied it on November 1, 1996. The Snohomish County prosecutor, vindicated in the matter of delivery, was now free to pursue execution.

January 31, 1997

The defense team again asked for a change of venue; the court again denied the motion. Final jury selection would begin within thirty days, but not before the defense and prosecution would skirmish over another important issue—potential surprise evidence.

"We had the strong suspicion that the defense had Mr. Clark examined by mental-health professionals while he was in jail," recalled deputy prosecutor Fine. "The defense stated 'the defendant has not pled insanity or has he asserted any other mental defense for the trial phase of these proceedings'. They didn't say anything about the mitigation phase. The only way to know that for sure if the defense had Mr. Clark examined or tested by psychiatrists and/or psychologists was to find out who visited him while he was in the Snohomish County Jail. The legal question was simply this: does the Snohomish County Prosecutor's Office, as a criminal justice agency, have access to jail visitation records?"

Richard Clark's defense attorneys, Bill Jaquette and Errol Scott, argued that such jail visitation records were the equivalent of "private paper and affairs."

Deputy prosecutor Ronald Doersch responded that jail records were kept confidential and only made available to "criminal justice agencies."

Any criminal justice agency, including the Prosecutor's Office, has full rights to jail visitation records. There is nothing secretive nor private about such visits. In fact, as these visits take place in clear and unobstructed view, anyone from a correctional officer to an inmate trustee could easily observe what person or persons visited a particular defendant. Doersch, in addressing the court, portrayed the defense's position as one designed to ensure that the defense expert witnesses could conduct comprehensive psychological examinations of Richard Clark, keep the results of such examinations and evaluations secret, and thereby prevent the state from being able to rebut the defense experts' testimony.

The state requested that its own expert, pretrial, evaluate the defendant and that the results be sealed. Only if the defendant introduced psychological mitigating evidence in the penalty phase would the state have grounds to obtain both the defendant's psychological evaluations and the sealed examinations by the state's expert.

"When a defendant delays in disclosing his penalty phase psychological evaluations and witnesses until after he jury finds the defendant guilty," said Doersch, "the state is severely prejudiced.

"The state is unable to rebut such expert testimony. Therefore, the state requests that its own expert, pre-rial, evaluate the defendant and that the results and reports of the examination be sealed. If the defendant introduces mitigating psychological evidence at the penalty phase, the state would then gain access to the sealed evaluation and thereby have the ability to present rebuttal expert testimony. When a defendant raises his mental condition as a mitigating factor, the state is enti-led to a fair opportunity to refute that claim. The state's equest is designed to ensure that the jury is presented with comprehensive mental examinations conducted by experts chosen by both parties."

With access granted to Snohomish County Jail records, he state saw that the defendant was visited by at least two psychologists, noted Ron Doersch—Wendy Marlowe, Ph.D., and Natalie Novick. "Ms. Marlowe is a neuropsychologist who contacted the defendant for a professional visit on January 21, 1997. Ms. Novick is a psychologist who contacted the defendant on January 3, 1997. There may have been another psychological interview of the defendant on January 23, 1997, by a third psychologist."

The state believed that the defense consulted these witnesses for expert testimony in the penalty phase of he trial. The rules of discovery were designed to enhance the search for truth, and the process always has been considered a two-way street with the court acting as traffic controller. The goal was to ensure a fair trial.

The defense first refused the state's request for any of he psychologists' reports on Clark, and the prosecutor's office wanted the court to compel the production to the expert findings and/or notes of Novick and Marlowe.

The State wanted copies of all psychological reports and evaluations, regardless of whether or not the defense

intended to endorse the psychologists as witnesses. I
deputy prosecutor Jo Vanderlee's view, the defense woul
most likely call the psychologists as witnesses to testify re
garding the defendant's neurological functioning i
general and on the day of the alleged crimes in particula
With less than two weeks until trial, Vanderlee entreate
the court to compel disclosure of the reports no later tha
February 18, 1997.

"She was really ticked off," recalled Tim Iffrig. "Afte
all, if the jury was gonna hear a bunch of psychologica
stuff, they should get the opinions of experts from bot
sides. I mean, I don't think you can have the defens
keep secrets and pull out something at the last minut
that the prosecution isn't prepared for. That wouldn
make sense. Of course, there were lots of things tha
didn't make sense anyway, like all the stupid-ass demand
Clark tried to make about media coverage of the trial."

February 12, 1997

Richard Clark, via his court-appointed defender, sup
plied the court with a laundry list of requests, entreatie
and motions. Under the heading of "Conduct of Trial,
Clark requested multiple restrictions on media coverage
Everett's newspaper, the *Herald*, immediately file
objections with the court.

"Of the nine requests the defendant enumerates in h
motion, The Herald objects to Nos. 2, 3, and 4," wrot
the *Herald*'s legal counsel. "The defendant's requests see
to prevent the press from questioning and photograph
ing the defendant outside the courtroom, a limitatio
that goes beyond the state's rules for limiting press acces
to criminal proceedings and impermissibly restricts fed
eral and state constitutional rights. Accordingly, thes
requests should be denied."

Roxanne Doll, a bright-eyed child with her life ahead of her. (Courtesy of Snohomish County Prosecutors Office)

Gail Doll and Tim Iffrig, Roxanne's parents, in happier days. (Courtesy of Tim Iffrig)

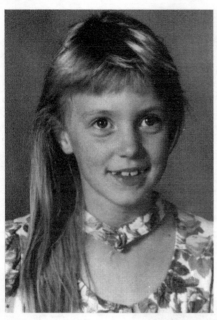

This picture of Roxanne Doll at age was used on the "missing child" flyers created by her mother and posted across the entire United States.
(Courtesy of Snohomish County Prosecutors Office)

The three youngest Dolls: Roxanne, Nicholas, and Kristena.
(Courtesy of Snohomish County Prosecutors Office)

The Doll-Iffrig residence in Everett, Washington. Richard Clark entered through the bedroom window on the left.
(Courtesy of the Snohomish County Prosecutors Office)

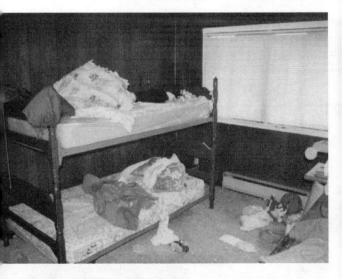

Roxanne was taken from the upper bunk while her sister slept next to her.
(Courtesy of the Snohomish County Prosecutors Office)

Baby photo of future child rapist and killer Richard M. Clark. *(Courtesy of Snohomish County Prosecutors Office)*

Officer Lloyd Herndon, then Senior Detective for the Everett Police Department, investigated the case. *(Author's photo)*

Richard Clark and his aunt, Vicki Smith, came to the historic Everett Police Department. *(Author's photo)*

Clark and his old pal Michael Jaaskela hooked up in the parking lot of the Buzz Inn, but Clark never mentioned the missing child. *(Author's photo)*

Detective Burgess located Richard Clark's van on Lombard Street sealed the doors with evidence tape, and had it impounded. The FBI then searched it.
(Courtesy of Snohomish County Prosecutors Office)

Gail Doll gave police a record of Roxanne's fingerprints, which had been made at her elementary school.
(Courtesy of Gail Doll)

These socks, found in Clark's van, were used to restrain Roxanne Doll. Tests revealed a mixture of blood, semen and saliva that linked Roxanne with Richard Clark. *(Courtesy of Snohomish County Prosecutors Office)*

Two young girls ran screaming when they saw Roxanne's foot protruding from brush and debris.
(Courtesy of Snohomish Country Prosecutors Office)

Police cordoned off the area surrounding the site where Roxanne's body was discovered and began a meticulous search.
(Courtesy of Snohomish County Prosecutors Office)

Law enforcement personnel combed the heavy brush where Roxanne's body was discovered.
(Courtesy of Snohomish County Prosecutors Office)

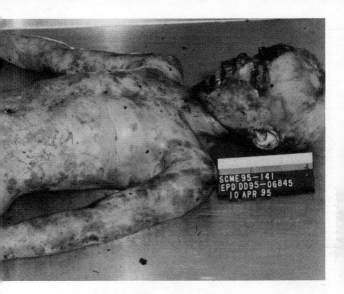

Roxanne Doll's body was carefully removed from the dump site
and thoroughly examined.
(Courtesy of Snohomish County Prosecutors Office)

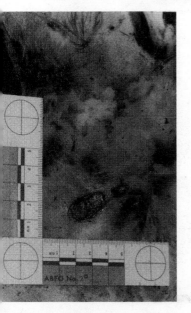

Roxanne died from at
least seven stab wounds
to her neck, including
one that severed her left
internal jugular vein.
The wounds were
consistent with a small,
single-edged blade
such as a pocketknife.
*(Courtesy of Snohomish
County Prosecutors Office)*

Roxanne's hands showed obvious defensive wounds sustained when she tried to protect herself from Clark's attack. *(Courtesy of Snohomish County Prosecutors Office)*

The people of Everett erected this shrine at the body recovery site as a spontaneous act of love. *(Courtesy of Snohomish County Prosecutors Office)*

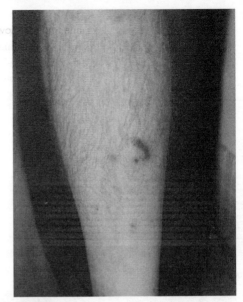

Scratches on Clark's legs from the thick bushes at the dump site. *(Courtesy of Snohomish County Prosecutors Office)*

Seth Fine, now Chief Deputy Prosecutor, won the yearlong battle before the State Supreme Court concerning the death penalty notification. He also argued before the State Supreme Court in opposition to Clark's appeal. *(Author's photo)*

Snohomish County Superior Court Judge Richard Thorpe presided over Clark's trial. *(Courtesy of Snohomish County Superior Court)*

IN MEMORY OF
ROXANNE DOLL
APRIL 21, 1957 TO APRIL 1, 1995

Roxanne's classmates at Fairmont Elementary School established this memorial in her honor. *(Author's photo)*

The Girl Scouts at Fairmont Elementary also dedicated their efforts to keeping Roxanne's memory alive. *(Author's photo)*

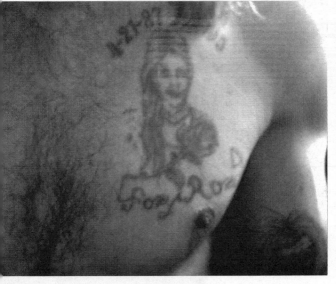

Iffrig had the image of his beloved daughter and the inscription "Foxy Roxy" tattooed on his chest. *(Author's photo)*

Jurors heard of Clark's 1988 incident with Feather Rahier. This is Clark's original 1988 booking photograph. *(Courtesy of Snohomish County Prosecutors Office)*

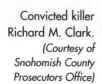

Convicted killer Richard M. Clark. *(Courtesy of Snohomish County Prosecutors Office)*

Guard tower at Washington State Penitentiary where Richard M. Clark, if spared execution, will spend the rest of his life.
(Courtesy of the Washington State Department of Corrections)

The only view of life outside prison—trees on the other side of the wall. This is the Big Yard at the Washington State Penitentiary.
(Courtesy of the Washington State Department of Corrections)

Tim Iffrig remarried in 2003. Gail and he remain close friends.
(Author's photo)

Roxanne Doll's grave at Everett's Evergreen Cemetery.
(Author's photo)

He also wanted the press excluded from the jury section process, again showing no reason why the press
hould be excluded.

In a typical case, a defendant will seek a court order lim-
ing press coverage only inside the courtroom. In this
ase, Clark wanted the press further restricted, even so far
s they could not attempt to engage him in conversation.

This request by Clark had no precedent. In fact, Washington State previously ruled that "an order that forbids
future communication is a prior restraint on the exercise
f free speech." As such, the prior restraints proposed by
Clark were unconstitutional.

The defendant actually wanted the press prohibited
rom even asking him questions. "The defendant does
ot want to speak to any member of the print or broad-
ast media. Consequently, there is no legitimate reason
hy reporters should attempt to speak to him," stated
he motion on his behalf. Not wanting to be asked ques-
ions by the press is not a constitutional right, and is
nsufficient to justify prior restraint on speech.

The *Seattle Post-Intelligencer* newspaper, part of the
Hearst Corporation and represented by Hearst's legal
ounsel, joined in opposition to Clark's emphatic de-
mands. The *P-I* asserted that the motions must be denied
ecause they violated the First Amendment to the United
tates Constitution as well as the Washington State Con-
titution. Both constitutions guarantee public access to
udicial proceedings and other public places. Clark's request for the court to control media access to the trial
nd public areas near the courtroom were, in the final
nalysis, ruled overbroad and without any justification.
Most importantly, Clark's request would deny media out-
ets their constitutional rights as assured in both federal
nd state law.

There is a presumption in favor of access to judicial pro-
eedings under the First Amendment to the United States

Constitution. Further, the United States Supreme Co
has explicitly recognized the public's right of access
criminal trials. The Washington State Constitution al
supports this well-established right: "Justice in all ca
shall be administered openly." This separate, clear, a
specific provision entitles the public to openly admin
tered justice.

There was more at stake than the rights of free pr
and free speech. These guaranteed freedoms share a co
mon core purpose of assuring freedom of communicati
on matters relating to the functioning of government. T
United States Supreme Court had previously ruled, "T
press does not simply publish information about trials, b
guards against the miscarriage of justice by subjecting t
police, prosecutors, and judicial processes to extensi
public scrutiny and criticism."

The *Seattle Times* chimed in with a letter of support f
the *Herald,* and KING-TV addressed the defendant's m
tion restricting the access of cameras to the proceeding
and forbidding reporters from asking questions of th
defendant.

The ability to observe the conduct of judicial pr
ceedings is particularly important in cases where the
are highly charged public issues involved. "Resolution
the criminal proceedings in this matter is of significa
public concern," wrote Jessica Goldman on behalf
KING-TV, "and television access is critical to securin
the public's right to observe this criminal trial."

The rights and freedoms that assured the America
people free speech, free press, and the free flow of info
mation would not be denied by Snohomish County in th
case of Richard M. Clark. There were other motions, ho
ever, governing what could and could not take place in th
courtroom that the court approved. Amongst them we
rules to which Gail Doll and Tim Iffrig were compelle
to obey.

February 25, 1997

Two days prior to the rigorous process of jury selection, Gail Doll and Tim Iffrig signed their agreement to abide by the court's rulings affecting witnesses. "The pre-trial rulings," explained the deputy prosecutor, "are exactly that—rules. The violation of any of them, and there were six in total in this particular trial, could have serious ramifications."

The six rules for witnesses in the trial of Richard M. Clark were as follows:

Witnesses shall not mention the term "polygraph" during their testimony, nor shall any witness testify about, mention polygraph tests or polygraph test results.

Witnesses cannot discuss their testimony with each other until each of them has testified and been excused from further testimony by the court.

Witnesses cannot discuss their testimony, their feelings regarding testifying, or related topics with members of the press or other media, except upon order of the court.

All witnesses shall be excused from the courtroom until they have testified, with the exception of Detective Lloyd Herndon and members of the Doll-Iffrig family.

No witness shall testify regarding prior crimes of the defendant, except upon order of the court.

No witness shall testify regarding the ruse attempted by detectives and the FBI agents wherein the defendant was told that Agent Vanderberry was "counsel."

No witness could mention the Vanderberry ruse but the word was already out. The Washington Association of Criminal Defense Lawyers heard about this ruse and was infuriated that chief criminal deputy prosecutor Jim Townsend actually knew of the investigators' plans but did not stop them.

Association president Mark Muenster contacted Washington State governor Gary Locke, objecting to

any consideration of Townsend for appointment t
Snohomish County judgeship. "If I were the governo
counsel, the guy who advises the governor on a
pointments, I would want to know about any potent
skeletons in the appointee's closet," he said.

"Law officers never should be encouraged to prete.
to be lawyers," Muenster said. "This kind of ruse that w
used by the FBI agent and approved by Mr. Townsenc
very corrosive of the trust between lawyers and th
clients."

Despite possible corrosion or blatant deception, t
trial process was under way. The final days of Februa
saw the first days of jury selection, and the final da
of DNA analysis of evidence by forensic scientist I
Raymond Allen Grimsbo, director of Intermounta
Forensic Laboratories in Portland, Oregon.

Grimsbo attended Portland State University, grad
ated in 1973 with a major in science, and minor
biology and psychology. In 1984, he went back to scho
and graduated in 1987 from the Graduate School
Union Institute with a Ph.D. in forensic science.

"My dissertation and research," said Grimsbo, "was
the area of analyzing bloodstains for genetic marker
Currently I hold a teaching appointment in Portla
State University, and I held appointments at the Heal
Science University in Portland and several of the small
colleges in the area. Currently I do case work and c
rect the laboratory. I direct the day-to-day activities in th
laboratory, just the overall running of the laborato
dictate policies, which procedures are to be used ar
general directions."

As for expertise in forensic science, Grimsbo's speci
ized training bespeaks volumes. "Prior to becoming
forensic scientist, I was a medical technologist in a clinic
laboratory in Portland. In 1975, I went to work as
trooper for the Oregon State Police, and was assigned

e crime laboratory in Portland. Over the next nine and half years, I was trained by the state police in general iminalistics—which is evidence collection—everything om hit-and-run accidents to murder scenes, to analyzing ace evidence—which would be like hairs and fibers— nd from that to serology—dealing with biological uids—toxicology to firearms, and just a broad spectrum ea, more like a general practitioner. The specialty that I ravitated toward was serology or biological analysis. I was ained by the state police and took classes at the univer- ties, classes with the FBI and various other groups to xpand that, joined several associations—for example, I'm fellow in the American Academy of Forensic Sciences."

In 1985, Grimsbo left the state police, established a rivate practice that was incorporated in 1987, as Inter- iountain Forensic Laboratories. "Right now," he said, our laboratory does testing all over the country.

"We are a clinical laboratory," explained Grimsbo, "be- des being a crime lab, in that we can do analysis for hysicians that want to diagnose disease in people. Our pecialty area for that is toxicology—drugs and poisons. Ve have a specialty license in that, and we adopt the uidelines that are required of the clinical laboratory. he guidelines of the professional associations in the orensic area are all incorporated into our laboratory ractice."

Ray Grimsbo is also no stranger to the courtroom as n expert witness. "I've testified in court regarding PCR nd DNA analysis in Oregon, Washington, Indiana—I elieve, Hawaii—Montana, Florida, and probably some nore. I don't recall them all, but quite a few."

For those unfamiliar with polymerase chain reaction PCR), Dr. Grimsbo happily explained his work and the igh standards utilized in evaluation of evidence submitted o him for examination.

"PCR is an amplification process for typing DNA,"

Grimsbo explained. "We have a separate room that is s
aside, that the only thing that's done in there is the a
plification and the typing of the DNA itself. We ha
other areas in the laboratory that we will examine e
dence, take cuttings from the evidence. And then
have a biological area, where we will extract the DN
and do setup. And from there, it will go into the PC
room and be worked up in there."

Techniques are utilized in the laboratory to minimi
the possibility of contamination when conducting
PCR/DNA test. "We have very stringent protocols," co
firmed Grimsbo. "In fact, sterile technique begins whe
we are just cutting or taking our samples, one item a
time, on the deck, new paper every time. After we ha
taken cuttings from the sample in an area of interest-
let's say we identified some blood on an item, we did th
with forceps and tweezers that we use, which get rinse
in Clorox, water, and ethanol, then dried. Then we cut
clean control area, where there is nothing, so you ca
gauge background and that. Aside from wearing glove
scrubbing the decks, what I consider normal in a clir
cal or in a DNA laboratory, we are pretty much steri
in that area."

On February 26, 1997, Dr. Grimsbo received his se
ond batch of evidence from Detective Lloyd Herndon
the Everett Police Department, evidence that had alread
been tested previously by Genex Laboratories. Include
was the laundered shirt given to detectives by Care
Clark. As to whether or not Grimsbo would recover DN
from Clark's shirt, the jury was still out.

Part 3
TRIAL

Chapter 12

"In the coming weeks," Judge Richard Thorpe told the over 150 potential jurors crowded into his Everett courtroom, "some of you may be asked to decide whether Mr. Clark should receive the death penalty."

Each potential juror completed a fifteen-page questionnaire asking detailed information about their knowledge of the case, their families, education, and work experience. "One of the things we need to know," Judge Thorpe explained, "is how much you know about the case and whether you've formed an idea or opinion about it."

In preparation for the trial, over eight hundred county residents were summoned for jury duty. Many of those who did not show up in court on the February 27 were previously excused due to hardship.

"We expect to spend the next two to three weeks interviewing and screening the potential jurors, individually and in groups," explained deputy prosecutor Ron Doersch. "Picking a jury is critical in a death penalty case," added deputy prosecutor Jo Vanderlee. "It only takes one juror to stand between the defendant and a death sentence."

The jury selection process launched with the sluggish speed and weary efficiency of Gutenburg's printing press. By the end of the first day, six people had been questioned, and Judge Thorpe dismissed two potential jurors.

"Once we hit our stride," said Thorpe, "things may go more quickly."

In the Portland laboratory of Dr. Ray Grimsbo, the progress was efficient and significant. "There were sleeping-bag cuttings that had been taken and then sent to me," recalled Grimsbo. "The typing results obtained from the bloodstain from the sleeping bag were consistent with Roxanne Doll's DNA type." In fact, test results on the plethora of evidence items indicated DNA consistent with that of Roxanne Doll, and/or the bodily fluids of Richard M. Clark.

"It would be reasonable that the laundered item would have the weakest test results," said Grimsbo. "If it was laundered, much of the material on there is going to be laundered away, leaving just enough to get weak results, that would be expected."

Despite its degradation over time, or in the rinse cycle, test results indicated, in Grimsbo's opinion, that Roxanne Doll's blood was on Clark's shirt, and these were equally valid as the results showing the child's saliva on the socks allegedly stuffed into her mouth.

"It was amazing to me," admitted Detective Herndon, "that Grimsbo got results from the shirt washed in bleach by Carol Clark. The bloodstain on that shirt, once tested, gave results that indicated that her DNA could not be excluded by any scientific process."

The ongoing process of jury selection, however, excluded several individuals because of their strong feelings against the death penalty. Among those was Margaret Jobe, despite her clear statement that she could abide by the law and make the penalty decision. She did indicate, however, that she didn't think that she could be fair to both sides, despite her best efforts to do so.

More definite in her stance was Jane Schwamberger, who opposed the death penalty for philosophical and religious reasons. "I probably would avoid finding the

defendant guilty to avoid havin[...]
penalty at a sentencing phase," sh[...]

Prospective juror Scott Koch sa[...]
could make the decision to impose t[...]
but he didn't know if he could make th[...]

Daniel Roczynski was another prospec[...]
readily admitted that he would have trouble i[...]
death penalty and that his reluctance might affe[...]
determination. On being told by the prosecutor th[...]
people had been excused because of their strong fe[...]
about the death penalty, Roczynski stated, "Right n[...]
think I would be affected to the point where I wouldn't [...]
able to make that kind of decision."

The court denied defense challenges of a number of
prospective jurors who, unlike those individuals previously mentioned, had strong views in favor of the death
penalty. Bill Hefley, for example, said that if Clark was
proven guilty beyond a reasonable doubt, "he don't deserve leniency." Hefley affirmed at least ten times that a
death sentence would be a foregone conclusion.

Gerald Johnson, in a manner similar to that of Hefley,
responded several times that if Richard M. Clark was
found guilty of premeditated first-degree murder, he
would feel "morally bound" to impose the death penalty.
Gertrude Carlson likewise said she would be "inclined or
compelled to impose the death penalty" and it would be
hard for her to presume that Clark warranted leniency.

"I can be just as impartial as the next person," said
Carlson, but she indicated later that she knew some of
the police officer witnesses, and that knowing them
would influence her, and that even after hearing the reasons to keep an open mind from the prosecutor, she
would still be inclined to vote for the death penalty.

Bessie Baker Thompson, another possible juror, said
that if Clark was found guilty, he "deserved the death
penalty" and it would be the defense counsel's job to

mpson said that
artial juror and
tion prove the

firmly stated
se, his or her
the taxpayers

ty," Pintler
ty." He also ad-
urely open to mitigating
believe that somebody was raised
the child, that gives the right later on in their
to take a life. I don't agree with that philosophy."

More extreme was Richard Lippincott, a prospective juror who stated numerous times during voir dire that if Richard Clark was proven guilty, then the death penalty should follow automatically. "Mr. Lippincott continued to be confused," recalled appellant's attorney Suzanne Lee Elliott, "about the two phases of the trial and the state's burden of proof at each phase."

The defense was forced to use four of its twelve peremptory challenges to excuse Hefley, Pintler, Carlson, and Thompson. In total, the defense used eleven of its twelve possible peremptory challenges. In other words, eleven potential jurors were excused by the defense.

When these challenges were exercised, both the defense and the prosecution were aware of which juror would replace the one removed. Had the defense exercised a twelfth, Lippincott would have been on the jury panel. The defense would have had no remaining peremptory challenge to remove him.

"Because the defense didn't challenge him, Lippincott was the first potential alternate," explained Elliott. There are three challenges available for alternate jurors. "In effect," said Elliott, "the defense was able to remove

Ir. Lippincott from the jury by not using its final peremptory challenge."

Over the next few weeks, 114 potential jurors were questioned regarding their views on the death penalty and their prior knowledge of the case. Ninety-seven of the 114 acknowledged hearing about the case in the media or from conversations with other people. Only seventeen people expressly denied any prior knowledge of the case, and only nine people who were not excused for hardship or for their views on the death penalty had not heard of the case through pretrial publicity.

"Clearly," attorney Suzanne Lee Elliott later commented, "the overwhelming majority of prospective jurors were aware of the case and the publicity surrounding it." In fact, 84 percent fell into that category, and when the final jury was seated, only one juror expressly disavowed prior knowledge of the case.

"And you folks," said Judge Thorpe to those not selected to serve, "breathe a sigh of relief again, and you may be excused. And thank you very much for your patience." The jury and the alternates retired to department jury room #8, and Judge Thorpe turned to the attorneys.

"My understanding," began deputy prosecutor Doersch, "is the defense may have an objection to the visual/memory aid that I intend to use in my opening."

"Yes, that's correct," said defense attorney Errol Scott. "I want to object [to] not only what I anticipate is the remarks of the prosecutor, but the poster that is going to be used by the prosecutor. The purpose of the opening statement is to inform the jurors in a summary fashion what the evidence will be, but what he intends to present is clearly a closing argument."

The prosecution's visual display and attendant commentary were objectionable, Scott said, because they were designed to "appeal to the emotion, sympathy, and prejudice of the jurors.

"It seems to me that the court should not allow that," said the defense. "That is for the final stage of the proceedings, after the jury has heard all the evidence—that's when the prosecution may be able to make those arguments, but not here, not at this time."

Judge Thorpe pointed to Doersch's elaborate poster display. "Are you objecting to the use of that?" Scott nodded emphatically.

"I do object to the use of that, and I'll object if I believe the prosecutor has overstepped the line in preying upon the jurors' emotions. In looking at that [poster], it's clear that is the prosecutor's intention."

Thorpe gave Doersch opportunity for response. "I've heard opening statements described as a road map," Doersch began. "When I take a road map and I unfold it, I see lines; I see all kinds of details, contours, all kinds of things on road maps."

The deputy prosecutor motioned toward Scott as he continued. "Counsel seeks to restrict the use of the English language to the barest recitation of facts. That's not an opening statement. You might as well have handouts and have a machine spit them out here. I intend to use the English language as I see fit—not to argue, but to paint for the jury a picture of this crime, the investigation, and the results. I am not required to stand up here mouselike and recite facts in the order Mr. Scott wishes."

"This," said Doersch, referencing his poster, "is a memory aid, this is something that will help me use the language effectively. There is nothing here that is argumentative. I would anticipate objections during my opening statement, but I would also anticipate that they will not be well taken."

Judge Thorpe studied the poster critically, then gave his decision. "Without some idea of how this amounts to a road map, the defense objection will be sustained. How much of this you can use during the language of your pening statement we will have to see as it goes along, but he opening statement will not be a closing argument. I am not inclined to allow this to be shown to the jury while you re making your opening statement for an hour or so."

Doersch, displeased, only replied, "Very good." Scott had another matter of emotional impact from which he wanted the jury shielded—the proposed testimony of Eugene Hillius, witness for the prosecution. Scott intended, he told the court, to object to the anticipated testimony. He wanted the court not to allow "any reference to the things he might testify to mentioned in the prosecution's opening statement."

The court asked Doersch to explain exactly the content of Hillius's proposed testimony and its relevance. He related that Hillius and Clark, both incarcerated, were watching a television program in which a murder was being committed.

"The murder victim was a young girl," said Doersch. "During that presentation, Mr. Clark apparently said, 'Fuck her before you kill her; fuck her before you stab her.' That was not the only remark that Mr. Clark made in Mr. Hillius's presence," Doersch continued. "One had to do with Mr. Clark telling Mr. Hillius, 'They got my DNA out of her butt.' This was done on a different occasion, but also in the jail. There is also a conversation in which he indicated his anger at his brother Elza for not lying for him. These three remarks are the ones we would seek to present to the jury. Mr. Clark made these three remarks in the jail, without any pressure of any kind from Mr. Hillius, without Mr. Hillius operating as an agent of anyone."

Judge Thorpe pondered the situation for a moment; Doersch added further commentary. "They were ill-advised remarks by Mr. Clark," he said, "but they can't be unrung at this point. They are clearly relevant to the case, and there is no legal reason that I can see, except of course the discretion of this court, to keep them out."

"When did this occur?" asked Thorpe.

"Sometime in May or June of 1996," Doersch answere

"I am not persuaded that his frame of mind fourtee months later," said the judge, "while he is in jail awaitir trial on a crime that occurred fourteen months earlier going to be relevant to the trial phase. I'm not ruling this time that you may not use it, but I am ruling th there will be no mention of it, and the evidence will n be introduced without prior leave of the court."

"Thank you," said Doersch, who had nothing at th point about which to be thankful.

"Now," Judge Thorpe asked the prosecutor, "you expe your opening statement to be how long?"

"Well," responded Doersch, "it will be shorter now."

"Ladies and gentlemen of the jury," intoned Judg Thorpe following a fifteen-minute recess, "will you pleas stand and raise your right hand to be sworn to try the case

With the jury duly sworn, the long-awaited trial (Richard Mathew Clark was under way.

"You are not to be sequestered during the trial," Judg Thorpe informed the jury. "You will take your recesse in the jury deliberation room, and when we recess f(the noon period and for the day, please proceed direct off the floor. And when you return, please proceed d rectly into the jury room, thus avoiding any inadvertel contact with anyone who may be a witness whom you al not able to identify by sight.

"Do not," emphasized Thorpe, "attempt to determin what the law is on your own by reading about or re searching the law in any manner. And because you mu: decide this case only on proper evidence admitted in th courtroom, you should never seek out any evidence o your own, nor inspect the scene of an event involved i a case, as conditions may not be the same.

"These instructions continue to apply to conduct throughout the trial and at every recess, until the matter is submitted to you for decision," said the judge. "I will repeat or refer to these instructions again, not because I have any doubt in your integrity or your ability to understand, but just so that if any of you does something inappropriate, I'll be satisfied that if sanctions should be imposed, you will have been sufficiently warned.

"The attorneys have the right and the duty to make any objections that they deem appropriate. These objections should not influence you and you should make no assumptions because of objections by the attorneys.

"It is the judge's duty to rule on the admissibility of evidence," he explained. "Please do not concern yourselves with the reasons for these rulings.

"You should disregard any evidence that is not admitted or that is stricken by the judge. The law does not permit a judge to comment on the evidence in any way.

"A judge comments on the evidence; the judge does not offer a personal opinion as to the weight or believability of the testimony of a witness or of other evidence. This is because you are the ones whose duty it is to make those decisions, not mine. Although I'll not intentionally do so, if it appears that I have made a comment on the evidence, you must disregard the apparent comment entirely. And if I lean back in my chair and stare at the ceiling, or close my eyes, it is not a comment on either the testimony of the witness or of the questions being asked by the attorneys."

Judge Thorpe gave the jurors another important instruction regarding possible interpretations of his personal demeanor. "I have an active imagination and a strange sense of humor. If I am seen to be smiling up here, don't try to figure out what just happened in the courtroom that caused me to smile, because it may be something that had absolutely nothing to do with what is going on in the courtroom. That is not meant to be a

comment on the evidence. The attorneys' remarks, state
ments, and arguments are to help you understand th
evidence and apply the law. They are not evidence, how
ever, and you should disregard any remarks, statement
or arguments that are not supported by the evidence o
by the law as given to you by the court.

"The only evidence you are to consider consists of te
timony of witnesses and exhibits admitted into evidence
Sometimes exhibits will be marked, will be carrie
around, will be talked about and that sort of thing, bu
unless they are admitted into evidence, they won' t g
back to the jury room with you. So just because some
thing is marked as an exhibit, don't figure you can tur
off because you can see it again, you might not.

"It is important that you listen carefully to the witnesses
testimony during the trial. During your deliberations, yo
will not be provided with a written copy of the testimony
but will have to rely upon the collective recollection o
the twelve of you." A few jurors looked at each other wit
ill-concealed disappointment.

"For this reason," continued Thorpe, "your ability t
accurately recall the testimony is important. Any exhibit
admitted into evidence will go to the jury room with yo
during your deliberations. You will be allowed to tak
notes during the taking of testimony, but not durin
opening statements or closing argument.

"Please pay attention to the testimony and don't le
note taking so consume you that you miss important ev
dence. You may not take the notepads with you from th
courtroom, so just leave them on your seats when yo
leave and they'll be on your seats when you return. You
notes will be confidential. No one else will read them
and after the case is concluded, they'll be destroye
again without having been read.

"And on the subject of note taking," said Judge Thorpe
"I'll be taking notes up here on my computer. Don't b

distracted by that. My notes are to record what is said so that I can make legal rulings on issues that come up. Your job is to decide credibility of witnesses and the weight to be accorded to the evidence. Since we are performing different functions, don't think that because I am taking notes, you should be also. You are the judges of the evidence. I have to make the legal rulings to make the evidence. I have to hear what is said, but I don't have to make any judgment with respect to credibility or weight and that sort of thing.

"And on the subject of evidence rulings," Thorpe explained, "there will be times when we have to excuse you into the jury room while we discuss evidentiary issues. Although it has been a while since this matter was begun, it has not been rehearsed or polished like a TV show. A trial is more like a play being written.

"The court of appeals and supreme court are looking over my shoulder to make sure that I don't let in any evidence that should be excluded, or exclude any evidence that should be included," said the judge. "Your being back there in the jury room not hearing testimony bothers me almost as much as it will you, so be sure I'll keep the interruptions as short and as infrequent as I can.

"You are to keep an open mind and not decide any issue in the case until it is submitted to you for your deliberation," the judge reminded them. "You are officers of the court and must act judicially with an earnest desire to determine and declare a proper verdict. Throughout the trial, you should be impartial and permit neither sympathy nor prejudice to influence you. We will now have opening statement by counsel, first for the plaintiff, Mr. Doersch."

Chapter 13

Deputy prosecutor Ronald Doersch stood from his table, collected his notes, and addressed the jury. First impressions are important, and Doersch was determined to make a strong impression indeed.

Describing Roxanne Doll's murder as an act of infinite cruelty, her victimization resulting from a combination of her vulnerability and availability, Doersch's opening statement mesmerized the jury. "Everyone was riveted," recalled Roxanne's mother. "You could see the shock and dismay on their faces when he described the horrible things done to my little girl."

The prosecutor detailed the multiple stabbings that plunged deeply into Roxanne's neck, nicked her spine, and finally transected the jugular vein on her left side. "She bled to death," Doersch explained, and then told how the child was dumped beneath piles of grass clippings, yard waste and a tree on Everett's East Grand.

The prosecutor allowed respectful silence as the backdrop for jurors' personal mental images of the crime's horrific nature. "We expect the evidence—physical, forensic, scientific, direct, and circumstantial evidence—will show that there is no mystery as to who committed this crime, who did these things to Roxanne Doll. As I'll describe to you, the evidence will show that this man committed the crime, the man seated at counsel table in the striped shirt, Richard Clark."

Jurors' eyes predictably shifted to Clark, then back again to Doersch, who related the story of nine-year-old Siobian Kubesh and her friend Sheena finding the body of Roxanne Doll. "Siobian does not know that the foot belongs to Roxanne Doll, a seven-year-old girl who has been missing for a week, that people have been looking for all over Everett, and all over Snohomish County, a girl who is two years her junior. All she knows," said Doersch, "is that she sees this foot and that it belongs to a person. Siobian screams and Sheena takes hold of her and says, 'Let's get out of here.'"

Uncomfortably enthralled, jurors listened as Doersch told them of the police arrival, Roxanne's body being taken for autopsy by the medical examiner, the damage inflicted upon her body, and the different types of tests performed by DNA forensic specialists.

"Roxanne is found on April eighth," he explained. "It is the body of a young Caucasian female, showing early to moderate decomposition, an identification bracelet around her right wrist, and it has an inscription on both sides, and it includes the name Roxanne Doll. There are disposable training pants on the child," continued Doersch, "that are torn at the left seam, an undershirt or training bra is also present. They secure the scene overnight. It's getting too dark, too late, and they rope off and tape off the scene. Guards are brought in to protect the integrity, as far as they are able, of the scene on East Grand. The next day, they commenced to picking up evidence and moving Roxanne out of there.

"They take her, put a sheet over her, and they roll her over and they take her out of there and transfer her to the medical examiner's office. They look at her in the van," he said, "and they see that the animals have been at her and so there are bite marks and there is damage to her face and to some other parts of her body from animal activity. But this animal activity is distinguishable from other

marks that will be found by the medical examiner—
wounds, injuries, and effects.

"The examination is conducted the next day. And
what they find," said Doersch, and he prepared the jury
for the unpleasantness of his following statements by saying, "I'll be as brief as I can about it. . . . There are
multiple stab wounds to her neck. There is something
called a transection of the left internal jugular vein. That
injury or defect comes out of one wound that has two
tracks, so that there is a wound track in one direction,
and then in another direction, which severs the jugular
vein. This, more likely than not, is the wound that actually killed her. There are a number of other stab wounds,
eight in total around her neck."

He emphatically detailed the prosecution's evidence
linking Richard Clark to the murder of Roxanne Doll.
"Blood samples taken from Roxanne at the autopsy, and
samples taken from Mr. Clark pursuant to warrant, are
tested. What they find is that Roxanne had a very rare
blood type that only one out of one thousand Caucasians
has. They find that blood not only on that shirt, but also
on the sleeping bag. DNA typing is later done on the
bloodstains from that sleeping bag, the socks, and the
carpet. Roxanne's DNA is on the sleeping-bag bloodstain and on the bloodstained socks; the defendant's
DNA is on one of the socks. The defendant's shirt is examined," continued Doersch. "Human protein tests are
done on the blood stain. The bloodstain turns out to be
human. Later DNA typing shows the DNA from the
bloodstain is consistent with Roxanne's DNA.

"Testing was done on the sperm retrieved from the
anal swab," Doersch told the jury, "and it was found to
be consistent with Richard Clark's genetic profile. DNA
from the sperm on the vaginal wash was found consistent with Richard Clark's genetic profile. DNA from the
sperm of the vaginal swab was consistent with Richard

Clark's genetic profile. DNA from the bloodstained shirt was consistent with Roxanne's genetic profile, in addition to the standard blood typing and testing. DNA from the bloodstained sleeping bag and sock seized from the van is consistent with Roxanne's DNA. And DNA from that sock also indicated a mixture of blood, semen, and saliva were present, and the results show that those were consistent with Richard Clark being the source of the semen.

"Aside from the DNA results," noted the prosecutor, "there are pieces of traditional evidence. Carpet fibers are found inside Roxanne's training bra—fibers that are microscopically similar to the fibers from the light brown carpet seized from the defendant's van. And there is one more piece of traditional evidence," he said. "It is seized, but not from the van, nor from Roxanne's body or the place that she was—let's face it—dumped, but from the window of Roxanne's room.

"Detective Kiser dusted for fingerprints," Doersch told the jury, "and he found a fingerprint. And that fingerprint is of a certain individual. Examining and comparing leads to the inescapable conclusion that the fingerprint on the window belongs to the person whose known fingerprints have been examined, and that person is Richard Clark."

By the time Roxanne's body was discovered, the prosecutor told the jury, the defendant was already in jail. "And he remains in jail and time passes and he is up with other individuals in the jail, including a fellow named Eugene Hillius. Eugene Hillius is what most of us would describe as a very bad man. He has multiple convictions for all kinds of stuff. And at the time I'm going to speak of, he is facing sentencing for a number of counts of first-degree child rape. Mr. Hillius is a scary-looking guy, as you will see when he testifies.

"In return for absolutely nothing," said Ron Doersch,

"Mr. Hillius agrees to testify. And what he will tell you is this: Sometime in late May and June 1996, Richard Clark tells him that he was kind of pissed off at his family, specifically at his brother Elza, because Elza wouldn't back up his story about the animal blood being in the van. He was upset because his brother wouldn't lie for him, wouldn't back up his story. Later on, June 22, '96, after Hillius has told the police about this and after he goes back to jail, he has another conversation with Richard Clark. He and some friends are standing around the television set and they are talking about DNA. Eugene Hillius walks by and the defendant asks Eugene if he's got a candy bar. He says, 'Yeah, I got one, but you have to come back to my room.' As they are going back there, the defendant says to Eugene Hillius unexpectedly, 'They took my DNA out of her butt.'"

Several jurors' expressions showed ill-concealed disgust at the defendent's remark. "Well, it is disgusting," agreed Tim Iffrig. "It's more than that. That's my little girl he's talking about—my little girl that he murdered."

"Seven-thirty in the morning, Nicholas wakes up and he tells his mother that Roxanne is gone," said Doersch, continuing his narrative. "That's about eight o'clock before he tells that to her. And what happens then is basically the nightmare that continues until Roxanne is found, and to this day, because Roxanne is gone. Kristena, at some point when the light is graying outside, awakens and Roxanne is not there; she can feel with her body that she's gone and goes back to sleep. So when did Roxanne disappear?

"What's interesting is this, about twelve forty-five to twelve-fifty A.M. on East Grand Avenue, right at the place where Sheena and her friend would play in another seven days, Janice Cliatt is driving home. She is thinking about the fact that it's April Fools' Day now, because it is early in the morning. She is thinking about the fact that she won't have to work the next Friday because she's had a scheduling change. She works for Safeco in Seattle. She leaves Safeco about twelve-fifteen A.M., where she is working without fail. . . ."

The prosecution sequentially prepared jurors for the orderly appearance of witness after witness, each more damning than the next in producing seemingly irrefutable evidence that Richard Mathew Clark brutally raped and murdered Roxanne Doll.

The defense, despite the all-American presumption of innocence, had an uphill battle. Interestingly, Gail Doll and Tim Iffrig have the highest regard for Richard Clark's defense team.

"I respect them tremendously," said Gail, "and some people are shocked to hear that. But this is important, because this is America. Everyone is entitled to the best defense and the presumption of innocence until proven guilty beyond a reasonable doubt. Bill Jaquette and Mr. Scott had a rough job, and they did it well. They worked hard. I hold no animosity against them at all."

"Yeah," agreed Tim Iffrig. "I believed in my heart that Richard Clark killed my daughter. And I also believe that if you don't have fair trials, you make a mockery of everything this country stands for. Yeah, I wanted to kill that son of a bitch, but that wasn't my decision—that's up to the jury to decide, based on the evidence and the law as instructed by the judge. I don't know if the defense really thought that they could get a not guilty verdict, but I sure as hell know they worked their ass off to keep him alive."

"Usually, the defense calls its witnesses after the prosecution completes their case," began defense team attorney Errol Scott in his opening statement. "However, we provided the prosecution with a list of who we would call as our witnesses for the defense. In this case, we anticipate the prosecution will call most, if not all, the defense witnesses in the prosecution's case. That means that intermixed with the prosecution's case will be people who would otherwise customarily be called by the defense, and they will outline for you the facts of the defense case.

"The effect of that is, is that you are not going to know when a witness testifies whether technically that witness might otherwise have been called by the prosecution or called by the defense. But what that also means for you is that you obviously have to keep an open mind in listening to the evidence."

Scott told the jury that they would hear, in Gail Doll's own words, that she "turned on their light, saw the two heads in bed, shut off the light, and closed the door. In another statement made May 1, 1995, she told Detective Herndon that what she had said in the earlier two statements that I quoted you [was] accurate. She declared that under penalty of perjury. We have a transcription of that statement. So," reiterated Scott, "I have three statements by Gail Doll that she saw both children in bed at around midnight when she returned home.

"Richard's aunt Carol, who you heard about, will testify that Richard arrived at her house about twelve-ten A.M., and saw a stain on his shirt," continued Scott. "When asked about it, Richard said it was from a deer that his brother Elza had poached. Richard cleaned up there and left there about twelve forty-five A.M., and apparently went to the Dog House in downtown Everett. Linda Hein and Cheryle Galloway will testify that they saw Richard twice that night, once around eight or nine P.M., and again around one o'clock in the morning. Tim Iffrig will tell you that Richard arrived at their home again round one o'clock A.M. And the evidence will show that after that time, Richard was continually in the company of Tim and Gail, or Tim and Patrick Casey at the neighbor's from approximately one o'clock A.M. until six-thirty in the morning; I believe between midnight and around one o'clock, Mr. Iffrig and his wife were at home. Richard arrived at one o'clock.

"Tim and Richard went over to the neighbor's house, Mr. Casey's. They stayed there at Casey's home until around six-thirty A.M. They then went back to Mr. Iffrig's home and packed for the camping trip. They left the house about seven-thirty A.M. It was about eight-ten A.M. that Nicholas reported to his mother that he could not find Roxanne, and that was the start of the inquiry about where she was and eventually calling the police.

"With regard to the stain on Richard Clark's shirt and the claimed statement by Elza that Richard asked him to lie for him," Scott explained, "testimony from Toni Clark and George Clark, Richard's parents, will show that there was in fact deer meat and deer blood in their home on the night this happened.

"George Clark the second, Richard's brother, will tell you that he heard a conversation between Richard and Elza that the bucket of deer blood had spilled in Richard's van. We are hopeful that Elza Clark will in fact tell you when he testifies that he did poach a deer and that some of its remains spilled in Richard's van.

"Let me turn now to the scientific evidence," said Scott. "The prosecution intends to offer a number of items of scientific evidence and testimony from a number of experts on blood typing, DNA testing, and carpet fiber comparison. Let me respond briefly to what he said.

"DNA testing is still a relatively new procedure, which requires a great deal of scientific control and care in preparation of the test and reporting the results. The defense will challenge the DNA evidence," asserted Scott, "on a number of grounds that I'll briefly outline for you."

The defense sharply criticized the interpretations of DNA test results, stating, "When there is a mixture of DNA, it's difficult or impossible to identify which DNA is which." If the control feature for a particular test has failed, and where there are multiple results when there should be only one, "in that situation," he said, "that test should be disregarded as unreliable."

Scott also advised the jury that the results of carpet fiber comparisons and blood group testing had problems as well. "If the samples of blood are correctly taken, preserved, and grouped, the conclusions are nonetheless based on calculations of the frequency of the blood group in a particular population. That means that all you can say is that this person is of one among a number of persons in a population group that has that blood characteristic. They can *not* tell you," he insisted, "that the person in question did in fact contribute that blood. As for the carpet fiber and comparisons," he said, "the same statement applies to both of those items.

"I believe the evidence will show that two fibers were recovered from Roxanne Doll's body and compared with carpet fibers from Richard's van. Let me tell you how that happened," he said, "and why they are reported to have similar characteristics.

"The evidence will show," said Scott, "that the comparisons do not specifically identify the fiber found on Roxanne Doll as having come from the carpet in the van. In fact, the comparison is done by taking ten or twelve fibers from one of these carpets samples and determining whether any one of them match the evidence sample. In many situations, one or two of those fibers will match, and on ten or twelve of them, the rest of them won't.

"So," Scott clarified, "from the same carpet sample you can have fibers which match the suspect sample, or suspect evidence and some that do not. And what is reported to you is those that match. And therefore we have no way of knowing whether the carpet that is the sample is in fact the contributor of the carpet fibers that were found on her body, or they could have come from some other place. The similarity of the hair, which is done in a much similar way, and the carpet fibers is of limited value because it can not be the base of claiming a match between the known and unknown samples.

"In conclusion," Scott said, "let me ask you to keep an open mind on all the evidence and not to expect a distinct and separate defense. It is our position that the abduction of Roxanne Doll could only have occurred after midnight, after Gail Doll saw two heads in the bed, those of Roxanne and Kristena, that we can prove to a near certainty where Richard Clark was between midnight and six-thirty in the morning. Thank you."

Errol Scott took his seat next to his conservatively dressed client, and Judge Thorpe asked the prosecution to call their first witness.

Chapter 14

"We screamed and we ran home on our bikes," said one of the two young girls who saw Roxanne's body on a brushy north Everett hillside. In her soft voice, the nervous child told of their innocent fun coming to a tragic halt upon the grisly and nightmarish discovery. Wesley Coulter, the man who actually summoned police to the scene, also testified.

Kristena Doll, Roxanne's sister, wearing a purple flower-print dress, sat poised within the framework of perceptible unease. "Does Roxanne live with you anymore?" asked deputy prosecutor Ron Doersch. "Yeah," responded Kristena seriously, "but she is up in heaven."

"Much of the first day was spent setting the scene, more or less, for Roxanne's disappearance and the discovery and recovery of her body," recalled Herndon. "There were detailed maps of the Iffrig home, the bedroom that she was taken from, and the site where the two young girls found her body."

The jury was also shown the Barbie pullover Roxanne last slept in and the dolls she kept in her room. "Several photographs of the body recovery site were shown to them," Herndon said, "and that included some where you could see Roxanne Doll's partially buried foot."

Tim Iffrig and Gail Doll gave detailed accountings of the hours from the early afternoon the of March 31 through April 1, 1995. "Richard Clark's attorneys," recalled Herndon, "really questioned Gail about the statements she gave to us in which she indicated that she saw Roxanne and her sister asleep in bed at about five past midnight, April first. They wanted her to have actually seen Roxanne in bed when she came home, but she didn't. As she testified, she expected to see two heads in the bed, and that's what she thought she saw."

The parents, pals, relatives, officers, pathologists, investigators, scientists, and significant passersby, by virtue of their overlapping testimonies, were as brick and mortar in an interlocking and fiercely impenetrable fortress of facts.

Dr. Eric Kiesel described in lurid detail the tragic injuries that violated young Roxanne, and those that caused her death. "If you are looking at the vagina with a person laying on their back," he said, "and set up a clock, this tear, the gape, the gaping laceration, would extend from about the four to eight o'clock position, through the six o'clock.

"There is another laceration. And this is on the left wall of the vagina," said Kiesel, pointing to large, illustrative photographs. "You can just see a hint of it. You clearly can see the full length of it. This one was from where the laceration began to the apex, or the top, of the laceration, which is in what's called the left fourchette; that's the space in the vagina adjacent to the cervix. That laceration also gapes to about two centimeters, as I measured it. And that's at the widest point. There is considerable amount of hemorrhage in the deep, soft tissues."

Asked by the prosecution to explain what that meant, he replied, "Well, by definition the laceration is a blunt-force injury. She tore and bled. I was not able to tell if there had been penetration to the anal area. The anus is dilated. But that can occur as postmortem artifact. So whether or not the anus is dilated enough from insertion of something or due to this postmortem artifact, you can't tell in part."

The way to tell if it is associated with sexual assault, he explained "is if spermatozoa or semen could be found in there, but considering the condition, the location she was on the hill, drainage would be from the vagina. She is on her back, and if the anus is dilated, there could be some cross contamination if spermatozoa is found in the anus or rectum. So basically I can't tell, but there is no trauma to the anus or rectum. So spermatozoa found on the anal swab could have drained from the vagina itself.

"There is really no way to tell how much force caused the injuries to her vagina, but sufficient force to tear the skin and from a stretching force, enough force to create disruption of blood vessels. But there is also going to be disruption of those blood vessels as the tissues stretch. So, there is no scientific way that I'm aware of to truly be able to measure that in this individual. You can do experiments, measuring how much force does it take to tear, but there is enough individual variability that I don't think we would be significant here."

Prosecutor Doersch turned attention away from Roxanne Doll's torn and stretched vagina, and focused on the fatal stab wounds. "First of all," Doersch asked Dr. Kiesel, "how much stab wounds to the neck in total?"

"Well, [there] were a minimum number of seven," Kiesel said. "The reason that there is a minimum number is because some of these wounds are multicomponent, and it's not possible for me to tell whether that's two wounds or if the second wound was created by the motion used to create the first."

On the right side of Roxanne's head, by the right ear, were more wounds. "There is a large irregular wound, which is the one furthest over to the side, and then there are two other wounds toward the center, or toward the middle part of the neck," Kiesel testified. "This upper wound, the small wound at the top of the series of three wounds, is a stab wound. It's three-eighths by one-quarter inch. It's a multicomponent stab wound. It's not a pure stab wound—it is not a wound from a knife going in and coming out. [It] has multiple cutting components to it, so that it suggests that either there are two wounds to the same area or it's a wound where there is movement on the part of the deceased, or there is movement on the part of the person creating the wound.

"Twisting of the blade could do this," he explained. "A shaky hand could do this; hesitation could do this. This wound is through the skin and it's relatively superficial, it's into the subcutaneous tissues. Subcutaneous tissues are those tissues immediately beneath the skin. It doesn't go into the muscles of the right neck, it's just into the skin. It goes slightly under the skin and has an estimated depth of half an inch; so measured from the skin surface to the apex or the end of the wound track, it was approximately one-half inch. The wound traveled from front to back, it went upward, and it went from left to right. So, this wound is heading from the . . . the injury to the skin itself, upward and essentially toward the back of the head. This wound is located, if you will, if you measure from the top of the head, this one is nine inches below the head. Just below it is a three-quarter-inch wound. These wounds also are gaping. Part of this is due to the elasticity of the skin, part of this is due to the decomposition changes. This lower wound is three-quarters of an inch long. It's almost transverse, or horizontal. The body is standing in an upright position—that would be the horizontal position. It's three-quarters inches right at the midline. And if you measure from the top of the head, it's nine and a half inches below the top of the head. This wound track is deeper; it's one and a quarter inches deep. It goes through the skin and through the strap muscles of the neck."

The neck has numerous muscles beneath the skin that attach to the neck organs. The neck organs being the larynx, or voice box, the trachea, or the cartilages there, the hyoid bone, which is a movable bone up at the top of the neck where the tongue attaches, and they also attach to the jawline. These strap muscles give control of the neck organs.

"If you turn your head and stretch your neck," explained Dr. Kiesel, "there is a large muscle that goes from the midportion of your collarbone, and it actually goes up to what's called the mastoid process. There is this bony lump behind your ear, and it's a pretty good size muscle. This wound is just center, toward the center of that, so it's in front of that muscle and to the side, the inside of that muscle. It doesn't really hit that muscle, but it goes through all these smaller muscles there. The significance of this is, if you feel your voice box, that big muscle, in the groove between the two is where your major inner-vascular bundle is, the major nerves coming from the brain down to the body, but your carotid arteries, major arteries that supply the brain, run here, and also the large vessels, the jugular veins, are also in this area. So this stabbing goes through the skin, into those strap muscles, but it does not hit the nerve vascular bundle.

"This wound is going again, from front to back. It's going just slightly left to right. In other words, it's almost straight on, but it's just slightly left to right, and it is upward, so it's going from bottom to top as it goes back.

"What's not shown well in any of these photographs," he told the jury, "is that there is a very significant wound just above the voice box. It's a multicomponent wound. There is more than one cut associated with it. It's horizontally oriented or transversely oriented. On the right side is a sharp edge. This—and because the wound margins are also smooth, this is telling us that we are dealing with a single-edged weapon creating that, most likely a single-edged knife. It's centered just a quarter of an inch of midline. Actually, in state's exhibit seventeen this wound is just barely showing upright at the edge of the ruler. This wound has two components and actually has two wound tracks. So it indicates there are two stab wounds essentially in the same hole; or the knife is in, comes partially out, and goes back in. One wound track goes through the skin in the muscles of the neck. It incises the left lateral or the side of the thyroid cartilage on the left or actually hits the bones of the cervical neck or cervical spine. There are seven vertebral bodies and this actually nicks number four."

Realizing that the stab wound pierced little Roxanne so deeply that the blade actually nicked her spine added additional disgust and revulsion toward whoever perpetrated such a horrid deed.

"The thyroid cartilage is, when you look at the voice box, the voice box is the larynx. In it, the very bottom edge of that, is another band of cartilage called the thyroid cartilage and immediately below that is the beginning of the trachea, which is the windpipe. So, this is a small piece of cartilage there at the bottom. This wound track, the first wound track, is nearly straight in, doesn't go up or down, doesn't go side to side; it's pretty much straight in."

With elaborate photographs detailing the wounds that took young Roxanne Doll's life, Dr. Kiesel testified to the autopsy's details, the determination of knife size, and the length of time her body was exposed to the elements.

Each subsequent witness, from the plethora of forensic scientists to the Dog House bartender who fixed Clark's final appearance at that popular watering hole at prior to midnight on March 31, appeared in sequence. Each participant, from Neila D'alexander recalling who consumed what while awaiting Tim and Gail's return home on Friday afternoon, to Elza Clark and his parents' discussion of deer remnants, easily eradicated any reasonable doubts concerning the culpability of Richard Clark in the kidnapping, rape, and murder of Roxanne Doll.

Concerning deer blood in the van and on Richard's shirt, Toni Clark testified that there was a deer poached by Elza and his friends a few weeks prior to March 31.

"Oh, gee, at least two weeks before March thirty-first," said Toni Clark. "It was only a hindquarter. I think Elza might have brought it over, because him and his two friends are the ones who poached it. It was just the bone, the fur, and a hoof. It was starting to stink, and we asked Richard to go put it in the van or just get it out of here. And so he picked it up—it was in a white bucket—he walked out of the patio with it, got to—I never seen him put it in his van. But he came back in and he got mad and started screaming and saying it got spilled, the blood got spilled. Well, there wasn't that much, just what little bit had dripped off the bone, because it was just the hindquarter. And so my husband says, 'Oh, just forget it, Richard,' and he doubled bagged it and he threw it in our garbage and the garbageman took it. It was just no big deal, you know, there was just no big deal."

Although Richard Clark was asked to take away a small portion of deer remnants, the event was the Sunday prior to Friday, March 31. There was no deer blood on Clark's shirt—it was the blood of Roxanne Doll.

Dr. Grimsbo detailed the DNA linkage of Clark to the crime, including the recovery of Roxanne's DNA from the bloodstained shirt given detectives by Carol Clark. That shirt became the focal point of an emotional firestorm when Carol Clark took the witness stand for the prosecution and completely contradicted her taped statements to detectives.

Prior to Carol Clark taking the stand, Detective John Burgess testified that a tearful Carol Clark gave him the gray-and-white pullover on April 18, ten days after Roxanne's body was found and after Richard Clark already had been arrested and charged with the killing.

Carol Clark was weeping uncontrollably when she first

came into the courtroom, and testimony was delayed while deputy prosecutor Ron Doersch and others helped her calm down. Once on the stand, the tearful and emotionally distraught Ms. Clark gave testimony that completely contradicted her taped statement to police.

Carol Clark originally told detectives, "I asked him how he got that on his shirt and he said, 'Well, I've been out poaching a deer.'"

On the stand, however, Carol said, "I noticed the stain on his shirt, and I stood at the sink washing some dishes and he told me at that time that Elza and his two friends had poached a deer, and at that time I thought the stain was from a deer."

"Is it your testimony," asked a surprised Ron Doersch, "that you didn't ask him where the stain came from?"

"No. That's what he told me. That's what he said. I didn't say anything."

"Why did you tell the cops on April eighteenth that [you] had a conversation with Richard, if it wasn't so?"

"I don't know."

"Is it because you did have that conversation?"

"No, I don't remember the conversation."

"You don't remember the conversation. Do you know if you had such a conversation and just don't remember it now?"

"I was being put through a lot of misery then," Carol said.

"That's not what I asked you."

"And I was going through—"

"Excuse me, ma'am," Doersch interrupted, "I'm asking you to respond only to the questions I ask you. Why would you tell the police that you had such a conversation with Richard, if it didn't happen?"

"Probably because I was so upset."

"Why were you upset on April eighteenth, ma'am?"

"Because of all the people that was always hounding

me, trying to find out things," she said. "People following us everywhere we would go; Herndon coming in and accusing me of knowing everything, knowing something about what was going on."

"And so it's your testimony that because of that, you told the police about a conversation with Richard that did not ever take place?"

Doersch turned to Judge Thorpe and asked permission to treat Carol Clark as a hostile witness. Defense attorney Errol Scott objected.

"I don't think there is any showing that she is hostile with the prosecutor," said Scott. "She's been cooperative."

"Objection, Your Honor," said Ron Doersch, and Thorpe sent the jury out of the courtroom.

"The state's position," Doersch explained, "is that we have been subjected to unfair surprise by the testimony of the witness. The witness has not testified as she said she would downstairs in speaking to me. The witness obviously favors the defense, and should be treated in a manner to cross-examine her as to statements she has previously made and testimony she has previously given."

"Has she testified," asked Thorpe, "the same way she told you she would?"

"She has not," Doersch explained. "She has previously indicated that this was indeed the shirt and now we are hearing something entirely different. She previously told us that she asked Clark where the blood on his shirt had come from, or words to that effect. When she testified here, she indicates that she asked no questions; she only looked at the stain on the shirt and that the defendant volunteers this information.

"When she spoke to me in my office downstairs, we discussed the issue of whether or not there had been drugs involved. In her recorded statement, she said, He looked like he'd been drinking. I don't know if he was on any drugs, 'cause I never took drugs myself. See, I never knew what anybody looked like when they're on drugs. On the stand, she said that he appeared to be on drugs. These are just two examples of what we are dealing with here," said Doersch.

"I object," said Scott. "First of all, the motion should have been made out of the presence of the jury. Second of all, I don't believe Ms. Clark was ever told or asked or confronted with her statement about whether she asked Richard about what was on his shirt and what his response was. I don't ever recall that exchange between the prosecutor and Ms. Clark. She said we didn't have a conversation; he volunteered it. The prosecution asked her several questions about whether it came out of the air, and she said yes. But he never asked her, 'Isn't it true you asked Mr. Clark what was on his shirt?' and whether it was a bloodstain, or whatever?

"And I also object," Scott said, "to the tone of voice that the prosecution uses toward Ms. Clark. I think it is oppressive and is certainly having some effect on the witness and we are certainly noticing it here. It's a tone of great authority and demanding an answer, and I think he should modulate his tone more equitably."

Judge Thorpe put a quick end to the debate. He told Doersch that he'd noticed "a wee bit of edge" in his questioning of Carol Clark, but he also granted the prosecutor's motion to grill his own witness.

"You told detectives that Richard said he got blood on his shirt from a poached deer, isn't that what Richard said?"

"That's what I said on here," she replied, referring to the transcript of her statement to detectives, "but he didn't say that."

"Is there any reason you would have told the detectives that, if it wasn't so?"

"I assumed he was with Elza and his friends when they poached it, and I thought it was that night."

Doersch, somewhat exasperated, held up his copy of the transcript. "You don't mention Elza and his friends anywhere in this statement, do you, of nine pages plus the signature, and that would be the entire statement of ten pages?"

"No, I don't."

"Now, you were asked again by Detective Herndon, were you not, with regard to that conversation you had with Richard. You were asked again by Detective Herndon about that, weren't you?"

"What are you talking about now?" Carol asked. "I don't remember saying that."

"Well, actually, ma'am, weren't you being taped at the time you made these statements to the detectives?"

"I may have been being taped," she replied, "but that doesn't mean [I] know what to say every time they ask me a question. I am not a smart person to know what to say to people."

"So why is it, ma'am, that you didn't mention anything about Elza and his friends to the police?"

"Because I probably forgot about that part."

Doersch paused, sighed, and collected his thoughts. "When you called the police on April 18, 1995, you were aware that there had been blood found in the van, right?" Carol Clark agreed and he continued.

"Okay. You had already thought about the fact that it might be Roxanne's blood on that shirt?"

"Yeah."

"And yet you did not mention, knowing all this stuff, knowing there was blood in the van, knowing that there was blood on the shirt, knowing that Roxanne was gone, and in fact had been found by this point, and was dead?"

Clark answered again in the affirmative.

"Knowing that in your heart you thought that might be Roxanne's blood on that shirt, when the police come and interview you, you don't mention anything about Elza and his friends, do you?"

"I didn't think about it then, probably."

Doersch, as calmly as possible, took Carol Clark back to April 18 when she tearfully invited the detectives to her home.

"Okay, you are there, you are being taped, right? You are just being asked questions, right?"

"Yeah," Clark answered.

"There is nothing threatening in there, in that situation, except you are talking to these guys, right?"

"Right."

"And no one is harassing you, right?"

"Right."

"And no one is mad at you, right?"

"No," said Carol Clark, "because I called them up."

"Exactly," said Doersch. "So, there you are, you are in your living room, at that point, you aren't under any of those pressures, are you?"

"Well," she said, "there was a lot going through my mind. I may not have been under any pressures then, and you don't know how I felt at the time."

"No, I don't," Doersch agreed, "but when you are being asked these questions by these officers, there is nothing in the way they are asking those questions of you, or the situation that you are in, that would cause you to say things that weren't true, is there?"

"No, there is not," she said firmly.

"Okay. So perhaps you can explain to me then," said Ron Doersch, "or explain to the jury, why it is that today you don't remember, or you say certain things didn't happen?"

"Because I was under a lot of stress then," she answered.

"There is the temptation, is there not, to want to say everything that comes into your mind at the current time, right?"

"That's true," Carol Clark acknowledged, "yeah, that is true."

"You don't know whether any part of that Elza deer story is true, do you?"

"No," she admitted. "No, I don't."

Doersch, further eroding the credibility of his own witness, asked her about the visit she and Richard Clark made to Elza, the visit during which both she and Richard requested Elza tell detectives that there was deer blood in Richard Clark's van.

In response, Carol Clark testified that the only reason Richard Clark went out to where Elza lived with his parents was to repay a loan to his grandfather.

"So, it's your testimony," asked Doersch, "that the only reason you folks went out there was to talk to Grandpa Smith?"

"He was there to pay him some money that he had borrowed," answered Carol.

"Is it your testimony," he again asked, "that that's the only reason you folks were there?"

"Yeah," Carol confirmed, "he went to pay him what he owed his grandpa."

Jurors, of course, heard otherwise from Elza Clark, consistently insisting that Richard and Carol asked him to confirm the poached-deer story to detectives.

Carol Clark had one more big contradiction for the prosecution. When they showed her the shirt she gave detectives on April 18, the shirt from which Roxanne Doll's DNA was recovered, she insisted that it was not the same shirt she laundered for Richard Clark. "That isn't the same shirt," said Carol. "The shirt had stains on it, and that one doesn't.

"I wouldn't cover up for someone if they murdered a little girl," said Carol Clark, knowing that it appeared as if she were attempting to do exactly that.

"Have you lied here today?" asked Errol Scott.

Carol Clark gave careful consideration to her phrasing, then replied, "I try not to lie."

The unsavory Eugene Hillius, a man whose criminal credentials included convictions for child molestation and rape, shared details of his prison conversations with Richard Clark. He described Clark barking, "Fuck her before you kill her," at a television villain stalking a young female, complaining of Elza's refusal to lie about the deer blood, and bemoaning the recovery of his DNA from the body of Roxanne Doll.

Hillius was not allowed, however, to share with jurors the fact that other prisoners didn't want Clark as a cellmate due to his "personal habits"—habits obviously unpleasant to the jail's more cultured and refined residents.

One witness Doersch desperately wanted to take the stand was Feather Rahier, the thirteen-year-old girl who ran away rather than again confront Richard M. Clark.

Significant legal wrangling took place in Judge Thorpe's courtroom on allowing so-called "child hearsay" evidence—letting police officers and others testify, in her absence, as to what Feather told them following her 1988 imprisonment at the hands of Richard Clark.

The defense argued that there was absolutely no legal rationale for bringing up a resolved case from 1988, a case for which Clark had already paid his debt to society, during this trial concerning the alleged kidnapping, rape, and murder of Roxanne Doll. The prosecution argued that the two cases were part of a "common scheme or plan."

Following intensive argumentation by both sides, Judge Thorpe made the following commentary. "The similarities between the two incidents are remarkable," he said. "A young child in one case, age four, in the other case, age seven, was removed from their family home and concealed. Knotted-up socks were used to gag

the child, the socks in the mouth knotted up. There
were other knotted-up socks in both areas. The one
child was seen with the knotted socks used as bindings to
hold her hands behind her back. There had been
grooming of both children by the defendant by giving
gifts. Each was, as I indicated, young children, one four
and one even, known to the defendant and to whom he
had access. In the one case, by reason of being friends of
the family, and the other in being next-door neighbors,
or at least neighbors across the alley from one another.

"The charges before us are kidnapping, rape, and murder," Thorpe continued. "Clearly, the prior incident was
a kidnapping. And the state suggests that the evidence is
relevant and admissible for two reasons. Number one, on
the issue of identity and the other on the issue of common plan, scheme, or design. With respect to identity,
this is the area in which we discuss whether or not it is a
signature crime. When Roxanne's body was found, it was
not bound in any way with socks. We just know that there
were socks in the defendant's van. And it seems to me
that when weighing the evidence that the state has presented and is able to present on the issue of identity, as to
whether or not it was Mr. Clark that committed these
crimes, that evidence is so great and persuasive. The fact
that Roxanne's body was not found with socks and that
sort of thing militates against the idea that the prior incident would be admissible as probative of the identity of
the person who abducted, raped, and murdered Roxanne, except for the fact that there is the outside
possibility that Jimmy Miller was in the van when it happened. From some of the testimony, I think it's very clear
that, from the scientific evidence, that he didn't have anything to do with this, and therefore the prior incident is
not necessary and is not particularly probative on the
issue of identity. On the issue of common scheme or
plan, it's my understanding that that rule requires that

the two acts be in furtherance of the same common scheme, plan, or design. When we consider the passage of seven years . . . I am not persuaded that the prior evidence is so indicative of a common scheme or plan, or of the same plan, common scheme, to render it admissible.

"If it had occurred a few weeks before or a few months before," Thorpe said, "it possibly could have been admissible, except for the fact that this sort of evidence is to be used very sparingly in sex cases, because if the evidence is too good, the jury might reason that if the person is of such low character as to commit the previous crime, he surely is of low-enough character to commit the current charged crime and therefore convict him on the basis of that, rather than on the evidence.

"So," concluded Judge Thorpe, "the evidence will not be allowed."

Ron Doersch wasn't giving up. He made one more plea. "Your Honor, may I remind the court," he said, citing case law, "that when an individual devises a plan and [it is] used repeatedly to perpetrate separate but very similar crimes, that's not quite the same as common scheme, plan, or design, and the passage of time is relatively irrelevant."

Thorpe was unmoved. "Had there been another similar event between the two . . . I just don't think that the two events, seven years apart, that there is sufficient similarity to warrant its admissibility in the trial phase. We may have to argue about it again later. So that means we have no more witnesses for today?"

"That is correct," said Doersch.

"Bring in the jury," said the judge, "we will work them harder tomorrow. My understanding is that the defense has perhaps one witness tomorrow, if indeed the state rests."

The jury returned to the courtroom, and Judge Thorpe assured them that neither he nor the attorneys had been idle in their absence. "We have honest-to-God been working ever since you went out, just ask my reporter, who is complaining about it. I have good news and bad news. The bad news is we won't work you anymore today. The good news is you may leave. We will be in recess until nine-thirty tomorrow morning."

The following morning, and for reasons that William Jaquette firmly believed were more than sufficient, the defense moved for the complete dismissal of all charges against Richard M. Clark.

Chapter 15

"My understanding," began Jaquette, "is that the state has rested, and we would be moving at this time to dismiss every one of the charges in this case. I don't have extensive argument to present to the court. I think the court has to, in making this decision, determine if the state has provided sufficient evidence to conclude that the crimes were committed beyond a reasonable doubt. It would be our position that they have not done so."

The defense then focused on the most significant issue: premeditation. "In order to convict Mr. Clark of aggravated first-degree murder they would have to prove, as the court is aware, that the killing was premeditated. There was really no evidence in this case, as to what occurred after the child went to bed until the body was found. There is evidence as to what occurred in that interim period, but no evidence to indicate who did what, when, and why, or what happened in what order, or what exactly occurred. And therefore it would be our position that the state has not established its obligation to prove premeditation."

Ronald Doersch anticipated Jaquette's motion, and his response was both immediate and fluent. "The mere obtaining of a weapon to kill someone presumes premeditation," he insisted. "The moving of a victim from one location to another to commit rape upon her, in this case, proves premeditation. Again, we have evidence that the defendant was at the residence prior in the day, at least snooping or hanging around, that indicates premeditation. The fact that she is secreted and hidden indicates premeditation. The method of obtaining her without essentially leaving any trace, by his fingerprint on a window, indicates premeditation. The state submits that premeditation has eminently been established in [this] case."

Judge Thorpe, carefully considering each point from both attorneys, turned again to Bill Jaquette. "Your Honor," said the defense, "all of those things that Mr. Doersch points out establish only an intent to commit the other crimes of kidnap and rape. Sufficient evidence of deliberation prior to the decision to execute the killing—sufficient to constitute premeditation—is not established by the fact that the rest of the crime appears to have been a part of a series of events."

"No," countered Doersch, "in order to kill this person, the knife had to be obtained, had to be employed, stabbing this person seven or eight times in a series of multiple stab wounds around her neck, that certainly indicates premeditation. It does not indicate, for example, the kind of second-degree murder, where a gun that was drawn in the heat of a moment and discharged, it does not—say a brick is picked up and in the heat of anger and smacked against the side of one's head. These are the wounds that killed her and they occurred after the rape."

Thorpe nodded in apparent interest and possible agreement before offering Jaquette the floor. "Again," insisted Jaquette, "there is no evidence as to what actually happened in the moment of the death, and a knife that was employed for purposes of threats is not proof of premeditation for killing."

Judge Richard Thorpe, wanting to make sure he understood Jaquette's position, asked, "Are you suggesting that all of the evidence that could persuade a jury that the kidnapping and the rape were intentional has to be more or less set aside, and that there must be additional, clear evidence that the decision to kill was formed far enough in advance of the killing to be premeditation?"

"Yes," Jaquette responded. "Yes, that is exactly correct."

"And you," said Thorpe, turning his gaze to the prosecutor, "suggest that having a knife there meets that criteria?"

Doersch nodded. Jaquette buttressed his position. "I can create a scenario in which a knife used for a kidnap and rape would not be involved in an intent to kill. Something could happen—a struggle or some other event—that triggers an instantaneous decision to kill. I think the prosecution must present evidence that proves premeditation, and they have not done so."

"Oh, I agree," said Judge Thorpe. Had he stopped there, Jaquette would have emerged victorious. His Honor, however, continued. "But I don't think your ability to come up with some scenario that would negate premeditation is the criteria. The criterion is whether or not there is sufficient evidence, sufficient circumstantial evidence. Obviously, that is all we have is circumstantial evidence in this case, to persuade a finder of fact of premeditation beyond a reasonable doubt.

"I am not persuaded that there isn't sufficient evidence," said the judge. "She obviously wasn't killed in her bedroom. She obviously was removed from there, granted it could be for the purpose of kidnapping and for rape, but that along with the circumstances of the abduction, with the circumstances of the disposal of the body and that sort of thing and the fact that there was weapon all taken together, I think there is sufficient circumstantial evidence from which an independent trier of fact could find this beyond a reasonable doubt that there was premeditation. The motion will be denied."

That settled that. Jaquette simply responded, "Your Honor, we have one witness to call. It will be very brief. Linda Hein was a patron at the Dog House Tavern. We will then be done with the testimony that we have available. We would like to reserve an opportunity to formally rest on Monday. We don't anticipate anything, but we want to be completely sure that everything that we can and want to present can be presented. I would anticipate this would not affect scheduling of events that we sort of come up with for Monday."

"Well," responded the judge, "unless you got yourself a blockbuster. In that situation, they might be tempted to put on some rebuttal."

"You can bet money on that," said Ron Doersch. "If there is a blockbuster, then all . . ."

". . . bets are off," Jaquette said, completing Doersch's sentence for him. "But I can give the court very strong assurances that will not happen."

"Any overwhelmingly and persuasive objection to that, Mr. Doersch," asked Thorpe.

"I guess not," he replied.

With that, defense attorney Errol Scott called their only witness.

"I've known Neila D'alexander ever since we were in grade school. We pretty much grew up together," testified Linda Hein.

"Do you recall where you were on the night of March 31, 1995?"

"Yes, I do. I was at the Dog House Tavern on C twenty-second and Colby," she testified. "I got there about seven in the evening, and Neila came in between seven-thirty and eight P.M."

"Concerning Richard Clark," asked Scott, "and about what time did you see Mr. Clark in the Dog House?"

"Approximately nine or so," said Hein. "I'm not real certain, but that's pretty close."

"Is there anything that happened that night around that time to give you an idea of what time it was?"

"Well, yeah," she replied, "the gentleman that was standing next to Richard Clark was arguing with the barmaid about not being drunk, when he really was drunk. The barmaid wasn't going to serve him, that's why I noticed him. I'm not a clock-watcher or anything, but I happened to glance at my watch just before the incident occurred."

According to Hein, she saw the two men—Richard Clark and Jimmy Miller—talking to the barmaid. The condition of Clark's companion, she said, was "not good. He had trouble even standing up. He was not standing too straight, he was having a hard time standing. That's because I believe he was drunk—not just intoxicated, I mean drunk."

"What was Mr. Clark doing?" asked Scott.

"He was standing there next to the fellow that was complaining."

"Did you see them leave?"

"No, I don't remember them leaving at all."

"Now, did you talk with Ms. D'alexander anytime later that night?"

"I carried on a conversation with her until she left," Hein said.

"Now, anytime later that night, did you see Mr. Richard Clark?"

"Yes," she answered. "I think I saw him around midnight. That was about an hour before I left."

"Now, you were obviously in a tavern. Were you drinking alcohol then?"

"Yes, I was. I hadn't had that much to drink. At most, I had two beers the entire evening. Sometimes I don't drink alcohol at all, but drink Pepsi instead. I was there from seven P.M. until closing. Richard Clark came in about an hour before Neila left, and she left around one-thirty A.M."

The importance of Linda Hein's testimony can *not* be overstated. If she were correct, Richard Clark had enough of an alibi to create reasonable doubt. He could not have been at the Dog House and committing the crime at the same time.

On cross-examination, Ronald Doersch had few questions, but they were also of vital importance. "What is it that drew your attention to Richard Clark when he supposedly came back at twelve-thirty?"

"Just the door opening," she said. "I turned and looked."

"At that time you had what, two beers to drink?"

"At that time? Well, maybe three beers," said Hein.

"Maybe more?"

"I don't drink all that much at all," she said again. The expression on Doersch's face expressed his opinion, unverified by evidence, that Hein was mistaken by virtue of alcohol ingestion.

The testimony concluded, the defense and prosecution prepared for their ultimate arguments for the guilt or innocence of Richard Mathew Clark.

"We will now have closing argument of counsel," said Judge Thorpe. "First for the plaintiff, Mr. Doersch."

"It's every parent's worst nightmare," began Doersch, and he brought that nightmare vividly to the courtroom. "You have been introduced to the dark side, the underside of the world you live in. It's a world where grandparents outlive their grandchildren. It's a world where a parent is too tired or too drunk to do anything to save his daughter. It's a world where the friend of a seven-year-old's parents gives her stuffed animals, lets her play with his puppy and smiles and smiles. And he's a villain. He takes her away, he rapes her, and he kills her.

"You see how close evil is. And you see how commonplace evil can look. Take a good look, right there," he said, pointing to Richard Clark. "Commonplace, evil, brutish, nasty, and as this case overwhelmingly demonstrates, stupid.

"You know what he did, and how he did it, and how badly he did it. In this case, evil has already won. Roxanne is dead."

Doersch then reminded the jury of the state's extensive physical evidence, including the controversial bloody shirt. "Consider what was done to that shirt in an attempt to keep that away from you, to prevent you from considering it as evidence," said Doersch. "It's laundered; it's kept away from the police for eighteen days after the occurrence. Carol Clark tries to tell you that it doesn't look like the shirt. Two police officers testified that's certainly the shirt she gave us, and we know, not just because we recognize it, but because we wrote down all the identifying characteristics of the shirt, and we got it from her—the defendant's shirt that has Roxanne's blood on it.

"Do you really think there was a crisis of conscience that caused that shirt to be turned over?" he asked rhetorically. "Or was it more a fear of being somehow more deeply involved in this homicide, in its cover-up?"

A litany of evidence, recited by Doersch, kept the jury tight-jawed and attentive. "Van evidence, pieces of carpet, blood is detected, two socks removed—there is saliva on one, probably from Roxanne—in fact, on both of them, spermatoza and blood on them, brown sleeping bag, clean, large bloodstain on it. PGM ST and EMG testing, consistent with Roxanne Doll's, her blood is on the sleeping bag. That's Urness's sleeping bag, as you will recall, the one the defendant borrowed the day before. There is blood on the yellow pillow, some blood on the blankets, an air mattress."

There were more charges against Clark than murder, and Doersch dealt with each of them. "One of the counts involved here is one in essence of forcible rape," he remarked. "And you know from the damage to Roxanne, and from the damage to that pair of pants, that she was forcibly raped. Greg Franks examines and sees sperm cells on the anal swab, the vaginal swab, and the vaginal wash. Hair evidence is examined. Long, light brown hair is found on one of the socks.

"There is fiber evidence from the training bra and the diapers, fibers from golden brown carpets. Using a microscope much more powerful than they use to compare rifling characteristics on fired bullets, photographing the results, this is what it comes up with. Note the similarities. Remember the testimony. Similar microscopic, chemical, and color characteristics to the van, the brown van carpets, and it could have originated from the gold brown carpet and from the other carpet as well, and that's as strong as you can get apparently in fiber testing."

Doersch piled on fact after fact, test result after test result. "The DNA from the sperm on the anal swab is consistent with Richard Clark's genetic profile. You heard the numbers," said Doersch emphatically, "only one in fifty-four-hundred Caucasians have that genetic profile. Other people are excluded, including Iffrig and Miller.

"In the excess of caution," he reminded the jury, "testing is done on people in order to exclude them, to show that it can't be them. The DNA from the sperm in the vaginal wash is consistent with Clark's genetic profile. Again, Iffrig and Miller excluded. The DNA from the bloodstained shirt that Richard Clark wore the night Roxanne Doll was murdered is consistent with Roxanne's genetic profile—not Clark's, Iffrig's or Miller's. Only one in twenty-nine hundred people have that same genetic profile.

"The DNA proves the defendant's semen was in the victim's vaginal area, and trickled down into the anal area. And it proves her blood was on a sleeping bag in the defendant's van. How did it get on the defendant?"

he asked rhetorically. "When he was stabbing her, she bled on him. Kiesel talked about there being some spatter, expecting to find blood somewhere. Well, that is exactly where you would expect to find it. Someone stabbing a little girl, it's on the front of the person stabbing her, that's how it got there, not by some bizarre transfer mechanism, the sleeping bag to the defendant."

The forensic evidence, Doersch asserted, was as good as or better than a fingerprint. "Scientific tests don't lie, they don't have an agenda, and all the scientific evidence points to the defendant. They tell us for certain Roxanne was raped by the defendant and they point overwhelmingly, with the other evidence in the case, to the defendant having killed Roxanne as well." Having recapped the forensic evidence, Doersch turned the jury's attention to Richard Clark's erratic behavior.

"Look at Richard Clark scrambling that night, that following week, trying to set up an alibi, trying to cover. He's everywhere on that night, and yet there are still times that are unaccountable. You recall who we are getting these times from. Look at what he does, the scrambling that he does, trying to get his alibi together, covering himself, conceal evidence. It starts, I submit to you, when he takes her—when he takes Roxanne. He knows, I submit to you, that he is never going to bring her back."

At this point, deputy prosecutor Doersch did everything in his power to convince the jury that the murder of Roxanne Doll was premeditated. "Why is he never going to bring her back? Because she is seven years old, and a seven-year-old talks. They speak."

Knowing that sexually violated children are often frightened into silence, threatened never to reveal the identity of their violator, one would question the imperative nature of murdering the victim. Doersch, curious as to the answer, consulted the FBI and shared the explanation with the jury.

"Even if the victim was too scared to tell who did ex
actly what to her, the one responsible knows that if she
even pointed her finger at him in any way, even indi
rectly, detectives and FBI agents would be after him in a
heartbeat.

"Recall too," continued the prosecution, "that after he
does these things, other witnesses remark upon his change
of appearance, because they notice that he's shaved off his
mustache. And suddenly we have the black-rimmed glasses
that, according to some witnesses, have never been seen
before.

"I submit that he goes as many places he can, running
around here and there. And then there is the Jimmy fac
tor," said Doersch with a note of sarcasm. "He picks up
Jimmy. Jimmy is leaning on a lamppost, as one witness
said. Is he hitchhiking? All we know for certain is that
Jimmy was at the Dog House earlier in the evening and
that he was on the reservation sometime at eleven o'clock
that night, and whenever the defendant brought him
there.

"When did Richard Clark really pick him up?" Doersch asked. "We don't know—and the reason we don't
know is because the defendant is the only one who tells
us, or anybody else."

Richard Clark's eroded credibility took further hits
as Doersch continued in the same vein. "He tries to get
Elza to cover for him, the deer blood again. What's it
come down to really? 'The detectives call you and ask
you about blood in the van, tell them it's deer blood.'
Let's forget this story about deer guts spilled in the van.
It's nonsense. When tests are done on the inside of the
van, it's not deer blood at all. Nobody else is scrambling
for an alibi either, only Richard Clark."

Addressing the contradiction between the recollections of Dog House customer Linda Hein and bartender
Cheryle Galloway, he said, "Are you going to believe the

bartender or the person drinking? The two people that address that issue, and I submit to you that Cheryle Galloway is far more believable in terms of when Richard Clark reappears at the Dog House.

"Scientific tests don't lie, they don't have an agenda, and all the scientific evidence points to the defendant. Except for the Urnesses and Gail and Janice Cliatt, all these people have been drinking. They are not clock-watchers. The testimony that we have as to the time line outside of Cheryle Galloway, Gail, Janice Cliatt, and the Urnesses," he insisted, "is largely that of people who are drunk, partyers, and barflies—people whose credibility is very much at issue.

"So the net is closing around him," stated Doersch dramatically. "The cops are starting to ask questions. They seize his van, and he is out there trying to secure his alibi. He goes out to Vicki, and she asked him point-blank: 'Did you do anything to that little girl?' What is the indicated response? The response is the same as you hear right now, silence. He picks up his dog, without a word, gets in the car and goes away.

"What does he tell to Toni Clark after he is in jail? Well, the first thing he says to Toni is, 'If I get the death penalty, don't mourn for me, don't grieve for me.' Okay. 'Did you kill her?' 'I don't know.' 'Did you rape her?' 'Don't know, might have.' 'Did you kill her?' 'Don't know, can't remember.'"

"Where in the statements to FBI agent Lauer and to Kiser is there any mention about blacking out? What does he tell Lauer? Clark tells him, 'I didn't hurt her, I didn't hurt her, I didn't hurt her,' vain repetition, as it turns out. And to Hillius, he said, 'They got my DNA out of her butt.'

"When the defense speaks, you are undoubtedly going to hear about a time line," said Ron Doersch. "You are undoubtedly going to see, pointing to the time line, that

Clark couldn't have been here, couldn't have done this, couldn't have done that. Okay. Perhaps Mr. Clark was then the victim of some huge frame-up; perhaps Mr. Clark was the victim of tremendous circumstance; perhaps in the turning of the earth, everything lined up just right to put her DNA on his clothes and the sleeping bag, with his DNA in her body. Don't you believe it. Instead, think about the people who have testified as to that time line. I submit to you the only really reliable testimony that we have, with regard to that, *is* probably Janice Cliatt. Working, not drinking, not carrying on, who sees Richard Clark's van at the site where Roxanne's body is found.

"Let's talk about something else. Remember Tim Iffrig telling us that in essence the defendant never had any reason to be behind the house; that when they road motorcycles, Tim brought the motorcycle around the front of the house. No evidence that the defendant ever worked on the house in any way, yet his fingerprint is on the outside window to Roxanne Doll's bedroom. Oh," he suddenly added as if it just popped into his mind, "look whose fingerprint is on the girl's window on the outside. Recall one of the panes is not secure. It's open far enough to get your fingertips into. The other may or may not be locked, but we know for sure it's got the defendant's fingerprint on it in a place where he should not have been, where no one ever saw him, where he had no reason to be, unless he was trying to open a window. It's clear that he could have opened the other pane, tested the one that has his fingerprint on it, or if it wasn't locked, open that one as well, or closed it on his way out."

He then turned the jury's attention back to DNA. "DNA is used for a lot of things. In this case," he explained, "you are looking for the source of evidentiary items; you are looking for or trying to find out where saliva or spit comes from, or blood comes from, or semen comes from. You are testing it against known samples. What do we find? The DNA testing can accurately disclose patterns, reflect DNA difference among humans. The testing that is used to free the innocent and identify the guilty. In this case, it points straight as an arrow toward Richard Clark.

"As for that shirt that Richard had Carol wash—there is no deer blood on that shirt. That's Roxanne's blood on that shirt; it's human blood; it's hers. Deer blood, my left eye! DNA typing shows the DNA from the bloodstain is consistent with Roxanne's DNA despite the attempts to destroy the evidence, I submit to you. The diaper, training bra, hair clips, bracelet, anal and vaginal samples from Roxanne's body, are sent to Greg Frank. Blood is detected on the hair clip, the diaper, and the training bra."

The primary issue Doersch repeatedly stressed was premeditation. "When you take this case and tear it down, pare it down to what the issues really are; the issue in this case is premeditation. So, let's talk about premeditation."

He referred jurors to instruction number eleven containing the word's definition. "Premeditation must involve more than a moment in time, it requires some time, long or short, in which the design to kill is deliberately formed. I submit to you that he knew he was going to kill her when he took her out of there.

"He knows when he takes her out of that house that he's got to take some steps to assure that she doesn't identify him," reiterated Doersch. "And I submit that he knows when he takes her out of that house, that he is going to kill her. So when he takes her, he is starting, he knows he is going to conceal it. He is covering even then. Not very well, as it turns out. Maybe the amount he had to drink has something to do with that. Maybe he's just not very smart. The evidence would point to both of those things, and in his actions during the rest of the week. When he kills her, he does that to conceal the foul things that he has done. Why does he kill her? I'm sure the defense can construct some scenario where this somehow becomes accidental wherein the heat of the moment. Don't you believe it.

"When he buries her in the dark on East Grand, concealment again. When he visits his aunt Carol, whenever he does that, to change, to shower, to shave, to have his blood-soaked shirt laundered, isn't that why he gives that to her? Aunt Carol, who, of course, is not mentioned to either the FBI agent or the detectives."

Then, taking a different tact, the prosecutor said, "But suppose I'm wrong, suppose he didn't know he was going to kill her when he took her out of there?" Doersch then approached the definition of premeditation within the context of the fatal stabbing.

"He has got to make a choice in there somewhere to keep on stabbing her, and that's just what he does. And that is premeditation. Whether that is some sort of conscious decision, verbally assembled in his head—'I have stabbed her and she must die, and so I must stab her some more'—or whether it's just some 'I've got to keep going, I've got to finish this.' Whatever the analysis is, it involves the taking of a human life and we have more than just a moment in time, we have premeditation.

"Look at her hands," pleaded Doersch. "Not only will blood tell, Roxanne's blood, but Roxanne's wounds speak to you. And what they will tell you is they took time to kill her, time in which a mind could be changed, and a time in which a choice was made to keep going. This is not a case where, in the heat of events, strong hands break her neck or crush her neck bone, and she dies. This is not *Of Mice and Men*, where Lenny squeezes just a little too hard without intent and someone dies. This is premeditation."

After the prosecutor engraved his perspective of premeditation on the jury's collective conscience, he turned to the concept of "aggravating factors."

"Those three aggravating factors are here for your consideration. You may find none. You may find one, two, or all three. I think we know, and I submit to you that you do know, that the reason Roxanne was killed was to conceal the commission of this crime. And that doesn't mean forever, that means for whatever time, in this case, a week, or to conceal the identity of any person committing the crime, to wit, Richard Clark.

"He killed her because she can talk, and that's what he does. Premeditation for this reason, for this motive, in this case.

"I want to briefly cover the elements, not because I think these things aren't important," said Doersch, "but because they are largely self-evident. Let's start with this, rape in the first degree. Regardless of whether penetration is achieved in the vaginal area or the anus or both, we have rape in the first degree.

"It is clearly forcible," he said, and a few jurors perceptibly winced. "The pants show that—the disruption of the hymen. Recall the doctor going back and checking, checked the sample, it was ruptured, it wasn't just absent. The damage to her inside, you heard that in length. I am not going to show that to you again. You can look at it, take it in the jury room and look at it. You heard what kidnap in the first degree [is]. Instruction fourteen, the defendant abducts Roxanne Doll with the intent to inflict bodily injury on her, with the intent to rape her. He sure did.

"He took her out," the prosecutor stated flatly. "She is a seven-year-old. She is a small child. He has to know what will happen, no matter what he does, if he rapes her. And that's if you ignore the fact that he took her out of there to kill her eventually. You know that, from the evidence, the intent to inflict bodily injury on her. What's that mean? Physical pain or injury, illness or impairment of physical condition."

Doersch dealt with abduction, clearly defining the word
in the context of this horrid crime. "Abducting means re-
straining a person by secreting or holding that person in
a place where that person is not likely to be found, in a
van, or some other place, on a hillside in Everett.

"And now," he continued, "murder in the first degree.
On or about the thirty-first day of March 1995, or the first
day of April 1995, the defendant stabbed Roxanne Doll.
How do we know that? She has been stabbed to death. His
blood is on her shirt. He lies by omission; he lies by affirmation to the cops, to the FBI. The intent to cause the
death is premeditated. I think we talked about that
enough. How could it be anything but, unless a fantastic
scenario was created?"

Chapter 16

Richard Clark's defense team was not about to create a fantastic scenario; they were about to push a boulder up a hill. In essence, the defense was fighting two battles at once. While defending the law, and the presumption of innocence that is so imperative to American justice, the defense had to also argue that even if their client did commit these acts, they were not premeditated.

Clark's primary defense was alibi. Through cross-examination of the state's witnesses, Clark sought to establish that (a) Doll-Iffrig saw Roxanne in bed after midnight on April 1, and (b) Clark was seen at so many different locations between 9:30 P.M. on March 31 and 1:00 A.M. on April 1 that he did not have time to commit the crime. The alternative theory was that the evidence presented by the prosecution was insufficient to establish premeditation.

"Let me say a few things before I get started," said defense attorney William Jaquette. He read his well-crafted closing argument instead of speaking from notes. "I apologize for not being more extemporaneous in this argument when it appears that I'm reading this. The reason is because I want to be precise in what I say, and I want to come to the point.

"I want to present to you the most thoughtful closing argument that I can. A trial such as this should be a search for truth, an attempt to secure justice under the law. We are advocates for Mr. Clark," he said, "and have attempted to vigorously represent him and present all the evidence and the facts to you that we believe are helpful in this case. The court has told that you are the judges of the facts.

"No one can tell you, individually or collectively, what to think or how to vote in this case," he reminded the jury, "because it is your conscience and impartial application of the law that will secure justice in a case such as this. Emotions run high, even two years after Roxanne's death. Remember, the law does not favor either a guilty or not guilty verdict."

Gail Doll's original statement to police that Roxanne was in bed when she returned from the theater should, Jaquette insisted, be taken as an unalterable fact because she was sober, and it makes sense that she would check on her children's safety in a smoke-filled house.

Richard Clark could not have kidnapped Roxanne Doll, insisted Jaquette, because Gail returned home at 12:05 and Richard was still at his aunt Carol's house until 12:45—a testimony that remained unchallenged.

None of the alibi witnesses, argued Jaquette, had a motive to help Richard Clark. All of them were deeply affected by the kidnapping, and none of them were strong advocates for Clark once he was charged with the crime, including his own family.

The defense then countered the prosecution's assertion that Clark's frantic movements that night were indicative of him searching for an alibi. The best way to establish an alibi, Jaquette told the jury, is to go to one place and stay there so you have witnesses. That is how one establishes an alibi, and preferably with people who are sober. Traveling from place to place in purposed search of alibi simply didn't make sense.

The most important aspect of Clark's alibi, according to Jaquette, was the information obtained by police investigators on the whereabouts of Richard Clark on the night of March 31st. None of the witnesses changed their version of events from their first statements made two years previous. The witnesses who made statements about the whereabouts of Richard Clark on that night did not know what facts would be helpful to him, or what facts would incriminate him. "They told the truth," said Jaquette. If what they said was true, he told the jury, Richard Clark could not have committed the crime.

The prosecution argued that Carol Clark was lying about the time Richard was home between 12:05 and 12:45, but Jaquette noted that all the other evidence of Richard's whereabouts that night was consistent with her testimony. More importantly, the defense pointed out, if she were lying about the time, why would she later call police and turn over some of the most damaging evidence in the case, the bloody shirt?

"She was not helping Richard when she turned over the shirt," said Jaquette, "and she did not lie for him when she told police where he was that night."

The erudite defense attorney then showed the jury a large illustration demonstrating what he termed the "consistency of the witnesses' time line statements." On the left side of the chart was the time; the middle showed location with the time it would take to move from location to location, and the far right indicated the witness who testified to this timeline. Jaquette, in painstaking detail, did his utmost to demonstrate that the times were not only accurate, but precluded that Richard Clark could not have committed the crime.

"I want to break the time period that night into two different parts," said Jaquette. "First, before midnight, and second, after midnight."

Defense attorney Jaquette proceeded to demonstrate that, according to his interpretation of events, Clark could not have committed the crime after midnight. "Richard is placed at his aunt Carol's at twelve-oh-five, and Gail Doll arrived home about twelve-oh-five. If Gail

Doll arrived at home at midnight and saw two heads in the bed, Richard Clark could not have abducted Roxanne Doll, because we know where he was after midnight until six-thirty in the morning."

This same timeline, argued Jaquette, demonstrated the improbability of Richard Clark abducting Roxanne Doll prior to 12:05. There was, according to the defense, no time or opportunity for their client to abduct, rape, murder, and discard the body of Roxanne Doll.

Time was also significant in the defense's argument against premeditation. "The law requires some time," stated Jaquette, "long or short, in which a design to kill is deliberately formed."

The general thrust of the prosecution's argument was that Roxanne Doll was kidnapped for the purpose of rape and the abductor knew she would reveal the crime, and therefore she was killed. This indicated deliberation from the very outset to take her life—that the murder was conceived as part of the plan from the outset. The defense, however, argued that premeditation needs to be of sufficient length that there is doubt that it was of a nature that justifies a finding of first degree murder.

"The known facts of the death of Roxanne Doll," said Jaquette, "do not prove that her death was premeditated."

While the prosecution would argue that the time it took to inflict the wounds constituted sufficient premeditation to constitute first degree murder, the defense insisted that "intent to kill is not the same as premeditation."

The intent to kill, acted upon without premeditation, is the definition of second-degree murder. Even if the jury determined that Clark was responsible for the three crimes of kidnapping, rape, and murder, they could find him guilty of second-degree murder. Should they reach that conclusion, Richard Clark would not face the death penalty.

"You can *not* infer from the facts proven to you that the

killing was premeditated," insisted the attorney. "The prosecution may, of course, claim that Mr. Clark should not benefit from having committed a crime, which he can conceal, or for which his whereabouts were unknown. That does not eliminate the prosecution's burden of proving all the necessary elements of the crime."

Contemplating the defense's argument years later, investigative crime journalist Jeff Reynolds found the presentation oddly compelling. "William Jaquette insisted that Clark didn't do it, and simultaneously argued that Clark didn't do it with premeditation. I must admire him for covering every possible angle to give his client the best defense, but the subtext was 'Let's not confuse the fact that my client is probably guilty as hell with the sanctity of the law.'"

Jurors were reminded that Clark was intoxicated on both alcohol and methamphetamines, and that he consumed as much as Jimmy Miller, possibly more. He drank heavily prior to picking up Miller, and Jimmy Miller blacked out at four or five in the afternoon. Tim Iffrig, Jaquette pointed out, was also intoxicated.

Hence, Jaquette reasoned, many "facts" of the case remained unclear. Not knowing when or where, or under what exact circumstances Roxanne Doll met her end, Jaquette told the jury, made premeditation impossible to prove.

"I apologize for all the time I have taken and let me make a few remarks before I close," he said. "Richard Clark was not trying to get Elza Clark to lie for him about deer blood. We have uncontradicted evidence that there was deer blood in Toni Clark's house. We have uncontradicted evidence that there was deer blood in Richard Clark's van. We don't have any proof that it was spilled, but it certainly was there. So when Richard Clark told Elza to tell the police, 'If there is any blood found in my van, it was from the deer,' what he was telling was the truth. And what happened was Elza Clark was so concerned about being arrested for poaching, he could not bring himself to back up Richard's story, which was true.

"Richard Clark never asked Vicki Smith to lie for him," asserted the defense. "He asked her if she told the police that she was with him that night and she almost indignantly replied no. And the prosecution suggests, well, with someone for a long period of time. Well, what Richard was really asking her, when she had seen the police, that she had seen Richard that night."

Tim Iffrig found these explanations astonishingly far-fetched. "Did he really think the jury was gonna buy that? I mean, c'mon. The guy was doing his job, but man—that was really stretching it."

The jury wasn't buying it. In the words of one wag, they were not even renting it or taking it for a test drive. Jaquette did everything within his oratory powers to raise reasonable doubt in jurors' minds. Three quick weeks after it began, the trial phase was over.

"Counsel," said Judge Thorpe, "we have been advised that the jury has reached a verdict. Are there any preliminary matters before we bring in the jury?"

"No, sir," replied both Ron Doersch and Errol Scott.

"Very well. While we are doing that, I want to compliment counsel on the good job they did in trying this case. I've had a lot of comments about how quickly the trial went. And on reflection, I attribute that to the degree of work, preparation, anticipation, and talent of the attorneys who are involved in it. And you are all to be commended for trying the case very well and very efficiently."

Judge Thorpe then turned toward the defendant. "And Mr. Clark, I can assure you that you had the best legal talent that I've seen defending you."

Whether or not Richard Mathew Clark appreciated Ja-

quette and Scott's efforts on his behalf remains unknown; the verdict, however, was widely publicized.

Once the jury was seated, Judge Thorpe addressed the
foreperson. "Sir, has the jury reached a verdict?"

Richard Mathew Clark was convicted of aggravated first
degree murder for the stabbing and strangulation death
of seven-year-old Roxanne Doll. The aggravating circumstances were that the murder was committed: (1) in the
course of or furtherance of Kidnapping in the First Degree and Rape in the First Degree, and (2) to conceal the
identity of the person committing the crime.

There was no delay between the jury's verdict and the
beginning of the penalty phase. It was now a life or death
battle.

Prosecutor Ronald Doersch began the penalty phase
with an unexpected and disturbing entreaty. "I received
a request from correction staff," he told Judge Thorpe
prior to the jury entering the courtroom, "that in light
of the defendant's conviction, he should remain shackled for the balance of the proceedings."

William Jaquette sighed; Errol Scott shook his head.

Chapter 17

Each charge was answered with a guilty verdict, and each juror was individually polled to ascertain the validity of the verdict. There was no doubt. Richard M. Clark was guilty, guilty, and guilty.

"What do you do with a guilty child murderer and rapist?" asked Lloyd Herndon rhetorically. "In Washington State, you have a special sentencing phase to determine if he should spend life in person, or be executed. Richard Mathew Clark was found guilty of all charges—first-degree kidnapping, first-degree rape, and first -degree aggravated murder. There was no delay between the jury's verdict and the beginning of the penalty phase."

It was now a life-or-death battle. Prosecutor Ronald Doersch began the penalty phase with an unexpected and disturbing entreaty. "I received a request from correction staff," he told Judge Thorpe prior to the jury entering the courtroom, "that in light of the defendant's conviction, he should remain shackled for the balance of the proceedings."

William Jaquette sighed; Errol Scott shook his head.

"I bring this to the attention of the court," Doersch said, "because they do have a legitimate security concern."

"Okay," Jaquette responded with a tinge of cynicism, "we better hear it."

"You just did," retorted Doersch.

"By shackles," asked the judge, "do you mean leg shackles?"

"Leather restraints," explained Jo Vanderlee.

"You plan on having leather restraints on his wrists?" asked Thorpe.

Before Vanderlee could answer, the court custodial officer quickly clarified the matter. "Just the legs, Your Honor."

"Well, we oppose that," stated Bill Jaquette firmly. "They need some particularized concern as to why it should be done, to overcome the presumption that it shouldn't be done. Mr. Clark has the same interests now," he said, "as he had at trial, which was to present himself to the jury in a fashion that would be favorable to him. And I think that is a factor that I'm sure he is considering as he considers his personal behavior in the courtroom. I mean, he sat through the whole thing so far, without demonstrating any efforts to escape or do anything, and therefore I think he has demonstrated over time his willingness and ability to sit calmly here to observe and participate in the proceedings."

"You said that there is a presumption that he *not* be restrained," commented Judge Thorpe, his inflection indicating an offer of proof should be forthcoming from the defense.

Jaquette brought up a previous discussion regarding restraints during the trial phase—a discussion Thorpe perfectly recalled. "I thought that had to do with the impact that it might have on the jury. I can understand that," said the judge, "but the defendant is no longer presumed innocent. He has now been convicted. And as long as there is no impact on the jury by the restraints, their being leather, they are quiet enough that they wouldn't be heard by the jury and they won't be seen by the jury, I don't see any prejudice to him.

"Well, the right is one that comes out of ancient English

common law, and the principle is that a man should not have to appear before the tribunal in chains. I think there needs to be some findings by the court to justify it."

"Well," countered Doersch, "Mr. Shawn Wells was sentenced this morning on assault in the third degree, and at that point, he was in shackles. He had presumably been found guilty by plea or some motion before the court, yet he was in shackles. Regardless of how uncomfortable it may be for Mr. Clark at this point, he has indeed been found guilty of the crimes charged. The risk is great," Doersch asserted, "despite the fact that he has not done anything up until now. Now he faces the certain prospect of life without possibility of parole and possibly death."

"Yeah," agreed Judge Thorpe, "I think that's a sufficient circumstance by itself to warrant shackles, leather restraints."

"I understand the court's ruling," said Jaquette. He understood it, but he certainly didn't like it. He also didn't care for the planned victim impact statement that Gail Doll would read to the jury, and he wanted to know exactly what use the prosecution was going to make of Toni Clark, current wife of George Clark Sr., as a rebuttal witness.

"We are in a particularly difficult spot in the penalty phase," said Jaquette, "because the issue of what can be introduced in rebuttal is an important matter because of the restrictions that exist. As a strategic matter, we don't want to open doors that would create evidence that's worse than what would happen if we didn't open that door. We would like to be able to make reasoned decisions on what to say in relation to what doors might be opened." What Jaquette wanted was Thorpe to rule on what the prosecution could, and could not, use as rebuttal arguments.

Thorpe merely ascertained from Jo Vanderlee that she would assuredly provide the defense with what she anticipated using as a rebuttal to the defense's evidence of mitigating circumstances. "I can have that by one-thirty," promised Vanderlee.

"That would be helpful, please," said the judge. He then did his best to deal with each one of the defense's new motions in orderly, efficient progression. "Mr. Jaquette's motions are pretty straightforward," he said. "Any objections to the first one?"

"Yes, Your Honor," replied Vanderlee. "There is no objection to the second and third, but to the first one, I would object. I mean, the defendant's criminal record is one of the aggravating circumstances that the state is permitted to put forth as evidence in front of the jury in the penalty phase."

Jaquette quickly agreed with his opponent and clarified the motion. "The motion isn't to exclude the record of criminal convictions, the motion is to prohibit the facts associated with those cases." In other words, the defense wanted assurance that the prosecution would not overstep the bounds of reciting Clark's previous judgments and sentences and go into details of his previous crimes.

"What convictions are we talking about?" asked Thorpe. Vanderlee had no difficulty reciting specifics.

"Specifically, what I would be trying to get in front of the jury for most of Mr. Clark's convictions is the information and the judgment and sentence. But," Vanderlee emphasized, "for the 1988 unlawful-imprisonment charge, I would be seeking to admit testimony from Detective Berglund and Officer Snyder. You want to know what the defendant's prior criminal history consists of?"

"Yes, please," said the judge.

"He's got an unlawful-imprisonment conviction; found guilty January 12, 1990, taking a motor vehicle without permission, and a second-degree burglary, sentenced January 18, 1990; taking a motor vehicle and eluding, sentenced January 22, 1992. And taking a motor vehicle without permission, sentenced September 17, 1992. He also has," she continued, "a juvenile conviction for fourth-degree assault, reduced from a second-degree assault. And he has two third-degree theft convictions that are obviously misdemeanors."

Vanderlee then presented her reasoning on delving into details of the Feather Rahier case. She argued that there was no law in Washington State that holds that underlying facts of previous convictions should not be admitted.

Jaquette was virtually drop-jawed. "The penalty phase has to be focused on mitigation. The one mitigating circumstance that is permitted [to the prosecution] is a record of prior convictions. We are way, way, way beyond the record of prior convictions if we are getting into all these assorted facts and details. I mean," he said, almost exasperated, "what is it that the prosecuting attorney is now going to be permitted to argue to the jury? Is it going to be able to argue that because Mr. Clark has a record of prior convictions that he is therefore someone who is worthy to be executed? Or are they going to say [about the Feather Rahier case], 'Oh, look, here's another case just like this one, only he didn't quite get so far, and therefore we got to be sure. . . . That is not what they get to do. That is beyond proper argument. . . ."

"Your Honor," countered Vanderlee, "we are not talking about dumping garbage here in terms of criminal history; we are talking about reliable information contained in police reports. . . ."

Judge Thorpe didn't see anything in the law restricting the plaintiff from putting on anything other than judgment and sentence. "So I will allow the testimony about the age of the child and that she was a neighbor, the judgment and sentence, and the police report."

William Jaquette was almost beside himself with

incredulity. "Your Honor, just a final dying gasp on this whole issue," he said, pointing out that case law clearly indicated that evidence to be presented relates to mitigating factors only. "This is not a mitigating factor, I can assure you."

Judge Thorpe believed it was his discretion as sentencing judge to allow the jury to hear details of Clark's 1988 conviction, including proposed testimony from Feather Rahier, the victim herself.

Feather, of course, had other ideas that included running away from home rather than participate in such courtroom shenanigans. Her motivation wasn't case law, but personal emotional pain. Indeed, it was the topic of pain and deprivation, both emotional and physical, that the defense would present as their first and most powerful mitigating circumstance.

Jaquette sat down at the defense table and let loose a long sigh. His odds of saving his client's life in this Snohomish Country courtroom were not worth a wise man's wager. It was his firm and unalterable conviction that allowing the prosecution to parade details of the Rahier incident for the jury's consideration was both a judicial error and prelude to the death sentence for Richard M. Clark—a sentence resultant from prejudice and emotion. William Jaquette held firm to his vow: give every client the best defense under the law. After all, it was the law that he defended, not the alleged act of the defendant. He would do everything possible to reduce the emotional aspects that could interfere with the jury's sober consideration of his arguments.

"We request," said Jaquette, "that the state be prohibited from introducing at any time during the penalty phase any in-life photographs of Roxanne Doll."

"Your Honor," said Jo Vanderlee, "I would point out to the court that the defense is admitting fourteen photographs of a cherubic-looking lad in mitigation, so I would submit what is appropriate for the defense would be appropriate for the state in this case."

"We obviously object," said Jaquette, and he argued that the in-life photos of young Roxanne were not appropriate—they were not required to prove the victim's identity, nor did they relate to any mitigating factor. "There is no basis to suggest that the state gets to put on a show here to show a bunch of pictures of the victim, because the pictures of the victim don't go to the question of victim impact, or the impact of the death of the child upon the family."

Vanderlee countered his comments by insisting that the photos illustrated Gail Doll's proposed victim impact statement. Doll's slightly truncated testimonial would form part of the prosecution's presentation. The defense, however, believed that Doll's statement should be saved until sentencing. "Your Honor, I am not denying that we are swimming up a pretty strong stream in that, because as a general proposition, the court has ruled that this type of evidence is admissible because of the Eighty-fourth Amendment to the Washington Constitution, which is essentially the victim's rights amendment. Again, it's our position generally that it is excludable, because it is something that should be heard by the court at the time that the sentence is imposed. Beyond that, I am of the opinion, and would urge the court, that the court has to take it in the context of the particular case. In other words, the state doesn't get to put on any victim impact testimony. I think it has to be deemed to be relevant and its probative value outweigh its prejudicial effect."

This case, Jaquette argued, had some unique factors to it. "The unique factor that I would point to is the fact that this particular offense had tremendous community impact," he said. "We moved for a change of venue, because of the impact that this case had upon the news and, in turn, the impact that all the news presentations had on the people in the community.

"Many people who were interviewed as possible jurors," he reminded Thorpe, "indicated that they had read about and seen it on television, read about it in the newspaper. A number of people were excused because they just couldn't get beyond that. In fact, we have one juror on the panel today who herself admitted at one point she read the newspapers and concluded that the defendant was guilty. So I think what we have *is* a situation where the impact, or the potential for abuse by victim impact, abuse to the question that's before the jury now, is quite high. Therefore, we generally move to exclude all victim impact statements and exhibits."

Judge Thorpe did not concur completely with either Jaquette or Vanderlee, and ruled that "some victim impact statement is permissible." One in-life photo of Roxanne Doll was to be selected to share with the jurors.

Prior to the jury being seated, Jaquette and Vanderlee skirmished over a few more important issues: the state wanted excluded from the mitigation/sentencing phase any testimony by Richard Clark's relatives in which they express their desire to have Richard Clark live because they love him.

"There is a federal case, Your Honor," said Jo Vanderlee, "that indicates it's improper for the defendant's relatives to get on the witness stand and say that they love the defendant, and in effect that they don't want him to be put to death. It's not a fact about the defendant, because most, if not all, relatives love their relatives regardless of [the] worth of that person, and it's not a fact about the offense. So it's not a mitigating circumstance, period, in *Coleman v. Saffle,* which I cited in my brief is authority for that position."

Jaquette was quick to counter Vanderlee's assertions. "It's our position that indeed whether an aunt and a brother have affections that are for the defendant is a factor that could be considered," he said. "The fact that he is loved by his aunt and his brother, that they don't want to see him die, that it would be painful to them, is a fact about the defendant which bears upon the decision."

"This argument," interjected Vanderlee, "is simply to get sympathy from the jury, and that is one of the reasons that it has been disallowed in the federal courts."

"Not in this case," Jaquette told Thorpe. "Obviously, sympathy is not the issue, mercy is, and mitigating circumstance is, and I think it qualifies as being under this definition that we will probably be using for mitigating circumstances, and indeed a definition the court has already read to the jury, or at least a portion of it has already been read to the jury, that it comes full square under that concept. It says something about the defendant—about the character of the defendant."

"Well, then," asked Vanderlee slyly, "can I also get into character evidence?"

"In rebuttal, sure," said Thorpe.

"Whoa," called out Jaquette, "we should talk about that. If they testify that they love him, is his rebuttal that they really don't love him?"

The three looked at each other, shrugged, and Thorpe noted that he had not yet heard the cross-examination.

"You said we could get into future dangerousness," said Vanderlee, changing the subject.

"I said you could argue it," Judge Thorpe corrected her, "but not put in evidence about it. I ruled that you may not put on any evidence, because you said you weren't going to in the first place."

"Right."

"Why should they not," asked Thorpe, turning toward the defense, "be allowed to argue future dangerousness?"

"Because they can only argue things for which there is evidence to support," Jaquette replied. "He will be imprisoned with adults and no one seven years old is going to be anywhere near him."

"Correct," said the judge. Jaquette nodded, as would a student passing a test, and the jury was brought in to decide the fate of Richard M. Clark.

Part 4
SENTENCING

Chapter 18

"You have been reconvened for this special sentencing hearing," stated Judge Thorpe. "At the conclusion of this hearing, you will have the duty to determine what sentence answering the following question shall impose:

"Having in mind the crime of which the defendant has been found guilty, has the state proved beyond a reasonable doubt that there are not sufficient mitigating circumstances to merit leniency?

"If you unanimously answer yes to this question, the sentence will be death. If you do not unanimously answer yes, or if you unanimously answer no, the sentence will be life imprisonment without the possibility of release or parole.

"The state bears the burden of proving beyond a reasonable doubt that there are not sufficient mitigating circumstances to merit leniency. A reasonable doubt is one for which a reason exists, and may arise from the evidence or lack of evidence.

"It is such a doubt as would exist in the mind of a reasonable person after fully, fairly, and carefully considering all the evidence or lack of evidence.

"Only if after such consideration you have an abiding belief that there are not sufficient mitigating circumstances to merit leniency, then you are satisfied beyond a reasonable doubt. A mitigating circumstance may be any relevant fact about the defendant or the offense, which although not justifying or excusing the offense, suggests a reason for not imposing the death penalty.

"You will be given a more specific definition of the phrase mitigating circumstances later on during these proceedings. You are to keep an open mind, and you shall not decide any issue in this sentencing phase until the case is submitted to you for your deliberation by the court.

"During your deliberations, you should consider anew the evidence presented to you in the first phase of this case, you should also consider any evidence offered and received during the sentencing hearing. We will now have opening statements from counsel, first for the plaintiff, Ms. Vanderlee."

"Your verdicts in the first phase of this trial bring us here to the sentencing phase of the trial," she began, "and as the judge just instructed you, the question that you will now have to answer is, having in mind the crime of which the defendant has been convicted, has the state proven to you beyond a reasonable doubt that there are not sufficient mitigating circumstances to merit leniency. That is the question you will be asked to answer in this stage of the case. The state is permitted, in this phase of the case, to only get into three areas of evidence. Those three areas are all of the evidence from the guilt phase or the first phase of the trial. The second portion of evidence the state will be able to admit to you is the defendant's criminal history or his record of convictions.

"You will hear about his prior convictions through certified copies of documents called judgment and sentences. The defendant's criminal history consists of several felonies and some misdemeanor convictions.

"You will hear about a May 28, 1988, unlawful-imprisonment conviction that the defendant has. Detective Diane Berglund will testify that that conviction involved the unlawful restraint of a four-year-old girl, a neighborhood girl known to defendant, who he restrained by tying her up in his garage.

"You will hear about a felony conviction from October 11, 1988, for taking motor vehicle. The defendant was convicted of that, and served time in the county jail as well. You will hear about a second-degree burglary conviction the defendant committed here *in* Snohomish County. You will also hear about a felony conviction that the defendant committed for the crime of attempting to elude a pursuing police vehicle. And also, as part of that crime, the vehicle that he was attempting to elude the police in was a stolen vehicle, so yet another taking of [a] motor vehicle. And Mr. Richard Clark also has some misdemeanor convictions for third-degree theft. He's got two of those and for vehicle prowling.

"You will also hear some evidence in this case about Roxanne Doll. You will hear evidence about what kind of child she was and why her family misses her so much. Mrs. Doll-Iffrig will testify that Roxanne was a trusting, friendly child, that Roxanne liked to ride her bike, that was her— one of her last accomplishments. In fact, she will testify that Roxanne liked to read, that she liked dressing up, and that she liked playing with her pets and her favorite pet was her cat.

"At the conclusion of the state's case, the defense may choose to put on evidence, but they do not have to. And after that, the state may, if necessary, put on witnesses to rebut evidence presented by the defense. And at the conclusion of the evidence, I submit to you, ladies and gentlemen, the answer to the question that you are asked to answer will be yes, the state has proven beyond any reasonable doubt that the defendant does not merit leniency, and that the appropriate sentence in this case is a sentence of death."

Vanderlee sat back down, and Judge Thorpe turned

toward Jaquette and Scott. "Does the defendant wish to make an opening statement at this time, or reserve?"

"Your Honor, we will reserve our opportunity to make an opening statement," replied Jaquette.

"Very well," said the judge, and he returned his gaze to the prosecution. "You may call your first witness."

Ronald Doersch arose. "The state calls Detective Diane Berglund." The entire 1988 case of Richard Clark's unlawful imprisonment of Feather Rahier was presented before the jury, beginning with Diane Berglund, and including Officer Dwight Snyder, Julie Gelo, and even Feather's mother, who was flown up from California. Feather was subpoenaed to appear, and a warrant was issued for her arrest, but she managed to elude all attempts to locate her.

Following the jury's total immersion in a matter resolved almost a decade earlier, Judge Thorpe intoned: "We will now have opening statement for the defendant."

William Jaquette stood to address the jury. "Thank you, Your Honor. Counsel, ladies and gentlemen of the jury, the night of March 31, 1995, Roxanne Doll suffered immeasurable terror and immeasurable pain. She lost her life and thereby lost the opportunity that a full life, full of experiences, would have brought her. She also was a great loss to her family, and you heard the evidence about the pain and suffering that her parents and her brother and sister have endured. I am not here to try to diminish that pain and torture, but what I am here however to do is to ask you to consider the question of mitigation.

"I'm here to tell you why it is that given that, Richard Clark does deserve leniency," explained Jaquette, "that there are sufficient mitigating circumstances to merit leniency, and that the sentence that Richard Clark should receive is a sentence of life in prison without the possibility of parole.

"You've heard about Richard Clark's itinerant lifestyle.

You heard about the events as they unfolded on March thirty-first into April, in the early days of April, including the amounts of alcohol and drugs that the defendant and many of the others involved in this case consumed. To that evidence, we intend to add some additional evidence this morning about Richard Clark's life.

"The memories of the witnesses are going to be varied," he said, "because it stretches over a period of twenty-eight years." For the first time, jurors would hear about the tragic upbringing of Richard Mathew Clark— an upbringing that the defense presented as a mitigating circumstance. Jaquette reminded the jury again that the defense did not need to prove mitigating circum-stances—they were presumed. The prosecution must prove the absence of mitigating circumstances.

"Richard Clark was born on August 18, 1968. His mother was named Kathy. And at the time of Richard's birth, she was married to George Clark Junior. Although George Clark does not believe that Richard is his natural child—and he has made that clear to Richard in the course of his upbringing. Sometime shortly after Richard was born, his mother, Katharine, took a job in eastern Washington driving a truck for a canning company, a vegetable-canning company or something in that order. And Richard and his brother and his sister, older brother and sister, were left under the care of Carol Clark, one of the witnesses who you already met in this case.

"That went on for a period of time, months, maybe a year or so, and then Kathy Clark came back to—from eastern Washington to western Washington—moved into the family home and began to take charge of her family. She had a couple of relationships in that period of time, but when Richard was somewhere around three or perhaps four, she met and married Bob Smith. Bob Smith came from Arlington and it wasn't long before the family moved back to the Arlington area, and there they lived for a period of time, either in Arlington or Darrington in two or three locations in that area. During this time, the family had a very hard time economically. Kathy Clark, Kathy Smith now, worked at the Reinell boat company, but she broke her neck and was disabled and unable to continue work.

"She received labor and industry payments, but that wasn't very much," he said. "Bob Smith did not work and the family had a particularly hard time in making ends meet. They did odd jobs and picked berries and cascara bark, and not surprising to you, I'm sure, they poached a deer or two in order to keep meat on the table.

"Both Bob and Kathy Smith were abusers of drugs and alcohol," he elaborated, "specifically marijuana and alcohol. This was something that was known to the children in the family. Bob Smith was an abusive father. He emotionally and physically abused the children, especially Richard and his older brother, George. He subjected them to humiliations. He made them do work out in the yard, which was meaningless, picking up rocks out of the ground, putting them into one pile, and when they were in one pile, moved the pile to another place."

Jurors listened in rapt attention, visualizing the severe physical and mental abuse suffered by the Clark children under Bob Smith's iron rule. Jaquette described brutal beatings that left bleeding welts and open sores.

"He beat them with a poker; he beat them with an electrical cord; he beat them so badly from time to time that they bled. One day, Richard went to visit his aunt Carol, who has always lived in Everett. Carol found that he was so badly beaten that he couldn't sit down, he couldn't lie down, he couldn't sleep for two days; he was bruised all over the back of his body. She called Kathy and Bob and said, 'If I see this again, I'm going to call the authorities.' Well, she didn't see it again, because Richard was not permitted to visit Carol for a period of two years."

Jurors, previously unfamiliar with Richard Clark's background and upbringing, listened intently to Jaquette's well-constructed, succinct, yet emotionally evocative narrative. "One month after Richard's fourteenth birthday, his mother was killed in a single-car accident on Highway 9." As this event was the prelude to the most pivotal moment in Clark's young life, the attorney allowed the heartrending implications to sink in before continuing.

"This was a devastating blow to Richard. He was crying—he cried every day about it. Then," said Jaquette with ominous finality, "at some point, he stopped. He simply closed himself in, never responded to that event again, and began his own career of alcohol and drugs."

He told the jury how the fragmented and emotionally fragile family members, deprived of the singular source of their united identity, drifted off in their own aimless directions. "Richard was only fourteen, and he got moved in with this relative and that relative. He stayed with George Junior, who was named for his father, husband of his mother at the time of his birth. He moved in with and stayed sometime with Carol Clark, and he spent sometime with his maternal grandparents, the Fellers, in Lake Stevens.

"Nothing was permanent," said Jaquette sadly, "and nobody took on the job of being a parent. Richard did not finish school, and has kind of been on the street ever since that time. We are going to bring in two witnesses to discuss Richard Clark's life. One will be Carol Clark, whom you've already met in the trial phase of this case, and the other will be George the second, not George Junior, the father, but George the second, who is the brother, the older brother of Richard.

"By your verdict in the trial phase of this case, you have removed the presumption of innocence," acknowledged the defense. "However, as we begin this penalty phase, and as it goes toward deliberation, Mr. Clark carries with him the presumption of leniency. I would ask you, at this point, to keep an open mind as you hear the rest of the testimony; as you hear the instructions from the court, and the arguments from the attorneys. Then I'll have another opportunity to come up here and ask you to sentence Richard Clark not to death, but to a life in prison without the possibility of parole. Thanks."

"You may call your first witness," said Judge Thorpe.

"Your Honor," said Jaquette, "the defense first calls Carol Clark."

The emotional Carol Clark told the entire story of Richard's life, confirming Jaquette's pretestimony remarks. She gave specific examples of the deprivation and discipline, acknowledging her own efforts to provide a healthier, stable environment for the children. Her testimony—emotional, sensitive, and heartbreaking—set the tone for Clark's penalty phase.

Following Carol Clark came Richard's brother George Clark II. In painstaking detail, and with great emotional pain to the witness, he related the beatings, bruises, and belittlement suffered by his brother and him at the hands of Bob Smith—the alcoholic tyrant who ruled the family with iron fists, electrical cords, and a fireplace poker.

George testified to the "marks that looked like cut marks, but they were welts that busted open" all over Richard Clark's body. "When I got to be in my teenage years," said George, "I got too old for the electrical cords and belts, as far as getting beaten. He then went to fists, and I believe Richard was hit with Bob's fists also."

George told jurors of the nonstop drinking and drugging he witnessed growing up, so much of it that he thought continual drinking was normal. As for marijuana, "I can remember him [Smith] smoking pot as long as I can remember wondering what it was," said George Clark II. All of this, he asserted, had a lasting impression on his younger brother.

"When I was married, my ex-wife and I lived down here in Everett. Richard would come over screwed up all the time." By "screwed up," George meant "drunk."

The prosecution, sensitive as anyone to the tragic lifestyle of George, Richard, and their siblings, did not consider it a mitigating factor. "Carol Clark has always been there for Richard, hasn't she? In fact, Carol Clark has always provided a home for Richard whenever he needed one, isn't that right?"

"I don't believe she's ever turned him away," confirmed George.

"From what you know of Richard's life," asked Vanderlee, "there was never a point where he was on the streets as a homeless kid because Aunt Carol and the grandparent Clarks were always there to give him a home, isn't that fair to say?"

"I would say he always had a choice to go there," said George Clark II, "because I don't believe he ever got turned away."

Jo Vanderlee did not want the jury's attention turned away from the horrid acts committed against little Roxanne Doll by Richard M. Clark. "We are here today about Roxanne Doll," said Jo Vanderlee, "and we are here about justice. We are here about murder and rape and kidnapping, and the concealment of an atrocity committed upon a child of this community.

"We are here about Richard Clark. Not the Richard Clark that sits there in that white shirt at counsel table, but the Richard Clark who went into a trusted friend's house—someone who trusted him—and took a child from that house, kidnapped that child, raped that child, and murdered that child.

"We are here about justice, justice for Roxanne, justice for Roxanne's family, justice for this community, and we are here about justice for Richard Clark."

The next comment by Vanderlee may have been over

the line: "In this trial, you are the conscience of the community," she said. "You are the law, and you decide what justice is and what that defendant deserves.

"What Richard Clark deserves is an answer on the verdict form of yes, that he does not merit leniency. The death penalty is reserved for the most serious crimes, and for the most dangerous offenders. You heard the evidence in the trial phase and you know, from your verdict, that the most serious crime has been committed, and that man, ladies and gentlemen, is the most serious, the most dangerous—"

"Objection, Your Honor," interrupted Bill Jaquette.

"Overruled," replied Thorpe.

"You have a difficult question ahead of you, a very difficult question," said Vanderlee to the jury. "That question is, has the state proven to you beyond a reasonable doubt that there are not sufficient mitigating circumstances to merit leniency?"

Vanderlee provided the state's unshakable conviction that no such mitigating circumstances existed to justify a sentence of less than death. "There is nothing about this crime, and there is nothing about this defendant, that merits leniency. Nothing can excuse this crime—not his crummy childhood, not alcohol, and not drugs. There is nothing that can excuse this crime.

"The defense is offering Bob Smith to you as a piñata—a human piñata—something to distract you away from the defendant," she said, "so that you will look at it and you will say that's really the bad thing. Let the defense take swings at someone who is not here to defend himself and bash Bob Smith, and they'll be looking at Bob Smith and they won't be looking at the defendant.

"I submit to you, ladies and gentlemen, Bob Smith did not rape and murder Roxanne Doll, he did not rape her, he did not kidnap her. The defendant did that, he did that all by himself.

"There were five kids that grew up in those circumstances, five kids who went from Everett to Lake Stevens, to Arlington to Darrington. It was a poor family, poor family that was living in the rural parts of this county, not unlike many, many children who grow up in this county, or grew up in this county during the '70s. And what do you know from hearing George talk or from hearing Carol and from hearing Toni?" she asked rhetorically. "You know that none of those other kids are child murderers or have raped children or are kidnappers.

"Let's talk about this crime for a moment," she said, and recounted the heinous doings of Richard M. Clark. "This was the premeditated killing of a seven-year-old girl, a little girl who has just learned how to read, to ride a bike, she just learned how to swim. This little girl just had hope in her heart when [she] went to bed that night on March 31, 1995. And she was taken from that bed, never to return to it."

Focusing again on the all-important issue of premeditation, Vanderlee approached it head-on. "Mr. Clark made three choices that night, three choices. He made the choice to kidnap her; he made the choice to take her in a van and conceal her. Once he even got her out to the van, he could have stopped himself; he could have said, 'I am not going to take her, I'm just going to put her back in the bedroom.' He didn't do that. He made a second choice; he made the choice to rape her.

"Even after he raped her, he didn't have to leave her in that injured condition. The defendant could have returned Roxanne to the parents' home, to a hospital, he could have even left her on a street somewhere, where someone could have found her. But he didn't do that.

"He didn't show very much mercy. After she was injured from the rape, he stabbed her seven times. It was a slow death, several minutes to half an hour. Whether she died in the back of his van or whether it was on that slope or anywhere in Everett."

From the time she was dying, said Vanderlee, he made a third choice: "And that choice was not to take her to a hospital. He made a third choice to bury her where he hoped she would never be found. Is there anything about that that could justify a sentence of less than death?

"If you sentence the defendant to life in prison," Vanderlee said, "the defendant will always have hope, because where there is life, there is hope. Roxanne is not going to get any more hope. The only hope that Roxanne Doll has is the hope for justice.

"The question that you have to answer," she told the jury, "is this: is there anything about the defendant that justifies a sentence of less than death?"

According to Vanderlee, people do not wind up in the penalty phase of a capital trial because of sheer bad luck or because of coincidence or because of a mean stepfather. They wind up in the penalty phase of a capital murder trial because of choices that they made.

"Richard Clark made choices in his life that got him here," she said, "like the choices he made in murdering Roxanne Doll. Some people in their lives leave legacies; they have families, they start a business, or they write a book; they leave behind a positive legacy. What is Richard Clark's legacy? His legacy can be summed up in these judgments and sentences that tell you about the crimes he's committed in his life. We know that Richard Clark is a burglar, a thief, a person who recklessly bribes and eludes the police, a person who commits the crime of unlawful imprisonment—tying up little four-year-old Feather Rahier in a garage in Snohomish County, Washington.

"Let's talk a little bit about his childhood," said Vanderlee. "He had a crummy childhood and he offers that to you as a mitigating circumstance. George Clark has a job. George Clark is dealing with his alcohol and drug abuse problems. He is in treatment. The girls have families, the girls have jobs. Those other four kids grew up in the exact same circumstances. I guess you could call it the phenomena of parallel lives, they all grew up in the same situation, and they did not turn out like Richard Clark, because Richard Clark chose his path. In truth, he chose to put himself in the position that he is in today.

"Do not blame Bob Smith," she said. "He's a bad guy, perhaps, for abusing his stepchildren, but Bob Smith cannot be blamed for this crime. It is sad that Kathy Smith died. It's always sad when a parent dies. There is no question about that. But consider that many children unfortunately have a parent who dies.

"A parent passes away, and the child turns to other relatives or perhaps the child turns to his church or some other thing in their life that they can rely on. This defendant, when his mother died, had a caring extended family right here in this county that he could rely on.

"So, when he is trying to say that [his] childhood should be an excuse for this crime, don't buy it, because his childhood, although not the greatest, was certainly one that had its support systems in it.

"I would like to talk for a second or two about these photographs," she said, approaching the defense exhibits. "There was some talk about Richard being beaten, about money being short. And that's probably all true. But when you look at these photographs, these photographs of a happy, smiling child, this happy kid with his Easter bunny, there is George Clark hugging Richard."

She showed the jury a picture of Richard Clark playing with some toys. "Does he look like he is really that deprived at this point in his life? This child," she said, referring to Clark, "got to grow up; Roxanne is not going to get to grow up. And this child," Vanderlee said, referencing the photo of a cherubic Richard Clark, "is not the person that you are here to decide whether he merits leniency or not. The person you are here to sentence is that twenty-eight-year old man over there, not that eight-year-old kid in those pictures."

Vanderlee reminded jurors that Clark was twenty-six when he committed the crime. "He had been away from Bob Smith for twelve years. He cannot blame someone for this crime when the crime happened twelve years after that person had completely passed out of his life."

Lest jurors conclude that Clark's horrid crime was attributable to his brain being under the influence of alcohol and methamphetamines, Vanderlee pointed out that Clark indulged in that stimulant primarily after committing the crime. "And the fact is," she continued, "that Richard Clark does not leave living witnesses to this crime. There is a lesson here that he did not leave a living witness. He took this kid and he did not want her to tell about what happened to her, so to protect his own self he killed her.

"There is no justification for this crime," Vanderlee asserted emphatically, "that would merit this defendant receiving a penalty of less than death."

There is a contention, held by millions of individuals, and the majority of nations in the world, that if a society uses capital punishment, the society is committing cold-blooded, premeditated murder. The prosecution sought to counter such contention by stating, "The death penalty is the law in this state, something that is in fact the law of the land."

"Objection, Your Honor," said Jaquette, "that is not accurate." Judge Thorpe agreed with Jaquette, and the objection was sustained.

Vanderlee, without missing a beat, continued: "Society does not make itself into a beast through using capital punishment. To argue that," she said, "would be to say that when society imprisons someone for burglary, that it's unlawful imprisonment, or when the state exacts a fine on someone, it's thievery."

The prosecution then addressed the topic of mercy, saying, "Mercy can be a mitigating circumstance. If you, as a jury, decide that mercy is a mitigating circumstance in this case, be sure that you are not applying that arbitrarily and be sure that you are considering the mercy to be appropriately given, if that's what you decide to do.

"It's been said that some people, because of the crimes they commit, because of the atrocities they commit, do not belong on this earth. I submit to you that this might just be such a case. And when the defense argues to you that Richard Clark deserves mercy, keep in mind the mercy he showed to Roxanne Doll on March 31, 1995, when the defendant had Roxanne Doll under his complete control, alone in that van and on that hillside. If you show this defendant the same mercy that he showed Roxanne Doll, it will be a just verdict."

Chapter 19

After prosecutor Jo Vanderlee sat down, Judge Thorpe said, "We will now have closing argument for the defendant, Mr. Jaquette."

"Thank you, Your Honor," said Bill Jaquette, and cut immediately to the unavoidable. "By your verdict in this case," he told the jury, "you have convicted Richard Clark of the most serious crime that exists under the laws of the state of Washington, aggravated murder in the first degree. Having done that, the law presumes what the sentence will be, the presumed sentence in this case, for someone who is convicted of that serious offense, is that they serve the rest of their life in prison. Richard Clark will be taken from here and taken to prison behind cement walls and steel bars, where every day of his life will be controlled by those who supervise him, what he eats, when the lights are turned out at night, everything will be controlled. That goes on today, tomorrow, the next day, and the next day, every day of the rest of his life.

"Richard Clark will not get out. He will not be released to furlough. He will not get to go visit a sick or dying relative. He will never go to a ball game or vote, go to a community activity, walk on the beach, or see a mountain. That's the sentence that is presumed Richard Clark deserves."

He then explained the circumstances under which the jury could order Clark to be killed. "Only if in those circumstances where you, the jury, decide that this crime is not just aggravated murder in the first degree, but the worst of the worst aggravated murder, can you bring back a verdict of yes on the verdict form and Richard Clark would be sentenced to death."

The jury must ask itself, he reminded them, "keeping in mind the crime of which the defendant has been found guilty, has the state proven beyond a reasonable doubt that there are not sufficient mitigating circumstances to merit leniency?

"That first sentence of that first phrase in the sentence is an important one, 'Having in mind the crime of which the defendant has been found guilty.'

"Having in mind the crime is not having in mind the crime and the cost that would be to you and I as taxpayers to support Richard Clark in prison for the rest of his life," explained Jaquette. "This is clearly a question of balancing this crime against the potential for mitigating circumstances. Other factors, like the fact that it's going to cost us money, are not the facts that you, the jury, are invited by the law to consider."

Of more concern to Jaquette than finances was the possibility that the jury could sentence Clark to death based on crimes other than the one for which they convicted him. "You have heard evidence about Richard Clark's prior convictions; you are going to be able to see the certified legal documents relating to those convictions. The sentence doesn't say, 'Having in mind the crime of which Richard Clark was found guilty and all of the other crimes.' You are not weighing whether he deserves to be executed because of his prior convictions. His prior convictions are proper consideration for you, but you are not punishing him for those things.

"He has paid the price for those previous crimes," said Jaquette. "You are not to put them into this; you are not to put them alongside of the current crime.

"Instruction number four tells you that the defendant is presumed to merit leniency, which would result in a sentence of life in prison without possibility of parole." Jaquette restated that the presumption of merited leniency, as with the presumption of innocence, must be overcome by the evidence beyond a reasonable doubt.

The scales of justice were tilted by intent toward innocence and leniency. Only if the state met its burden of proving to the contrary would the tilt be toward guilt.

"The state's burden," said Jaquette, "is to prove this case beyond a reasonable doubt. You hear a lot of talk about 'beyond a reasonable doubt.' You applied that principle in reaching a verdict. But I would like to say a couple things about it. I would suggest that reasonable doubt is a commonsense concept. It's something you do use in your everyday life, and it's something that I'm sure that you used in that same fashion in reaching your verdict in this case."

The erudite attorney again quoted the definition of reasonable doubt regarding mitigation. "Only if . . . you have an abiding belief that there are not sufficient mitigating circumstances to merit leniency are you satisfied beyond a reasonable doubt.

"I want to focus on that word, 'abiding.' The word 'abiding' means continuing without change, enduring and lasting—a belief that will not change—a belief that will endure for the rest of your life."

In the trial phase, a unanimous verdict was required. All twelve jurors had to agree on the answer to a question of fact: "Was there proof, beyond a reasonable doubt, that Richard Clark is the person who committed these offenses?"

Now, however, the jury was not asked to agree unanimously on the matter of sufficiency. It was a measure that appealed to one's individual and collective conscience. "Your individual moral sensibilities developed over your experience as a child," explained, "things given to you by your parents, things you learned on your own, learned at school, and things that happened to you from the time you became adults until now."

These moral sensibilities were the tools that jurors would use in measuring question of sufficiency. "You can't capture an individual's moral sensibilities by slogans," asserted the defense. "But the way you think about those slogans has in some way to illuminate what the moral sensibility is. We talked about, or I presented the notion of, 'an eye for an eye.' 'An eye for an eye,' in many respects, is an attractive moral principle, certainly feels good in a situation like this, where we have a young child who was taken and a family who suffers so much. It is certainly an understandable response. This is not an adequate principle; it's not a sufficient principle. It's not a sufficient principle, because when you think about what 'an eye for an eye' means, you realize that it doesn't really give compensation."

When you have given the life for a life, said Jaquette, "what has the person who has been wronged received? Well, they haven't got their daughter back; they haven't been put whole."

An "eye for an eye" is not reflected in our American system of justice. In fact, the first instruction to the jury stated that they were not to respond to, or be influenced by, passion, prejudice, or sympathy.

"Saying about Richard Clark that he's somebody who doesn't deserve to be on this earth is not treating a person with intrinsic value."

The question jurors faced, of course, was one of sufficiency of mitigating circumstances to merit leniency. "That term 'leniency' is an important one and one that you need to be careful of," said Jaquette, "because in some context it doesn't seem like Richard Clark could possibly deserve leniency. But you remember, we are not talking about leniency of a teacher whose student has failed to turn in the term paper on time. What we are talking about is a question of whether the death penalty should be imposed or whether that second most serious punishment, life in prison without the possibility of parole, should be imposed."

Richard Clark and several other adult participants in this tragic story shared an affinity for alcohol and other lesser intoxicants. The defense would never offer alcoholism and drug addiction as an excuse, but it was an issue for consideration in sentencing.

"We are beyond the question that excuses and justification," acknowledged Jaquette. "We are not asking you to say this is an excuse or a justification for what he did. Richard Clark had a fifth of whiskey and a twelve-pack of beer, which they started in the afternoon and they just drank and drank and drank and drank the rest of the day. Mr. Clark was described as being on his feet, but it's still a ridiculous amount of alcohol. Both alcohol and drugs were something that his parents used, something that he knew about, something that he began to use, and something that took over his life."

People who are not alcoholic or drug addicted think in terms of "choice." They are aware of choosing to drink or not to drink, to use or not to use. For people such as Richard Clark, argued Jaquette, they no longer perceive choices, only wants and needs. "Richard Clark has to have alcohol," Jaquette asserted. "It's not something that he chooses anymore.

"Yeah, there was some choices back there that he could have made, but it's not a choice that he can make anymore. And what does alcohol mean? We are not suggesting here that Richard Clark was so drunk at the time of the offense that he didn't know what he was doing. Mr. Scott did not make that argument.

"When alcohol is used as an anesthesia to any situation

that is stressful," he asserted, "any situation that causes emotion, you don' t learn how to control your emotions, don't learn how to deal with your feelings. . . . There is no control. You cannot turn your emotions to the positive moral force necessary to get along in the world. You cannot develop the moral sensitivity needed to make a reasoned decision, to make the same kind of decision on the night of March thirty-first that the rest of us can. Again, I am not saying this is an excuse. This is not a justification, it's an explanation, and I would urge you to find it a mitigating circumstance.

"Neglect, abuse, and tragedy," delineated Jaquette. "Richard Clark was subject to all of these. I am not going to detail them, and I am not going to say that he suffered the worst childhood on the planet. I am not going to tell you that his brother and sisters did not suffer similar abuse. But each person is unique, each person comes upon these things at a particular time in their life.

"George Clark, Richard's brother, was affected by the beatings. He cried out; he could not believe that Richard didn't. Richard just took it. Why? Well, there is four years' difference. It's a different situation, they are different people, and they are affected differently. So you can't say, well, just assume that it doesn't mean anything, because Richard's brothers and sisters got through it. It does mean something," he insisted, "it does have an effect on one's life. You cannot say that what happened to Richard Clark does not have an effect. Again, this is not an excuse, not a justification for what he did. It is simply an explanation, it is an explanation which is a mitigating circumstance.

"When people are subjected to that kind of abuse," insisted Jaquette, "that kind of neglect and that kind of a tragedy, they avoid reaching out to other people. They avoid the experiences that bring them so much pain. Why do I feel for somebody when I realize the person I feel most about dies and leaves me alone? Why do I want to reach out for people when although there is family available to take care of me, there is a place to live, there is nobody that's going to take up and parent Richard?

"Nobody that says, 'Richard, you get in here, you get to school, and you go to school every day, because I say so. I'm your new parent. I'm taking over and you do it.'

"'Well, he didn't want to go to school, so we just didn't have room for him, because it was kind of inconvenient because of all the people around.' That's the message you get, that's the message you learn, and Richard learned it and he essentially became a creature of the street. Without that kind of experience, with the touching other people, you lose the ability to develop the moral sensibility that is necessary to make the kind of decision that Richard Clark should have made on the night of March thirty-first, two years ago.

"You've heard the phrase 'It takes a village to raise a child.' That phrase really kind of simulates a political discussion, a debate of people who say, 'Well, it's the responsibility of our community to do something to raise children.' Other people say, 'No, this is a family responsibility.' I think the fact that the debate exists, tends to show you what you must all accept, which is 'We are what we are because of things that are beyond our control.'

"Our culture is filled with homicides," Jaquette reminded the jury, "In the news that we get, homicides with multiple deaths. I'm sure each of you can think of people whom you read about in the paper who were charged with and convicted of terrible killings. We have a trial going on in Denver about the Oklahoma City bombing, which I can' t even remember how many people died in that. This is not a multiple death; it's the death of a child—it's horrible, but it's not a multiple death.

"Second of all," he said, "there is no evidence that there was any torture in this case. It is clear that death occurred, according to Dr. Kiesel, probably the same day that the child was taken. There was no period of captivity where the child was kept, and any kind of acts repeated. You got the evidence; you know where Richard Clark practically was from beginning to end. You know that couldn't have happened. This had to happen in a very short period of time. And again, it's a terrible thing, but again, measured against the various shades of black, I would suggest that these facts mitigate this about this crime."

The death penalty is not something Clark would choose either, and it certainly would impact more than Richard Clark. "The death penalty, unlike war or self-defense, is the only one of these things that actually has as its objective the taking of a life—war is about taking land; self-defense is about preserving one's own life.

"The death penalty has its greatest effect upon the person who would be executed. But it has an effect on other people too. It has an effect upon the family of the people who are executed. The family of the accused who didn't commit any offense will suffer the anguish and the anticipation of the execution itself, and they'll suffer the loss when the execution is done," Jaquette said convincingly. "Even the officials of the Department of Corrections are affected by the death penalty, because they are put in the position of actually bringing about the death of another human being.

"This case does not have the malignant premeditation that the worst of the worst would have," alleged the defense. "Mr. Doersch, in his closing arguments, told you that this was an act of opportunism. It had to be an act of opportunism. Mr. Clark had no idea that Tim Iffrig was going to fall asleep on the night of March thirty-first. It created an opportunity. It was something that occurred on the spur of the moment. An opportunity arose and he took it. As Mr. Doersch described it, this was a stupid crime; it was stupid in its inception; it was stupid in its being carried out. Mr. Doersch offered as proof that there was premeditation because there were multiple stab wounds—that even after the first blow, there was time to think before making the second blow—but is this the worst of the worst?"

William Jaquette answered his own question, saying, "The worst of the worst is a crime that's premeditated, where the consequences are thought over carefully ahead of time and affirmed. Where the Oklahoma City bomber thinks about what he is going to do, purchases the nitrate fertilizer, purchases the diesel fuel, rents the truck, brings it into the vicinity of the building, the federal building, at a time that he knows there are the most people present. That's the kind of malignancy that makes the crime the worst of the worst.

"This is a stupid crime, this is an opportunist crime, and this is a crime where there is no evidence where there was some kind of plan as there was in Oklahoma City. It was developed as it went along, and that doesn't demonstrate the kind of malignancy, which is the worst of the worst."

Having hammered rational proofs and exercises in comparative "worseness," Jaquette next attempted prying mercy from the jury's collective heart. "Finally there is the question of mercy. A mitigating circumstance is something that in fairness or in mercy justifies a sentence less than death. There are two things we are talking about: What's just and fair on one hand. And on the other hand, we have mercy. So to say that it's not fair that Richard avoid the death penalty is not the end of the case, because you must consider mercy.

"The law is a very subtle thing, because it directs you to consider not just the question of fairness, but the question of mercy. Ms. Vanderlee said, well, show Mr. Clark the same mercy he showed to Roxanne Doll. Well, I would ask you not to do that. I would ask you not to put yourself into Mr. Clark's shoes. You are in the jury room

with your fellow jurors, you are making a sober and reflective decision based on your moral sensibilities, and
there is no obligation for you to do what Richard Clark
did when you bring back your verdict.

"What is mercy? Mercy is something beyond what is
deserved. The law permits you to give Richard Clark something that he really doesn't deserve. The appropriateness
of mercy, says the instruction, the appropriateness of the
exercising of mercy is itself a mitigating factor you may
consider in determining whether the state has proven beyond a reasonable doubt that the death penalty is
warranted. I would suggest to you that mercy is appropriate in this case, and something that you have to consider
in reaching your verdict.

"Members of the jury," concluded Jaquette, "there are
sufficient mitigating circumstances in this case. Not sufficient mitigating circumstances to avoid a sentence of
life in prison without the possibility of parole, that's already been decided. There are sufficient mitigating
circumstances, however, to avoid the sentence of death.
I would urge that you bring back a verdict in your verdict
form of no, that as a consequence, Richard Clark will be
taken from here and put in prison for the rest of his life,
which is the sentence he deserves. Thank you."

Chapter 20

At the conclusion of Jaquette's presentation, Judge Thorpe said, "We will now have rebuttal for the plaintiff. Ms. Vanderlee?"

Jo Vanderlee kept her remarks short, pithy, and pointed. "Thank you, Your Honor. I would like to address a few things that Mr. Jaquette brought up," said Vanderlee. "And one is that there is absolutely no evidence that his client, Mr. Clark, likes to do things like walk on the beach or go to the mountains. In fact, there was a lot of things that Mr. Jaquette brought up in his closing arguments which were simply not brought up in evidence.

"Some of the things that were in evidence," she said, "were the fact that Richard Clark was drinking the night Roxanne was raped, and killed and kidnapped. But not to the extent where he was having accidents, nor to the extent that someone would cut him off in a bar, nor to the extent that the people he was in contact with that night thought he was intoxicated. The Urnesses didn't think that he was unusually intoxicated. They said simply that he had been drinking. That is not a mitigating circumstance.

"I would also like to point out," continued Vanderlee, "that the reasonable doubt standard that you dealt with in the guilt phase of this trial is the same standard you have to deal with here. It's not a mathematical concept. You decide whether the state has proven beyond a reasonable doubt that there are not sufficient mitigating circumstances, you decide." There were, she insisted, no mitigating circumstances—not even mercy—to keep Richard Mathew Clark from receiving the death penalty.

The arguments ended; the rebuttals ceased. The hushed rustling in the packed courtroom echoed back from the high ceiling to the solid wood doors opening out into the clatter and din of the Snohomish County Courthouse. Jury room number 8 would be sole witness to the jury's final deliberations regarding the punishment and sentencing of Richard M. Clark. They decided upon the death.

April 25, 1997

"I'm sure he did it," said Judge Thorpe to newspaper reporters from the *Everett Herald*. "I will not hesitate to sign Richard Clark's execution warrant." As Clark had not yet been sentenced when Thorpe made this comment, the defense immediately filed a motion for Judge Thorpe to step down—to recuse himself from the case.

Thorpe gave his lack of actual bias against Richard M. Clark as reason for denying the motion, but several attorneys were somewhat surprised when Thorpe did not recuse himself. Among them was Suzanne Lee Elliott.

"Trial before a fair and impartial judge is a fundamental right," she said. "That right extends to sentencing." The Washington State Supreme Court previously wrote, "The principle of impartiality, disinterestedness, and fairness on the part of the judge is as old as the history of courts; in fact, the administration of justice through mediation of courts is based upon this principle.

"The fundamental nature of this right," insisted Elliott, "is demonstrated by the fact that not even the appearance of bias is tolerated. Our system of law has always endeavored to prevent even the probability of unfairness." A proceeding does not meet the requirement of the appearance of fairness, she explained, if a disinterested observer would be reasonably justified in thinking that the judge wasn't impartial.

There were other issues raised by the defense—issues that could either cause the sentencing itself to be stopped or for a new trial, or sentencing phase, to take place. On the day Judge Thorpe handed down the sentence, defense moved for an arrest of judgment.

"We are asking at this time for the court to enter an order arresting judgment and sentence Mr. Clark to the lesser penalty of life imprisonment without possibility of parole." The motion was denied. Jaquette, unfazed, spoke up immediately.

"Your Honor, we will then next ask the court to grant us a new penalty phase proceeding. The basis for this motion," said the defense, "is based upon matters that the court has previously considered. We ask the court to reconsider it."

The essence of the defense motion hinged on a familiar name—the name of a young girl who packed a backpack, strapped on her Rollerblades, and skated away from the home of Julie Gelo—Feather Rahier.

"The court permitted the state to introduce evidence in the penalty phase of the trial about the facts behind the 1988 conviction of Mr. Clark for unlawful imprisonment. The court, had ruled at the time of trial that that was not admissible. The court, however, allowed the state to bring in the facts behind the 1988 conviction.

"It's our position," said Jaquette, "that that goes beyond what is permitted to the state in a penalty phase. I've indicated I think the argument pretty completely in my brief. I have cited not only the circumstances of this case, but I cited to the arguments which counsel made to the jury, reflecting those facts. And it's our position that not only was the introduction of the evidence improper, but also the argument based upon that."

The defense attorney, gaining momentum in what he firmly believed was a valid argument, quoted from the prosecution's own statements to the jury. "From the transcript of counsel's closing argument, 'He preys on the young, he preys on the vulnerable, and he preys on the . . . ' And then there was an objection and the court overruled the objection."

Thorpe and Doersch remembered the words and the objection. "That was in their opening argument," said Jaquette. "In their rebuttal, counsel again went on to say, 'But she did not win because this defendant preys on the vulnerable and the weak and the small.'"

To make sure everyone knew exactly what he was referencing, Jaquette stated it plainly: "He brought up the matter of Feather Rahier directly to the jury. Your Honor, I think the evidence together with the argument is improper. In essence, what the jury is doing is not sentencing Mr. Clark for the crime that he was charged with. The jury was invited by the evidence and by argument of counsel to conclude that this is a man who should be executed because he preys on the vulnerable and because he preys on the young."

In short, Jaquette was advancing the theory that the jury was passing judgment not only on the matter of Roxanne Doll, but also on the matter of Feather Rahier. "I think under the laws of Washington, that would be improper," argued the defense.

Prosecutor Doersch disagreed, and countered by defining what he meant by the words referenced by Jaquette. "The evidence that this jury had is that this defendant preys on the vulnerable, the weak, and the small, to wit, a seven-year-old girl, to wit, Roxanne Doll."

"With regard to the admissibility of that evidence," Doersch said, "the court heard evidence at the time before the argument [to] the jury, weighed that evidence, and made a determination that it should come in. And I also note that there is no objection following the statements of Ms. Vanderlee, as you know of his conviction of little Rahier, *R-A-H-I-E-R*. There is no objection to that point. There is objection before to the vulnerable, the weak, and the small. And further, on the argument goes, you know, he goes into homes, he's a burglar, he's a thief, he's a criminal, that certainly is material."

Even if admitting the details of the Rahier incident was an error, countered Doersch, "and the state does not concede that there is an error. If anything, it's a harmless error, and it is not the kind to arrest of judgment, in light of the evidence against the defendant, both in the trial and penalty phases.

"The court made a well-founded decision," Doersch said to Judge Thorpe, "to admit the additional facts with regard to the 1988 conviction."

"The measure of this whole question," countered Jaquette, "is the prejudice. And the measure of what is prejudicial is what is contained within a judgment and sentence. It's the ordinary thing that the state is allowed to introduce information that is not prejudicial. In this case, we have a lot more than information. We have something that gives additional facts about the [Feather Rahier] case and the facts about that case is not an abstract conviction; it is something that is of a similar nature to what the defendant is on trial for now. Those things, I think, do create the kind of prejudice which I think would be improper under Washington law."

"You may be right, Mr. Jaquette," said the judge. "But I'm persuaded that there are no Washington cases [that] require the ruling that you seek. And in reading the United States Supreme Court decisions, it's clear that they speak in terms of criminal history of character of the defendant, as reflected therein, et cetera, and they don't speak in terms of judgment and sentence. They don't speak in terms of naked convictions. And I'm persuaded that the amount of evidence that was allowed with respect to the unlawful-imprisonment conviction was merely enough to give the jury a sufficient indication of what the conviction was so they could make some intelligent decision with respect to it."

The expression on Jaquette's face bespoke volumes of disagreement. "It must be borne in mind," continued Thorpe, "that there was a tremendous amount of information in that unlawful-imprisonment conviction that would have been tremendously prejudicial to the defendant and that was all kept out. I think the bare minimum that was put in was sufficient and was not unfairly prejudicial to the defendant."

No sooner had Judge Thorpe uttered the words "So, that motion will be denied," than Mr. Jaquette spoke up again. "Your Honor, finally the defense would move for a new trial in the penalty phase proceeding based on misconduct of the jury."

Thorpe and Doersch gave Jaquette a duet of raised eyebrows. "We have filed a brief with that," continued Jaquette, "which includes a declaration, and I would ask the court to consider that as a presentation of facts upon which the court might rule. Attached to and incorporated by reference to the declaration is a portion of the article appearing in the *Post-Intelligencer* on Saturday morning April nineteenth quoting from a juror who has asked that his name not be included. Having read the article," explained defense counsel, "we contacted the reporter in question and we have attempted to serve him with a subpoena. . . . I have been contacted by an attorney representing the *Post-Intelligencer,* who is present in court to represent his client's interest. It's our position; first of all, that the article itself is sufficient to get us what we want. It is our position that the article stands on its own, and that the court should take those facts as being facts upon which it should make its ruling."

The meat of Jaquette's argument was simply this: "The jury has committed misconduct, and that the verdict in this case is a direct result of that misconduct, and therefore the defendant should be granted a new penalty phase proceeding.

"I refer specifically to three comments that were quoted in the article regarding the jury deliberation process. First of all," he explained, "the jury apparently was very much concerned with the defendant's demeanor as he sat at counsel table. Mr. Clark chose not to testify. He did not present any evidence whatsoever personally in this case, and the juror was quoted as saying, I'm quoting from the newspaper article: 'In the end it was his lack of emotion during the trial that helped seal his fate. "It was difficult for us to have mercy," said one juror, who asked that his name not be used. "If he had shown his compassion and how sorry he was, showed us that he was a human being, but every time you looked at his face, it was blank with certain callousness."' The juror said Clark would have a better chance to receive mercy if he exercised his right to testify and given the jury some clue that he deserved mercy. '"We were told to look for some mitigating circumstance,"' quoted Jaquette from the newspaper, '"but he didn't show her any."'

The newspaper interview, according to Jaquette, revealed three things about the jury. "One is that they were concerned with his demeanor as he sat at counsel table. The second one is that it created the concept that he should have testified, and that he would have been better off if he testified. The court instructed them that they should not consider the fact that he didn't testify in any way in making their decision. Finally the quote from the juror suggests that the defense had some obligation to show that there were mitigating circumstances. 'We were told to look for some mercy,'" quoted Jaquette, "'but he didn't' help us find any.' And that suggests that the burden was shifted, at least in the jury's mind, from the state, where it belonged, to the defense to come up with some mitigating circumstances.

"Based on those facts," concluded Jaquette, "we believe that those facts are sufficient under themselves to give us a new penalty phase hearing. It is possible that the court may want to look further into this matter and resolve what in fact was going on in the mind of the jurors. If that is the conclusion, then we ought to have a hearing in which the jurors are summoned and a detailed understanding of what went on should be done. But we believe that we have enough facts now to get the court to make a ruling."

Judge Thorpe thanked Jaquette, then turned to the deputy prosecutor. "Mr. Doersch?"

In response, Doersch went politely ballistic. "He just asked the court to do precisely what the case law says it ought not to do, examine thought processes of a jury in coming to its verdict. How is this jury misconduct? I'm listening to this. 'We were told to look for some mitigating circumstance, but he didn't help us find any.' Who told him to look for that? I guarantee the state did not do so, the defense did that."

"I think the instructions of the court," said Thorpe dryly, "required them to do that." Doersch courteously nodded at the blunt, professional correction.

"We have to prove beyond a reasonable doubt that there are no mitigating circumstances," said the prosecution. "What I see here, these quotes the defendant gives us, what I see is a jury looking hard to find some reason not to sentence this guy to death and can't find it."

Doersch paused to collect his thoughts. "I'm getting ahead of myself here," he acknowledged. "What I'm telling the court is this, this is not jury misconduct. In the first place, even if the *PI* reporter comes in here and testi-

fies, that's hearsay. Even if he swears out an affidavit to
what he heard, that's not permissible. What the jury does
in the jury room in terms of its considerations, its thought
processes—the case law is absolutely clear on that."

The defense was also absolutely clear that they still
had another issue to address. "It would be our position,"
said Jaquette, "that making an effort to look over and
watch Mr. Clark as he sits at counsel table is akin to going
out to the crime scene and taking a look around during
the course of a trial, and it is essentially getting additional information, additional facts upon which to make
a decision."

This argument was a new approach, and both judge
and prosecution listened carefully to the defense's line
of reasoning. "The inferences that can be drawn by the
way Mr. Clark sits at counsel table, most of the things
that his lawyers tell him to do. He's heard the evidence
before, all about the evidence and countless pretrial
hearings about what's admissible, what pictures are admissible, what isn't, so it's not as if he's surprised by these
things, as this is not his first time through that. So the inferences are very misleading, the reasonable inferences
are very unfair. But be that as it may, it is simply evidence
outside the province of what was presented at court and
the jury went out of its way to look elsewhere for their
answer."

In the defense's opinion, "the jury was disregarding
directives from the court about whose burden of proof
it was and whether the defendant, whether any inference
should be drawn from lack of the defendant's testimony.
I think in this case, and I've indicated in my brief that we
are under the special circumstances of a death penalty
case where the Eighth Amendment to the United States
Constitution, and Article One, Section Nine, of the
Washington Constitution compel a particularly reliable
proceeding, and when the jury goes beyond what they

are told, or what they are presented with, when the jury uses things and creates inferences against what they were told, we don't have a reliable proceeding, and Mr. Clark should therefore get a new penalty phase trial."

Judge Thorpe leaned back and thought it over. In his response, he sided with Ron Doersch. "I don't think that that indicates that they did not follow the directives of the court or the instructions of the court with respect to the burden of proof. It was simply a question of fact for this juror in answering a question put to him or her by the reporter. The defendant had put some evidence on, and they found that that wasn't sufficient. And I'm inclined to agree with Mr. Doersch that the statements made here indicate to me a jury that undertook its duties very soberly, very judicially, very carefully, and were looking for mitigating circumstances and didn't see any.

"The second statement that he would have had, or might have had, a better chance if he testified," continued Thorpe, "well, they knew that he did not have to testify, they were instructed that they were not to consider the fact that he did not testify. And for the juror to say after it was all over with kind of a Monday-morning quarterbacking kind of a thing, which is what the reporter's inquiries generally prompt one to do. To say he would have had a better chance if he testified is that person's guess, certainly doesn't indicate to me that they talked about that during their deliberations, or that they did not heed the court's instructions, that they were to draw no conclusion because he didn't testify.

"The first thing you mentioned was the defendant's demeanor," the judge said to Jaquette. "It must be borne in mind that this trial took about three weeks, that there was some—well, there was a good deal of evidence that tended to implicate Mr. Clark in the crime, and the jury was sitting in a position where they could easily see Mr. Clark, and during some phases of the trial, I noticed they were looking at him a lot. I don't think that the defendant's demeanor is extrajudicial. It's not the same as the jury going out and driving through an intersection someplace that may be the subject of a suit, or going down and retracing the route that he may have taken from the site on East Grand to Lombard Street, or anything of that nature.

"It's something that happened within the courtroom, something that happened that was entirely under the control of the defendant. And as an example, if at the penalty phase, as Ms. Doll-Iffrig left the witness stand and went to take her place in the audience, if the defendant had flipped his middle finger at her, surely the jury could have taken that into consideration. And I wouldn't deem that to be something extrajudicial or improper for them to consider. Same too, if he had shown hurt. He doesn't have to show surprise, but if he had shown hurt or showed something that would indicate that he really was remorseful, really was sorry for this, surely the jury could have taken that into consideration. I don't think that the demeanor of the defendant while sitting in the courtroom is extrajudicial, or watching him is an extrajudicial activity that would vitiate the jury's verdict. That motion will be denied.

"Any others?" asked the judge.

"None from the state," replied Doersch.

"Just matters relating to offender score," commented Jaquette.

The court took a fifteen-minute recess, after which Gail Doll stood and read aloud the unedited version of her victim impact statement.

"The physical loss of having lost a child this way is that you are never able to see them grow up," began Gail Doll. She read the statement with an undeniable intensity tempered with tragic resignation.

"The emotional impact of this crime is that we all feel a hole in our lives. I feel lost every now and then. Mad at others, scared that if this could happen to her, who's to say it won't happen again.

"One of my biggest fears is that my youngest won't reach age eight. She just turned seven in January. I stayed up half the night worrying. For the first year, I didn't leave the house at night. I would call several times when I did. I didn't let them (the kids) leave the yard to play at neighborhood friends' houses. This last summer was the first time I let them go to friends' houses on their bikes or walking.

"I'm emotionally drained when I come back from the court hearings. I used to sleep about four hours at night. I have good and bad nights. It took over six months to get Nick and Kristena to sleep in their own rooms and Kristena still ends up in our bed sometimes. We went through grief counseling until the kids said no more.

"Nick and Kristena miss Roxy a lot. If we do something, like see a new movie, they say how Roxy would have liked it. They will say out of the blue how much they miss her. My son got behind in school because he couldn't focus. He still hasn't caught up.

"Roxy is truly and desperately missed by her family. We miss the way she laughed and the funny way her mouth moved when she was being silly. We miss just holding her; we miss her smile. The way you couldn't stay mad at her when she cried. We still goof and try to call her for dinner or in from outside. Sometimes we even call Kristena 'Roxy' by mistake.

"She's a part of us we can never get back. Though in our hearts she is always with us, it still cannot take away the fact that she is not with us. The holidays and birthdays that have been shattered by her absence; the eternal missing piece of our family." Gail Doll sat down and cried.

"Your Honor," said Bill Jaquette, "the court is compelled to enter a sentence of death. There is not much we can say at this point that would do any good. I would say that on behalf of Mr. Scott and myself, we would thank Mr. Clark for the understanding that he's had during these proceedings, for what we have tried to do, and that peace that he's had and shown during these proceedings."

Bill Jaquette paused a moment, and the courtroom's atmosphere was chilled by mutual anticipation of the inevitable. "Mr. Clark is not an animal, he's a human being with a soul. He stands here to pay the ultimate punishment, and Mr. Scott and myself are very sad about it. But we are here to take the verdict of the court."

Judge Thorpe looked directly at Richard Mathew Clark, convicted kidnapper, rapist, and murderer. "Mr. Clark, is there anything you would like to say before I pass sentence?"

"Yes, I do," he replied, and Richard Clark spoke his first complete sentence in Judge Thorpe's courtroom. "I have sympathy for the seven-year-old girl, what happened to her. But for the Iffrig family, they are the murderers." An audible gasp of collective disbelief punctuated his comment. Tim Iffrig, overwhelmed with outrage at Clark's statement, abruptly left the courtroom.

"I had to leave," said Iffrig, "I had a pocketknife on me, and right then I wanted to . . . Well, I had violent feelings toward him. I think the only thing that stopped me was that I didn't want my family to go through the pain of another trial."

A security guard confirmed that Iffrig left the courthouse with a four-inch serrated blade, and declared the court's metal detectors worthless.

"I can't believe that this is happening," said Richard Clark to Judge Thorpe. "I've been in shock for the past two years. And I'm here today. That's all I have to say. Thank you."

Judge Richard Thorpe sighed. "Mr. Clark, in view of what your life could have been, and in view of the tragedy of Roxanne Doll's final minutes of life, it is with profound sadness, but with no regret, that I sentence you . . . to death"

After being sentenced to death, any other matter would seem inconsequential and anticlimactic. Clark didn't seem much concerned when the judge advised him that he owed $100 in crime victim penalty, and registered no dismay when informed that he may no longer own or possess any firearm, and must surrender any concealed-pistol license.

"I assume you don't have a concealed-weapon permit on you," said Judge Thorpe to the man whom he had sentenced to death, "Also, you have the right to appeal this sentence. This right must be exercised by filing a notice of appeal within fifteen days."

Bill Jaquette already had the appeal papers prepared. Thorpe signed all appropriate forms; Richard Clark returned to prison. As Clark was led out of the courtroom, he ignored repeated questions from reporters asking him what he meant by calling Roxanne's family "murderers." Even defense attorney Bill Jaquette said he did not fully understand Richard Clark's comments. On his way out the door, Richard Clark called out, "See ya; wouldn't want to be ya."

The battle for the life and future of Richard Mathew Clark was then handed over to a higher power—the Washington State Supreme Court.

Chapter 21

Before a death sentence can be upheld, the state supreme court must ascertain if the sentence of death was brought about through passion or prejudice. If so, the sentence cannot stand.

Clark's appeal would argue, as did Bill Jaquette at the time of sentencing, that the sentence was indeed the result of passion and prejudice. The appeal would note several reasons for the sentence falling under that unwelcome classification.

The media coverage of Roxanne's disappearance and death, as previously noted, saturated the community over an extended period of time. In addition to the publicity, members of the community actively participated in the search for Roxanne, wore angel pins to support her family, and provided the funds for her funeral. Because Richard M. Clark's motion for a change of venue was denied, virtually all of the jurors were aware of the pretrial publicity and of the extensive involvement of their community in the response to the crime.

The jurors knew their decision whether or not to impose the death penalty might evoke strong community reaction. During the penalty phase closing argument, the prosecution told the jury that they were the "conscience of the community," that they "were the law," and that they "decide what justice is." The appeal would argue that in making these statements, the state improperly placed a burden on the jurors to either convict Clark or answer to their community and society at large.

The prosecution's argument also may have improperly described the jurors' role and power as something greater than and different from their sworn duty to uphold the law as provided to them by the court, and to vote for the death penalty only if the lack of mitigation had been proven beyond a reasonable doubt. Most importantly, this argument implied that it was the jury's duty to sentence Clark to death.

The United States Supreme Court previously ruled, "That kind of pressure (exhorting the jury to do its job by convicting the defendant) has no place in the administration of criminal justice." The prosecution's argument, the appeal would insist, pressured the jury to return a verdict based on passion or prejudice, instead of a reasoned decision based on the law.

It was the state's strategy at the penalty phase of presenting facts underlying Clark's conviction for the unlawful imprisonment of Feather Rahier that could be the most viable reason for granting a new penalty phase, if not a new trial.

The state argued, asserted the appeal, that Richard Clark should be executed, not because of the circumstances of the crime charged, but because of its unproved claim that Clark had lived his life preying on the young and weak and would continue to exhibit this character trait in the future.

The prosecutor argued that Clark was "the most dangerous of offenders, he preys on the young, he preys on the vulnerable." The prosecutor reminded the jury that Clark, in the past, had tied up Feather Rahier. "This clear request for a decision based on an unsupported characterization of Mr. Clark's life," stated the appeal, "and an unfounded and irrelevant prediction of future dangerousness invited a decision based on passion or prejudice."

"If the death penalty were not imposed, Richard Clark would live the rest of his life in prison," stated appellant's attorney Rita Griffith, "and there was no evidence of any kind that he would pose a future problem in prison.

"The evidence at the trial's penalty phase showed that Richard Clark, for most of his life, was the weak and the vulnerable victim of his stepfather and mother," said Griffith. "The prosecutor also improperly shifted the burden to the defendant by asking rhetorically if there was anything that could justify a sentence of less than death."

These arguments by the prosecutor, the appeal insisted, demonstrated that the state's strategy was to secure a conviction based on passion and prejudice.

The state filed a cross appeal, defending itself against the allegations. As with other cross appeals to the state supreme court, the man responsible was deputy prosecutor Seth Fine. One by one, Fine argued against each issue raised by the excellent attorneys assigned to represent Richard Clark's appeal to the state supreme court.

In our daily lives, no one ever wins an argument unless the argument is over matters of fact. Two people can argue about the correct spelling of "Mississippi," and the argument will end once the prolix disputants consult a dictionary. Should they argue, however, about which city in Mississippi has the most pleasing aroma, no one will win because the argument is one of personal opinion, not established fact.

In matters of legal interpretation, a covenant exists whereby all agree to abide by the decision of a third party empowered to render decisions of interpretation and application of the law. In an appeal to the state supreme court, the defendant states what errors of interpretation and application were made by the superior court. Legal precedents, previous rulings, and prior interpretations by the state supreme court and the United States Supreme Court back up these arguments.

The prosecutor, in response, will argue that there were no errors of interpretation or application in the specific instances cited by the defense. In Richard M. Clark's appeal, the defense attacked every issue from pretrial through penalty phase, beginning with a renewed challenge to the supreme court's previous ruling allowing the state to seek the death penalty.

"This court rejected that argument," wrote the state supreme court, "finding that Clark's trial counsel actually received notice of the intent to seek the death penalty within the statutory period for filing the notice. Clark invites us to revisit that holding essentially because, in his estimation, the court incorrectly applied the requirements. . . ."

The law, however, prevented Clark from seeking further reconsideration of the supreme court decision. "Where there has been a determination of the applicable law in a prior appeal, the law of the case doctrine ordinarily precludes redeciding the same legal issues in a subsequent appeal. It is also the rule that questions determined on appeal, or which might have been determined had they been presented, will not again be considered on a subsequent appeal if there is no substantial change in the evidence at a second determination of the cause. The supreme court is bound by its decision on the first appeal until such time as it might be authoritatively overruled."

Only if the holding of the prior appeal was clearly erroneous, or if the ruling resulted in "manifest injustice," would it be reconsidered.

"The court's unanimous ruling in Clark I is not clearly erroneous. Clark presents no new theory as to our purported error," wrote the supreme court, "and we cannot find one. While Clark argues that allowing the death penalty to remain intact in light of this issue is a manifest injustice, we noted in Clark I that 'it is not disputed the notice was received by counsel for Clark within the statutory period.'"

It was also argued on appeal that Clark's right to due process and a fair and impartial trial were denied because the trial court (twice) denied his motion for a change of venue. He contended the pretrial publicity affected the jury's ability to decide his case impartially.

"The decision to grant or deny a motion for change of venue is within the trial court's discretion," wrote the supreme court, "and appellate courts are reluctant to disturb such a ruling absent a showing of abuse of discretion."

"Abuse of discretion" is not a vague term. To demonstrate an abuse of discretion, the defendant must show "a probability of unfairness or prejudice from pretrial publicity." There are nine factors used to determine whether or not there was probable unfairness and/or prejudice:

The inflammatory or noninflammatory nature of the publicity.

The degree to which the publicity was circulated throughout the community.

The length of time elapsed from the dissemination of the publicity to the date of trial.

The care exercised and the difficulty encountered in the selection of the jury.

The familiarity of prospective or trial jurors with the publicity and the resultant effect upon them.

The challenges exercised by the defendant in selecting the jury, both peremptory and for cause.

The connection of government officials with the release of publicity.

The severity of the charge.

The size of the area from which the jury pool is drawn.

Clark's attorney strenuously urged that a large amount of inflammatory publicity, calculated to evoke strong emotional responses, saturated the community around Everett in Snohomish County.

Judge Thorpe previously ruled that "the media coverage itself didn't create the inflammatory publicity as much as the facts of the crime," and even Judge Thorpe, upon first entertaining the change of venue motion in December 1995, had thought the eight months elapsed since the crime had likely dislodged any impressions in the minds of prospective jurors.

The appeal also pointed out that only one of the seated jurors expressly disavowed prior knowledge about the crime. Seth Fine, on behalf of the state, quibbled with this assertion, arguing that most jurors who were excused expressed a hardship or strong views about the death penalty.

"Whether it was 1 seated juror, 8 prospective jurors, or 12 prospective jurors out of a panel of 114," decided the state supreme court, "there is nevertheless no evidence presented of such an overwhelming pretrial bias amongst the panel members that a fair and impartial jury could not be selected." In the supreme court's opinion, "Clark does not present persuasive evidence of juror partiality . . . nor do we here find an abuse of discretion."

Another issue appealed to the state supreme court was the allegation that the state introduced evidence of his prearrest silence in an attempt to persuade the jury of his guilt. Both Clark and the state agree that the Fifth Amendment prevents the state from commenting on "the silence of the defendant so as to infer guilt from a refusal to answer questions."

This rule equally bars the use of prearrest silence as evidence of guilt. The fact that an issue was made of Clark not showing up at the Doll-Iffrig residence with his aunt Vicki after leaving the Everett Police Department on April 1 was regarded as a violation of that rule—the message being "he didn't show up, therefore he had something to hide, such as guilt."

Characterizing Richard Clark's behavior as "prearrest silence" seemed a bit of a stretch to the state's highest court. He volunteered to speak with Lieutenant Hegge and Detective Herndon. He told Lieutenant Hegge he would go to the Doll-Iffrig house on April 1, 1995; he told his aunt, traveling with him, he did not stop because he had no license. The next day, he changed his story and told Detective Herndon he did not come out because he was low on gas. "When a defendant does not remain silent and instead talks to police," the supreme court wrote, "the state may comment on what he does not say."

False information given to the police is considered admissible as evidence relevant to defendant's consciousness of guilt, and in this situation, Clark spoke with police on two occasions prior to arrest and developed a conflicting account of why he did not follow Lieutenant Hegge's instructions to meet with detectives at the Doll-Iffrig house. "This is not apparently a matter of prearrest silence," decided the Washington State Supreme Court. "There was no error."

The courtroom appearance and testimony of child rapist and jailhouse informant Eugene Hillius also came under attack in the appeal. Hillius testified that Clark, after commenting on the retrieval of his DNA from the anal cavity of Roxanne Doll, "just looked at me, just—it was like I was looking like I could look right through him, which is unreal, like he didn't care, like there is no feelings there at all. I get kind of blown away."

The error, Clark's lawyers insisted, was that the trial court erred in denying him the opportunity to tell the jury the specific instances behind Hillius's convictions for theft and forgery. Clark essentially argued that if the jury knew what a dishonest crook Hillius was, they wouldn't pay any attention to him.

In both law and theory, Clark's argument was correct—except for one significant point: misconduct diminishes with the significance of the witness in the state's case. "Hillius was not a crucial witness," said Seth Fine, and the state supreme court agreed: "Hillius was impeached on direct examination by an enumeration of each of his 36 prior convictions, Judge Thorpe concluded further examination on the misconduct underlying some of those convictions would not be any more probative. That was not an abuse of discretion."

Using the same line of reasoning as Jaquette did in the courtroom, Clark's appeal asked the state supreme court either to dismiss his conviction for a new trial, or remand for sentencing for second-degree murder.

However, the supreme court had previously ruled that sufficient evidence to infer premeditation has been found where (1) multiple wounds were inflicted; (2) a weapon was used; (3) the victim was struck from behind; and (4) there was evidence of a motive, such as robbery or sexual assault.

Sufficient evidence to infer premeditation also has been found in cases where multiple wounds were inflicted by a knife procured at the site of the killing; the killing took place in a room away from the kitchen where the knife was found; and where the evidence indicated that the victim had engaged in a prolonged struggle.

"Roxanne Doll was killed with a knife and was stabbed at least seven times in the neck," noted the court. "Cuts on her hands indicated a defensive struggle, and she was sexually assaulted. The trial court properly denied Clark's motion to dismiss."

Another attack on the case was that there were so many errors, that when you added them all up, the cumulative errors were enough to overturn the conviction, or grant Clark a new trial. "The state claims any alleged errors, individually or collectively," argued Seth Fine, "were harmless in light of the overwhelming evidence of Clark's guilt beyond a reasonable doubt."

The state supreme court ruled in favor of the Snohomish County prosecutor. "As we have found no errors with respect to the guilt phase, we find no cumulative error to have denied Clark of a fair trial."

There was nothing fair, however, about Clark being shackled when the verdict was read, and also throughout the special sentencing proceeding. The appeal insisted that this violated both the United States Constitution and the Washington State Constitution.

"A trial judge must exercise discretion in determining the extent to which courtroom security measures are necessary to maintain order and prevent injury. That discretion must be founded upon a factual basis set forth in the record. A broad general policy of imposing physical restraints upon prison inmates charged with new offenses because they may be 'potentially dangerous' is a failure to exercise discretion.

"This court and courts of other jurisdictions have universally held that restraints should 'be used only when necessary to prevent injury to those in the courtroom, to prevent disorderly conduct at trial, or to prevent an escape.'"

Clark was shackled when entering the jury auditorium on the first day of jury selection, in front of the entire jury venire. Despite defense counsel's objection, the trial court found the jury venire would not be able to see Clark actually in shackles. However, the jury could infer shackling from Clark's stilted and restrained movement.

"The state concedes the trial court went through no individualized assessment of the need for shackling," noted the court. "The state directs us to no evidence in the record, nor do we find any, that would imply Clark posed a threat of violence, escape, or disruption. Nor was there evidence of anything other than decorous behavior during pretrial hearings. Therefore Clark's shackling at points during the guilt phase was constitutional error and therefore presumptively prejudicial. With respect to the shackling on the day the verdict was returned, and throughout the special sentencing proceeding, Clark was shackled throughout the sentencing phase."

Unlike prison clothes, physical restraints may create the impression in the minds of the jury that the court believes the defendant is a particularly dangerous and violent person. Therefore, in the absence of a compelling need to shackle the defendant during his sentencing hearing, such a practice is inherently prejudicial. "The crucial thing," states the court, "is the impact of the thing done wrong on the minds of other men."

First, Clark was not shackled throughout the two-and-a-half week trial. Second, the jury had already arrived at its verdict of guilt or innocence prior to the second time they saw Clark shackled. Because the impact of shackling on the presumption of innocence is the overarching constitutional concern, it would logically follow that in the minds of the jurors Clark's shackling on the first day of voir dire was more than logically offset by over two weeks of observing Clark in the courtroom without shackles.

Furthermore, the presumption of innocence was not at stake on the day the verdict was read because the jury had already judged Clark guilty. "Clark's shackling on the first day of voir dire and the day of the verdict was harmless error beyond a reasonable doubt," ruled the state supreme court.

The trial court made sure Clark was not moved in or out of the room in the presence of the jury, the shackles were taped to eliminate any noise, and the jury never saw Clark in motion during the guilt phase. A protective skirt concealed the shackles at counsel table, and Clark never moved from his seat during the penalty phase except to stand for the entry of the judge and jury.

"Although Clark's shackling during both the guilt and penalty phases was constitutional error because no appropriate individualized assessment took place," ruled the state supreme court, "we find he was not prejudiced and hold the error harmless beyond a reasonable doubt."

One by one, Seth Fine's command of law, logic, and application convinced the Washington State Supreme Court that the objections of the defense were rightfully overruled, but the biggest battle yet remained. The battle best summed up in two words: Feather Rahier.

Judge Thorpe ruled that the facts surrounding Clark's 1988 conviction for unlawful imprisonment were inadmissible in the guilt phase. In the penalty phase, however, the state was allowed to present full details of the abduction and unlawful imprisonment of little Feather Rahier. They heard all about the dark garage, the age of Feather, and that she was Clark's neighbor. The defense argued that it should not be allowed because it was unfairly prejudicial to Clark.

Countering that allegation, Seth Fine argued that the state only sought to evince a "few basic facts" surrounding the matter, and that such information was perfectly admissible.

In deciding whether leniency is merited, the jury may consider whether the defendant has or does not have a significant history, either as a juvenile or an adult, of prior criminal activity.

"Since the death penalty is the ultimate punishment," wrote the court, "due process under this state's constitution requires stringent procedural safeguards so that a fundamentally fair proceeding is provided. Where the trial which results in imposition of the death penalty lacks fundamental fairness, the punishment violates article 1, section 14 of the state constitution."

The law does not prohibit the introduction of additional information, that simply states the particular elements of the crime that was the basis for the conviction. What happened in the case of Richard Mathew Clark was quite different. Not only was a certified copy of the judgment and sentence for the conviction entered, but a police officer from the Everett Police Department was permitted to testify from a police statement that the victim of the unlawful imprisonment was a four-year-old girl who was a neighbor to Clark. Testimony was offered to prove more than the fact of a conviction and more than the elements of the offense.

"The trial court erred by admitting this testimony for two reasons," read the court's opinion. "First, it was inadmissible on its face because it went beyond the scope of the statute we have construed to allow introduction of only the record of conviction. If we allow narrative testimony of this kind there would be no foreseeable end to these trials within a trial. Second, it should have been excluded from evidence even if otherwise admissible because it was unduly prejudicial. Evidence of the unlawful imprisonment victim's tender age and relationship to Clark did not go to the elements of unlawful imprisonment—the knowing restraint of another person. One need not imprison a child, or be an acquaintance of the victim, in order to commit the crime of unlawful imprisonment.

"The prejudice is apparent when one recalls the offense for which Clark was sentenced to death. On the face of it, this may have been the most prejudicial evidence entered in the sentencing phase against Clark, a bit of evidence that the jury could not have possibly disregarded. Perhaps that is why the trial court did not allow the evidence to come out during the guilt phase, before paradoxically changing its position in the penalty phase. The prejudice of its admission became clear in the state's closing argument during the penalty phase that 'this defendant preys on the vulnerable and the weak and the small.'"

The Washington State Supreme Court feared such evidence was too likely to short-circuit the jurors' reasoning and inflame their passions. "We therefore hold the admission of the police statement concerning the previous false imprisonment conviction, over and above the mere judgment and sentence for that crime, was unfairly prejudicial, and requires vacating Clark's death sentence and remanding for a new special sentencing proceeding.

"We affirm Clark's conviction for aggravated first-degree murder, first-degree kidnapping, and first-degree rape. However . . . we reverse his death sentence and remand to the trial court where, if the state desires, a new special sentencing proceeding may take place."

Richard Mathew Clark was still guilty of all charges, and he still possibly faced the death penalty. The entire sentencing phase, deciding life in prison or the death penalty, must be conducted anew. "And with a new jury," said Gail Doll with a sigh. "It's amazing how long this has been dragging on." Doll's frustration was revealed in her latest victim impact statement.

"It has been over six years now since Richard Mathew Clark stole a very valuable piece of my life. Time has been marching on and changing everything except for the one photograph on my wall of the beautiful little girl who once loved us and trusted us to keep her from harm's way.

"It was on that one night, in a moment of comfort, that our guard was let down and this man who pretended to be a friend stole a part of me and my family that we can never get back.

"In the first victims statement I wrote of who Roxy was: a beautiful little girl with a heart of gold, an animal charmer, lover of books, movies and songs. How she worked hard to learn to ride a bike, [a] person with such potential and inner strength that you couldn't help but love her. But in this statement I would like to tell you what it has been like going on without her.

"Each day I see my children growing moody and I can't help but think if only she were here. Her brother is now in high school; her older sister in college. Her youngest sister, who's [*sic*] has now had to live over half her life without her sister, is beginning to blossom into the young woman Roxy was never allowed to be.

"I have had to watch with aching heart as my nieces, who are only months older than Roxy, grow and become [the] wonderful young people they were meant to be.

"It is hard to believe that it has been six years since Roxy has been gone. This trial and the Oklahoma Bombing trial started at the same time. The only difference is Oklahoma is going to receive closure soon and the lawyers here will still be fighting to make sure that Mr. Clark receives a fair sentence.

"Mr. Clark is the one who brought this action upon himself the moment he took my daughter from us. He used her like she was nothing and discarded her like trash. He took no more thought in how truly special she was than he did a piece of waste. He took something from my family we can never replace. Roxanne Christine Doll. And for this crime, he should die. He has lived on this earth longer than he should have. We have waited longer than we should have for the justice we deserve. We the loved ones should have the closure we deserve, and that this man be made accountable for the vicious acts he did to my daughter. That he [be] made to pay the price that he chose when he brutally raped and murdered Roxanne, and dumped her like she was nothing. Roxanne deserves justice; she deserves to have her killer's fate be finalized."

The finalized fate of Richard M. Clark was most likely sealed the day his mother died on Highway 9, or perhaps it was the day Carol Clark told him that she couldn't be his mother, the first time he was beat with a fireplace poker, or the evening meal where he choked down that cigar. Jaquette made a point that not everyone experiences or responds to hardship the same way. None of the other kids became child molesters or murderers, but none of the other kids was Richard Mathew Clark.

Clark was in Snohomish County Superior Court on December 18, 2002, for the setting of a time to start the new sentencing phase. Ron Doersch asked for a quick start, preferably the third week in January. Bill Jaquette, head of the Snohomish County Public Defender Unit, agreed that "the third week in January would be fine, as long as it is in 2003."

"It's apparent the defense tactic is to set this so far in the future that I'll be retired or die of old age," Doersch said. "Justice deferred in this case is justice denied. None of the facts will change, so there's no reason for so much extra time."

"The extra time is needed to develop a case that might convince a jury to not impose the death penalty," explained Jaquette. "The defense will hire an expert to do that, and the expert needs about a year. The defense won't be content with the same information that was presented in the first trial," Jaquette said. "That obviously wasn't enough to turn a jury to spare Clark's life." Clark's life-or-death judicial proceeding—an entirely new penalty phase—has been scheduled, but not for 2003. The new date is 2004.

The reason for the extensive delay is that William Jaquette, for whatever reason, opted not to represent Richard Clark again. New lawyers must review everything. There is no question of guilt or innocence. Clark is guilty. It is the mitigation, or sentencing phase, that must be held anew.

"Once again a jury will have to decide if he should live or die," said Gail Doll. "Of course, you already know how I feel about it. Life in prison is too good for him, and death isn't bad enough."

Epilogue

May 2003

Gail Doll and Tim Iffrig, although divorced, remained close. Tim worked for the same employer, now located in Mukilteo, Washington. Both he and his mother have stopped drinking.

Gail Doll continued to live in the same little house in Everett from which Roxanne was kidnapped. Carol Clark remained on Lombard Street in the same house where she washed Richard Clark's bloodstained shirt.

Lloyd Herndon was no longer senior detective for the Everett Police Department. For reasons both personal and professional, he returned to patrol duty in Everett's South Precinct.

Feather Rahier, violated at age two by her father, groped in the garage at age four, and vanished from the Gelo residence at age thirteen, returned home alive and well following Clark's conviction and imprisonment. She will not be called to testify, nor will her name be mentioned, at the 2004 penalty phase of Richard Mathew Clark.

Author's Note

In this author's analysis, Richard Clark ineffectually attempted to prevent himself from committing the initial kidnapping of Roxanne Doll. Even though Neila D'alexander made it perfectly clear that she intended to spend the night in town, Richard Clark asked her to return with him to the Doll-Iffrig residence. He also urged Vicki Smith to accompany him after returning Jimmy Miller to the reservation. Had either accepted his invitation, the kidnapping, rape, and murder would have been at least forestalled, if not prevented.

It is also highly probable that the coffee-drinking, glasses-wearing Richard Clark, who reappeared at the Dog House Tavern between 10:00 and 10:30 P.M., and asked about selling his van—a van he had only recently acquired—was a Richard Clark who was already past the act of rape, and into the mental act of "undoing."

This scenario, if valid, puts Jimmy Miller, unconscious in an alcoholic blackout, in the front passenger seat of Clark's van when Richard Clark kidnapped Roxanne Doll between 9:15 and 10:00 P.M. It also means Roxanne Doll was alive in the back of the van until just prior to midnight. Jimmy Miller was asked point-blank if this was possible, and he acknowledged that in his condition that night he would have never known.

None of these various interpretations of time lines and behavioral indicators alters the fact that Richard Clark kidnapped, restrained, raped, and murdered an innocent seven-year-old child named Roxanne Doll.

Each child—Roxanne Doll and Richard Clark included—is potentially the light of the world. Had Richard Clark's life been different, his basic at-birth biology balanced, his upbringing healthy, his emotions matured, the odds of him ever committing such a heinous act rapidly diminish.

If there is nothing learned from this nightmare beyond the unquestioned guilt of Richard Clark in the death of Roxanne Doll, her death does not rise to the level of sacrifice. If, however, her death compels a closer examination of the facts and factors that contributed to the creation of the mind-set and motivations of Richard Clark—an examination that saves future lives—then her death is not in vain.

Richard Clark appears to fit the profile of a "situational" child molester. "This type of individual doesn't really have a sexual preference for children," explains Dr. Stephen Rubin, "and the motivation is really more one of power or control over someone more weak than they are."

Quite often, abuse in the offender's own life sets the stage for his or her sexual abuse of young people. "These individuals usually have low self-esteem, lax standards of morality, and even though this type of offender doesn't have a primary sexual desire for children, they may react to a built-up sexual impulse or anger that, to them, is irresistible."

Childhood beatings, for example, interfere with the proper development of the hypothalamus, which regulates the body's emotional and hormonal systems. An excess of the hormone noradrenaline, or low levels of the brain chemical serotonin, may cause violent responses to various stimuli.

The main criterion for the victims is "availability." Unlike the pedophile who has a compulsive sexual desire for children, and thus pursues them fairly constantly, the situational molester may have many years between episodes, or only one sexually inappropriate act in his entire life.

Incarceration, devoid of comprehensive treatment, has no effect on altering their postrelease behavior. Comprehensive treatment, however, is of significant value. "Sex offenders are not as hopelessly fated to a life of deviant behavior as is widely believed," says Dr. Rubin.

Canadian psychologists R. Karl Hanson, Ph.D., and Monique T. Bussiere, Ph.D., recently reviewed 61 studies covering more than 23,300 cases of sex offenses and found that only 13 percent of the individuals identified in the studies went on to commit another sex crime. According to their study, published in the *Journal of Consulting and Clinical Psychology* (Vol. 66, No. 2, pp. 348–362), those who did re-offend had committed more diverse sexual offenses and more deviant sexual interests, and did not complete their rehabilitative treatment programs.

"The findings contradict the wide-held notion that most sex offenders inevitably repeat their deviant behavior," noted the researchers, who are corrections researchers at the Department of the Solicitor General of Canada.

"Treatment programs can contribute to community safety," they write. "We now have reliable evidence that those who attend and cooperate with treatment programs are less likely to re-offend than those who reject intervention."

"Child molestation, because of its large numbers of victims and because of the extent of its damage to the health of its victims, is a national public health problem," state Gene G. Abel, M.D., and Nora Harlow, authors of *The Stop Child Molestation Book* (Xlibris 2001). "To combat this public health problem we must focus on the cause. People with pedophilia molest 88 percent of child sexual abuse victims. Early diagnosis of this disorder, followed by effective medicines and therapies, has the potential to save children from being molested."

The Association for the Treatment of Sexual Abusers (ATSA) is a nonprofit, interdisciplinary organization founded in 1984 to foster research, facilitate information exchange, further professional education, and provide for the advancement of professional standards and practices in the field of sex offender evaluation and treatment. ATSA is specifically focused on the prevention of sexual abuse through effective management of sex offenders, and the protection of our communities through responsible and ethical treatment of sex offenders.

For further information on publications, seminars, and state chapters, contact:

The Association for the Treatment of Sexual Abusers
4900 S.W. Griffith Drive, Suite 274
Beaverton, Oregon 97005
Phone: (503) 643-1023
Fax: (503) 643-5084
E-mail: atsa@atsa.com

This author has found no confirming evidence that Richard Clark received any comprehensive ongoing treatment for his inappropriate behavior toward Feather Rahier other than being locked up in a cell. That behavior aligns symptomatically with those of children born of alcoholic mothers—children born with either fetal alcohol syndrome (FAS) or fetal alcohol effect (FAE).

"Children with FAS," stated Inez Serrano, information specialist for the Cowlitz County Health Department in Washington State, "often develop behavior problems that increase their risk of becoming involved with the criminal justice system. The most serious characteristics of FAS/FAE include a high probability of sexually inappropriate behavior, including the molestation of children. At least sixty-five percent of adult males with FAE manifest sexual behaviors that are repeatedly problematic, or for which the individual is incarcerated or treated."

It is thought that the actual incidence of inappropriate sexual behavior is much higher, and not always reported by the individual or the family due to embarrassment or fear of being reported to authorities. In addition to child molestation, problem sexual behaviors most common for those with FAS/FAE include indecent exposure, various sexual compulsions, voyeurism, masturbation in public, incest, sex with animals, and obscene phone calls.

Other symptoms of FAS/FAE include:

• **Mental Health Problems**
During childhood, 60 percent of children with Fetal Alcohol Spectrum Disorders have ADHD. During adulthood, most adults with FASD have clinical depression. Twenty-three percent of the adults had attempted suicide, and 43 percent had threatened to commit suicide. Richard Clark attempted suicide three times in a twelve-month period.

• **Disrupted School Experience** (suspension or expulsion or drop out)
By the time students with FAE reach adulthood, the rate of disrupted school experience peaks at 70 percent. Common school problems include: not paying attention, incomplete homework, can't get along with peers, disruptive in class, disobeying school rules, talking back to the teacher, fighting, and truancy. Following his mother's death, Richard Clark didn't return to school.

• **Trouble with the Law** (involvement with police, charged or convicted of crime)
Sixty percent of those age twelve and over develop criminal records. The most common first criminal behavior

reported was shoplifting, followed by property damage, possession/selling, sexual assault, and vehicular crimes. The criminal record of Richard Clark includes virtually all of the above crimes.

• Confinement

Inpatient treatment for mental health, alcohol/drug problems, or incarceration for crime is experienced by 60 percent of those ages twelve and over. Over 40 percent of adults with FASD had been incarcerated, about 30 percent of adults with FASD were confined to a mental institution, and about 20 percent had been confined for substance-abuse treatment. Richard Clark served time for criminal behavior, but never received comprehensive treatment for his alcoholism or drug usage.

• Alcohol/Drug Problems

Of the adults with FAE, 53 percent of males and 70 percent of females experience substance-abuse problems. This is more than five times that of the general population. Richard Clark's continual consumption of alcohol, the drug most linked to violent behavior, and other lesser drugs, is well documented. The massive amounts of alcohol consumed by Richard Clark following his mother's death certainly did him no good. Research at the University of North Carolina tested the sensitivity of the adolescent brain to binge drinking. The results, published in the November 2000 issue of *Alcoholism: Clinical and Experimental Research,* advanced the hypothesis that this damage is a component of alcoholism.

• Problems with Employment

Eighty percent of adults with FAS/FAE have significant difficulty in securing and maintaining employment. Richard Clark never had his feet firmly on any career path other than petty criminality.

• **Exposure to Violence** (sexual and/or physical abuse)

Seventy-two percent of individuals with FAS/FAE have experienced abuse. Those exposed to violence are four times as likely to exhibit inappropriate sexual behavior. There is no doubt that the violence inflicted upon young Richard Clark left an indelible mark on his psyche and his future behavior.

Craig Harris at the University of Massachusetts Medical Center in Worcester has asserted that adolescent experiences can determine how a person will behave for the rest of his or her life. Bullies, for example, are easily created. According to Harris, if you place an adolescent hamster in a cage for one hour a day with an aggressive adult hamster, it will grow up to become a bully who picks on smaller hamsters. When faced with a hamster its own size, it will cower in fear. Once again, research confirms that fear is the underlying component of aggression.

In the United States of America, over three percent of the population is currently in prison. In Canada, it is estimated that at least fifty percent of the prison population was possibly exposed to excessive amounts of alcohol prebirth. As of yet, no comprehensive studies have determined the percentage of FAS/FAE-afflicted population in America's rapidly expanding prison system. In the previous decade, the population of Washington State increased twelve percent while the Washington State prison population increased ninety percent.

The Fetal Alcohol Syndrome Family Resource Institute is an excellent source of further information. The mission of the FAS Family Resource Institute, a nonprofit organization, is to identify, understand, and care for individuals disabled by prenatal alcohol exposure and their families, and to prevent future generations from having to live with this disability. For more information, contact:

FAS Family Resource Institute
PO Box 2525
Lynnwood, WA 98036
Phone: (253) 531-2878,
or in Washington (800) 999-3429
http://www.fetalalcoholsyndrome.org

Life, including death, appears incomprehensibly unfair. Time heals all wounds except the fatal. Scars of the heart seldom fade, and comforting the bereaved is a temporary social obligation.

A natural desire for simplicity and certitude tempts us to sanctify the innocent and demonize the guilty, burying the depth of our pain in the shallow "It was God's will." No religion on earth includes rape and murder as praiseworthy acts. Indeed, mercy and compassion are the hallmarks of all faiths.

"Crime victims, their families and friends, deal with more than pain, grief, and anger," Gail Doll has said. "We must also cope with the complicated and often impersonal criminal justice system. Families and Friends of Missing Persons and Violent Crime Victims provided us with ongoing support in our time of grief, information and referrals in time of confusion, and advocacy by volunteers that made all the difference in the world to us."

Families and Friends is the oldest victim advocacy and support group in Washington State, and one of the first such groups in the nation. They offer services to crime victims, their loved ones, and the public throughout Washington twenty-four hours a day, at no cost. Peer support groups provide comfort, understanding, compassion, and coping skills.

Among the valuable services provided by Families and

Friends are educational programs to increase public awareness of the impacts of violent crime, and abduction prevention information. They have fingerprinted thousands of children and adults, and developed "Personal ID Packets" with dental charts, fingerprints, and safety tips. Families and Friends also offers a complete resource center with updated information on topics ranging from the criminal justice system to victim experiences. A newsletter, *The White Rose*, offers important insights into victim issues, pending legislation, and personal stories of victims and survivors.

Families and Friends works closely with national organizations such as the National Organization for Victim Assistance (NOVA), the National Center for Missing and Exploited Children, and the National Victim Center to provide further resources for assisting local crime victims and families of missing persons.

Prior to the trial, the organization familiarizes victims and survivors with criminal justice system terminology and procedures. During trials, transportation to court is provided, and victims are shielded from curiosity seekers, the news media, and confrontation with the alleged offender and/or family members of the accused.

"We also provide assistance and support to families searching for loved ones," added a dedicated volunteer, "and we monitor the conduct of judges, prosecutors, and other criminal justice personnel in an effort to help make the system more responsive to victims and the general public." For more information, write:

Families and Friends of Missing Persons and Violent Crime Victims
PO Box 27529
Seattle, Washington 98125

MORE MUST-READ TRUE CRIME FROM PINNACLE